CHINA STATION

To Fang Fang

CHINA STATION

The British Military in the
Middle Kingdom 1839–1997

Mark Felton

Pen & Sword
MILITARY

First published in Great Britain in 2013 by
Pen & Sword Military
an imprint of
Pen & Sword Books Ltd
47 Church Street
Barnsley
South Yorkshire
S70 2AS

ISBN: 978-1-78159-069-0

A CIP catalogue record for this book is
available from the British Library.

Typeset in 11/13pt Palatino by
Concept, Huddersfield, West Yorkshire

Printed and bound in England by
CPI Group (UK) Ltd, Croydon, CRO 4YY

Pen & Sword Books Ltd incorporates the imprints of Pen & Sword
Archaeology, Atlas, Aviation, Battleground, Discovery, Family History,
History, Maritime, Military, Naval, Politics, Railways, Select, Social
History, Transport, True Crime, Claymore Press, Frontline Books,
Leo Cooper, Praetorian Press, Remember When, Seaforth Publishing
and Wharncliffe.

For a complete list of Pen & Sword titles please contact
PEN & SWORD BOOKS LIMITED
47 Church Street, Barnsley, South Yorkshire, S70 2AS, England
E-mail: enquiries@pen-and-sword.co.uk
Website: www.pen-and-sword.co.uk

Contents

Acknowledgements   vi

Introduction   1

1   Foreign Mud   3
2   Harrying the Coast   19
3   The Arrow War   41
4   'Destroy the Foreigners'   62
5   Slaughter in Shangri-La   87
6   Showing the Flag   105
7   Christmas in Hell   120
8   Cloak and Dagger   143
9   'Am Under Heavy Fire'   158
10   The Immortal Memory   174

Appendix 1   Order of Battle – Anglo-Tibet War 1903–04   189
Appendix 2   Order of Battle – Shanghai Volunteer Corps
             21 November 1941   191
Appendix 3   China Command 1900–1997
             British Garrisons, Hong Kong   193
Appendix 4   Order of Battle – Hong Kong Volunteer
             Defence Corps, 8 December 1941   199

Notes   200
Bibliography   210
Index   212

Acknowledgements

The author would like to acknowledge the kind assistance of the following organisations and institutions: Custodians of the Zhapu Forts, China; Dr. Nicholas Hall at The Royal Armouries Museum; The British Library, London; The Imperial War Museum, London; The Royal Armouries Museum, Portsmouth; The National Archives (Public Record Office) Kew; The National Army Museum, London; The National Maritime Museum, Greenwich; MaritimeQuest; The Hong Kong Historical Museum, Kowloon; The Shanghai Library; The Museum of Coastal Defence, Hong Kong; Shanghai History Museum, and a special thank you to my wife Fang Fang for kindly acting as an unpaid researcher and translator.

Introduction

One hot and humid summer's evening in 2010, I was attending a function at the 'Seed Cathedral', Britain's extraordinary contribution to the Shanghai World Expo. The vast expo site was crowded with hundreds of thousands of people, all enjoying the fascinating exhibits and the air of international friendship and cooperation. A large Union Jack flew proudly above Britain's landmark building, itself an award-winning and dazzling profusion of light and colour. The special guests then marched in. To everyone's amazement in came the Band of the Royal Marines, immaculately turned out in white tropical service tunics, medals proudly pinned to their chests. It was not lost on me the significance of this event – for the first time since 1949, uniformed British soldiers stood under their own flag on Communist Chinese soil.

The Royal Marines, probably more than any other British military unit, had played an integral role in Britain's military campaigns in China, from the First Opium War in 1839 to the Yangtze Incident in 1949. I wondered as I stood listening to the music whether the other guests realised how significant a moment this was in Anglo-Chinese relations – such a thing would have been unthinkable even ten years before. And I wondered how many guests considered the enormous impact that had been made on modern China by not just the Royal Marines, but by the Royal Navy and British Army. Shanghai itself was a product of British military adventurism, and it seemed rather poetic to me that it should have been the Royal Marines, whose unofficial motto is 'The First to Land', were representing Britain before the Chinese public one last time.

Britain's involvement with China is truly epic. We launched huge naval and military campaigns on three occasions during the 19th and early 20th centuries, invaded Tibet, patrolled China's rivers for over four decades, fought a glorious last stand battle in Hong Kong, helped China to fight Japanese aggression, and got caught up in the Chinese Civil War. We gave millions of Chinese a fresh start in Hong Kong while defending the territory during the Cold War, and, although not part of this book, we fought the Chinese in set piece battles in Korea. For over 150 years Britain maintained a military presence in China, in both peace and war, and millions of British service personnel passed through our barracks, cantonments and campaigns. The bones of many of these soldiers and sailors lie buried today beneath Chinese soil.

As I listened to the Royal Marines playing 'God Save the Queen' at the Shanghai Expo in 2010, I couldn't help but wonder how it came about that Britain became a military force in China. This book attempts, in a necessarily limited way, to shine a little historical light onto this incredible story that began with an illicit drugs trade in 1839 and ended with the skyscrapers and financial markets of Hong Kong in 1997.

Chapter 1

Foreign Mud

If you will not surrender, we shall be obliged to use warlike measures for obtaining possession.

Commodore Sir James Bremer,
Chusan Islands, China, 1840

The first shots in Britain's most infamous conflict, the First Opium War, were not fired by a British warship at the Chinese but somewhat ironically by the Royal Navy warship at a British merchant vessel. On 27 October 1839 a British merchant ship named *Royal Saxon* attempted to run a Royal Navy blockade into what was then Britain's biggest trading post in China, Canton, located nearly a hundred miles up the Pearl River in the south of the country. HMS *Volage*, a fully rigged frigate, fired a warning shot across *Royal Saxon*'s bows, a shot that was to bring out a large Chinese fleet under orders to protect the British merchantman. That this confused situation even occurred had its roots in a pernicious drug that the British were then in the process of foisting upon the Chinese literally by the ton. The British government, in a move of breathtaking immorality, launched the nation into a war against China to protect ruthless drug traffickers and in so doing ushered in over a hundred years of British military activity in China and dragged China unwillingly from feudalism into the modern world.

The Opium Wars are generally agreed by historians to have been one of the less proud chapters in the history of Britain's ascent

3

to world hegemony. For the first and only time in history one nation used narcotics to dominate another, and for good reason today the Opium Wars are remembered in China as a national humiliation. Although morally difficult to justify, Britain's success in the First Opium War would eventually lead to China becoming a modern power in her own right, and it can be argued that China's prosperity today has its roots in its forcible opening to the world economic system in the 1840s, forced by the sort of gunboat diplomacy that the British used so successfully to usher in the first globalisation of trade and finance.

Although Britain's relationship with China had always been firmly rooted in trade and profit, it actually began quite differently. China, a vast underdeveloped empire and the oldest nation-state on earth with its teeming hundreds of millions, and self-satisfied contempt for all things 'foreign', was about to collide with a grasping, heavily-armed and belligerent nation of free-trading buccaneers busily adding ports and territories to its ever expanding empire with a determination unmatched even by the Romans.

The first ship from the British Isles had visited the south China coast in 1635. They were relative latecomers, for the Portuguese had already established a small colony at Macau a century before. Soon there were British traders in small communities at Zhoushan and Xiamen, but the most important trading town was Canton (now Guangzhou) at the mouth of the mighty Pearl River. A city of over a million souls, it was ringed, as was the Chinese style, by a massive town wall to protect it from the depredations of pirates and was at the time one of the largest cities in the world.

Between 1700 and 1842 Canton dominated the China trade, and it was the British who quickly became the masters of that trade. The British and other foreigners traded in China with the permission of the seldom seen divine emperor in Peking (now Beijing), under Chinese laws and at the behest of Chinese officials known collectively as mandarins. The ruling Qing dynasty, themselves foreigners from Manchuria who had seized power from the elegant Ming Dynasty in 1644, held an ambivalent attitude towards overseas trade and a Confucian disdain for merchants and traders. Chinese officials believed that trade incited unrest and disorder in the empire, caused piracy and compromised the nation's defences. In the case of the British they were to be proved right on all of these scores. The Chinese were not particularly interested in foreign manufactures and technologies, seeing no practical use for them, and they erected high tariffs and created rigid laws governing such imports, also inadvertently fostering widespread corruption among junior officials and provincial governors.

The Chinese trading system with foreigners had operated for centuries on an elaborate system of tribute. The Chinese emperor was 'The Son of Heaven', mandated ruler of the entire Earth, so all foreign rulers were expected to present tribute to him and acknowledge his superiority. Western nations were happy to play along, as the emperor's gifts, in order to demonstrate his munificence, were superior to the tribute given, and the emperor bestowed titles upon foreign emissaries and permitted them to trade. Trade for the foreigners was always lucrative but by the early nineteenth century European traders demanded more access to Chinese markets as their trade and wealth grew. At this juncture the emperor tried to turn back the clock, with disastrous results. The history of China in the mid- to late-nineteenth century is of successive leaders trying vainly to close the door to the foreigners, but finding that their former guests were not averse to kicking in the door to get what they wanted.

The Honourable East India Company, 'John Company', carried out British Far East trade under royal charter. It was a vast firm with a huge private army and navy that had conquered and administered great swathes of India. There was low demand among the Chinese for European goods but huge demand in Europe for Chinese tea, silk and porcelain. The problem for the Europeans was the Chinese demand to be paid in hard currency – and the only currency that they accepted was silver. The figures were astounding. For example, from the mid-sixteenth to the mid-nineteenth centuries the Chinese received 28 million kilograms of silver from Europe and America. The British especially did not like this arrangement because since the mid-eighteenth century they had used the gold standard, and in order to obtain the required silver they were forced to purchase it from other European nations and Mexico, thereby incurring fees that lowered their profits.

The East India Company first imported small quantities of the Indian narcotic opium, derisively called 'foreign mud' by the

Chinese, following the annexation of Bengal by Robert Clive in 1757. The Company needed a product that they could trade with the Chinese in return for tea. Initially they tried European clothes, but the Chinese preferred homespun silk. Then, despite moral objections raised at the time, the British chose to fix the trade imbalance by means of Indian opium. Widespread addiction among all classes of Chinese soon reversed the flow of silver back into British coffers.

The Chinese government banned the importation of opium when they realised the damage the drug was inflicting on their society and perhaps, more importantly, on their silver reserves. The East India Company circumvented the ban by establishing an elaborate trading system using both legal and illegal markets in China. British merchants would buy tea on credit at Canton. They would then buy opium at auction in Calcutta. The chests of opium would be sent on British merchant ships to the China coast, smuggled inland by local Chinese merchants, and the debts would be settled.

Then as now, the profits from drug smuggling were enormous, and the trade boomed. In 1730, the British sold 15 tons of opium in China, by 1773 this figure was up to 75 tons, by the 1820s it had reached 900 tons annually. At the same time the British government attempted to persuade the emperor to ease the ban on opium imports in return for certain concessions. In 1793 Earl Macartney was granted an audience with the Qianlong Emperor in the yellow-roofed Forbidden City, but he was soon politely shown the door. In 1799 and 1810 the emperor issued imperial edicts forbidding opium importation or smoking. But because of endemic corruption, the emperor was unable to effectively govern his southern provinces and between 1821 and 1837 there was a five-fold increase in opium sales in China, vastly increasing British traders' power over the region and its population.

The turning point came in 1834 when free trade reform in Britain ended the East India Company's monopoly in the Far East, ushering in hundreds of piratical and independent operators and freebooters. The Americans also began importing cheaper lower quality Turkish opium into China.

In 1839 the 56-year-old Daoguang Emperor, who had reigned for nineteen years, appointed a Manchu nobleman named Lin

Zexu as Governor of Canton with orders to stop the opium trade. Commissioner Lin banned the sale of opium, ordered all opium stocks to be surrendered and destroyed, and required foreign traders to sign a 'no opium bond' before they could moor their ships in the city. Any foreigner found with opium in his holds was to be put to death. Lin also closed the sea channel into Canton up a myriad of tributaries and creeks off the Pearl River, in effect holding the city's British traders hostage.

The man who was responsible for opening up China to foreign trade, at the point of a gun, was 37-year-old Royal Navy Captain Charles Elliot, British Superintendent of Trade. Elliot had joined the navy in 1815 and had served in the East and West Indies and West Africa before being sent to Canton in 1833. Importantly, he was firmly and vocally against the opium trade, though he followed his orders to the letter. Elliot held a meeting with the angry British traders. He managed to persuade them to hand over their opium stocks to Lin, in return for the British government promising to compensate them for their losses. However, the government had no intention of honouring this agreement because it rightly feared a backlash from the British public if it became known that Her Majesty's Government was protecting drug traffickers. The delighted Chinese commenced burning 20,000 chests of opium (each packed with 55kg of the drug) on 3 June 1839. There was so much 'foreign mud' that it took over twenty days to destroy. Lin wrote a 'memorial' to Queen Victoria, asking her to stop the opium trade, but this letter never reached Buckingham Palace and was conveniently ignored by the hawkish Foreign Secretary, Viscount Palmerston. The atmosphere all along the Chinese coast was tense during the summer of 1839.

The spark that opened general hostilities between Britain and China was an incident that occurred in the small fishing village of Tsim Sha Tsui (part of today's Kowloon, Hong Kong) in July 1839. At the end of June the skipper of the British tea clipper *Carnatic* had been arrested by the Chinese coast guard in Kowloon. On 7 July a large group of British and American sailors, many off the *Carnatic*, had gone ashore in Kowloon and discovered a supply of locally produced rice wine. Sufficiently liquored up, the mob of sailors had started a small riot in Tsim Sha Tsui, vandalised a local temple and murdered a Chinese man.

At the time, China lacked a jury trial system or evidentiary process. Britons were horrified at the mediaeval punishments that were dispensed by Chinese magistrates. The British government and Commissioner Elliot demanded that British subjects be granted 'extraterritoriality' for crimes committed in China, meaning that Britons would be tried by their own consular authorities and not subjected to local justice. Commissioner Lin demanded that the sailors suspected of murder be handed over, but Elliot refused. Instead, a British court in Canton tried them, found them guilty and transported them back to Britain, where they were promptly released.

On the issue of the 'no opium bond' that the Chinese demanded all foreign skippers sign, Elliot refused to agree and instead ordered that the British withdraw from Canton and cease trading with the Chinese. In order to enforce this order Elliot ordered two Royal Navy sloops, HMS *Volage* and *Hyacinth*, to lie off the Bocca Tigris, a narrow channel that runs between islands in the Pearl River Delta, to prevent British ships reaching Canton. The Chinese called the channel the *Humen* or 'Tiger Gate' and it was well named for the Chinese had fitted the islands with 'claws' – multiple forts well supplied with cannon.

Not all of the British were drug smugglers. Some ship owners refused to allow their vessels to carry opium for religious or moral reasons, and they saw no reason why their own profits should be damaged by Elliot's drastic measures to protect the drug traffickers. These owners and captains even agreed to sign the 'no opium bond' that the Chinese authorities demanded.

On 3 November 1839 the *Royal Saxon,* whose Quaker owners refused to take part in the opium trade, attempted to enter the Bocca Tigris and make her way upriver to Canton. Elliot ordered Captain Henry Smith aboard the *Volage* to stop the ship. The *Volage* fired a shot across the *Royal Saxon's* bows. Shortly afterwards a small fleet of Chinese war junks and other craft emerged from the mouth of the river under the command of 58-year-old Admiral Guan Tianpei, who was later admiringly described by the British as 'an altogether fine specimen of a gallant soldier'.[1] The Chinese naval commander moved out to protect the *Royal Saxon* from further illegal interference from the Royal Navy, triggering a full-scale naval battle between Britain and the Celestial Empire.

The *Volage* and *Hyacinth*, the latter a 106-foot long 18-gun Favourite-class sloop constructed in 1829, that had previously surveyed the northeast coast of Australia, went line ahead in battle formation and opened tremendous broadsides from starboard on the Chinese vessels. Gun ports stood open as British cannons mouthed great iron balls at the Chinese ships, or loosed off grapeshot that peppered the junks' sails and crew. The British ships were well armed and manoeuverable and they completely outclassed and outgunned Admiral Guan's junks.

The Chinese were facing the world's most technologically advanced and best disciplined navy, its ships officered by men who had fought under Admiral Nelson at Trafalgar or in a myriad other battles and landings from the West Indies to the Mediterranean, from the cold North Sea to the Cape of Good Hope. The Royal Navy bestrode the globe like a massive octopus; its men-of-war, frigates and gunboats protecting the sea-lanes for free trade, inserting military forces like projectiles onto hostile shores when required, and also mapping and exploring from Australia to the Arctic. Chinese naval warfare had scarcely evolved since the fifteenth century. It was the equivalent today of an F-15 supersonic jetfighter going head-to-head with a Sopwith Camel.

Within minutes one Chinese fire raft had sunk and a war junk blew up in a great cloud of fire and black smoke after a British shell tore into its magazine. It was a complete turkey shoot and a shocking display of British naval might. The action took place off Chuenpee Island, which was heavily defended by dug-in Chinese artillery and infantry in small forts and gun emplacements.

After an initial pass with all guns blazing, the two British warships came about and made a second pass firing port broadsides. Massive clouds of gunsmoke obscured the carnage as each deafening broadside did its grim work. Another huge junk blew up, three more sank, their hulls torn to pieces by solid shot, and several others were badly damaged and on fire. What was left of the Chinese fleet wisely retired upriver except for Admiral Guan's flagship, which bravely remained stationary and continued firing. Realising that the small Chinese guns were ineffective, Captain Elliot ordered Captain Smith to cease firing and Guan's damaged vessel retreated to safety. There was no honour in continuing to hit an opponent when he was already on the canvas, and the Royal Navy was nothing if not honourable.

HMS *Volage* had suffered some slight damage to her sails and rigging and the *Hyacinth's* mizzenmast had been holed by a Chinese cannon ball. One British sailor was wounded, while fifteen Chinese had been killed and four of their war junks sunk.

The *Royal Saxon*, the original catalyst of this ugly little battle, brazenly continued on her way to Canton while Elliot withdrew his ships to the nearby Portuguese colony of Macau as he knew that the Chinese would send fire boats down the river. This was the only real threat to the British wooden sailing vessels, tied as they were to the vagaries of wind and tide.

The first round of the First Opium War had decisively gone to Britain. China had revealed itself to be militarily obsolete and fundamentally weak – what some were already calling the 'sick man of Asia'. Such an easy victory only encouraged the British to press the Chinese further with the eventual goal of securing ports for their exclusive use. The seventeen battles that followed were as one-sided as those of the first. The British would manage to defeat the massive Chinese Empire for the loss of just seventy-four men. Chinese casualties were to be conservatively estimated in the tens of thousands and the ramifications of defeat were to be long and deep.

Foreign Secretary Lord Palmerston began hostilities to obtain compensation for the opium smugglers whose stocks had been burned by Commissioner Lin in Canton the year before. Opinion in Britain was deeply divided concerning the morality of such a war. The future prime minister William Gladstone denounced the war in the House of Commons as 'unjust and iniquitous', adding that Palmerston was too willing 'to protect an infamous centralised traffic'. There was also outrage in the British and American press, but regardless of public opinion the government was determined to press ahead with its punitive campaign against China and protect the drug trade. For it saw that as well as keeping the traders happy, land could be added to the growing empire. Niall Ferguson notes in *Empire* that 'whenever the British were behaving despotically, there was almost always a liberal critique of that behaviour from within British society.'[2] This is what set the British Empire apart from its European rivals, and such criticism was both consistent and loud in Britain against the Opium War, an important point that is often ignored today.

The twenty-nine British merchant ships that had evacuated Canton decided not to follow Captain Elliot's two warships to Macau, preferring the shelter of Hong Kong Harbour, then a largely uninhabited Chinese appendage. In early 1840, Elliot asked the Governor of Macau for permission for British ships to load and unload their cargoes in the Portuguese colony, offering to pay rents and duties. The governor sensibly refused, afraid that the emperor would cut off food supplies and other necessities to the enclave. Portugal had no desire to be dragged into a war with China.

On 14 January 1840 the emperor asked all foreigners to stop material aid to the British in China. The British government and the East India Company decided to take fast action by attacking the coast of Guangdong Province, the ultimate target being the capture of its capital city, Canton.

In June 1840, an expedition was outfitted in Singapore and sailed north for China. It consisted of fifteen warships carrying 4,000 Royal Marines and soldiers, four brand-new steam-powered gunboats and twenty-five smaller craft. A portion of this force first struck at Chusan (now Zhoushan) Island off Zhejiang Province in the middle of China on 5 July. In 1793 Lord Macartney had asked the Qianlong Emperor for 'a small unfortified island near Zhoushan for the residence of English traders, storage of goods, and outfitting of ships'.[3] The emperor had frostily refused, so now the British decided to take it anyway, and by force if necessary.

Four British warships arrived in the anchorage off Chusan Harbour on 4 July. The largest vessel was HMS *Wellesley*, a 1,745-ton 74-gun third-rate ship-of-the-line built in 1813. Aboard her was the expedition commander, Captain John Fletcher. Accompanying the *Wellesley* was HMS *Conway*, a 651-ton sixth-rate armed with twenty 32-pounders and six 18-pounder carronades (referring to the weight of the shells these guns fired), and two Atholl-class 28-gun sixth-rates, the appropriately named *Alligator* and *Rattlesnake*.

Negotiations were attempted on 4 July when Captain Fletcher boarded a Chinese war junk accompanied by Viscount Jocelyn,

secretary to Major General Lord Saltoun, and a Prussian missionary interpreter named Karl Gutzlaff. Fletcher delivered a written
message from Commodore Sir James Bremer, 53-year-old Naval
Commander-in-Chief and Brigadier General George Burrell, who
commanded the landing troops. Bremer was to figure prominently
in the coming war.

A Napoleonic Wars veteran, Bremer had seen extensive service
in English, Canadian, Mediterranean and East Indies waters and
had been involved in the colonisation of Australia. In 1836, Bremer
had been made a Knight Commander of the Royal Hanoverian
Guelphic Order and after the original naval commander in China,
Rear Admiral Sir Frederick Maitland, had died, he had succeeded
him to the post. Bremer alternated this position with Captain
Elliot.

The local Chinese governor of the Chusan Islands, Admiral
Chang, was requested to surrender immediately. 'If the inhabitants
of the said islands do not oppose and resist our forces, it is not
the intention of the British Government to do injury to their
persons and property'. The message further stated: 'If you will not
surrender, we, the Commodore and Commander, shall be obliged
to use warlike measures for obtaining possession.'[4] The Royal
Navy, scourge of pirates all over the world, was now applying
piratical methods with shameless alacrity.

After an hour of largely fruitless discussions, Admiral Chang and
some local officials from the capital city Ting-hai (now Dinghai)
were invited aboard the *Wellesley*. Chang and the others told
Bremer and Burrell that they were extremely annoyed with being
held responsible for the actions of Commissioner Lin in Canton,
stating 'those are the people you should make war upon, and not
upon us who never injured you; we see your strength, and know
that opposition will be madness, but we must perform our duty
if we fall in so doing.' Unimpressed, Bremer gave Chang until
daybreak on 5 July to surrender or military action would follow.

On the appointed day there was no sign of a Chinese surrender,
indeed lookouts reported over 1,000 Chinese troops manning
prepared positions on the beaches, surrounding hills and Ting-hai
city walls located one mile from the sea. At 2pm the brigs HMS
Cruizer and *Algerine* moved into position off Chusan Island and
the scarlet-coated landing troops began embarking in cutters. The

first division consisted of the 18th Royal Irish Regiment, Royal Marines, 26th Regiment of Foot and two 9-pounder guns. The second division comprised the 49th Regiment of Foot, Madras Sappers & Miners and a unit of Bengal Volunteers.

At 2.30pm the *Wellesley* suddenly opened fire on the Chinese beach defences as the landing boats were rowed towards the shore, the two gun decks blasting out broadsides for seven or eight minutes of concentrated firing. The effect on the Chinese was devastating – after firing a few desultory shots in reply the Chinese troops simply abandoned their positions and fled back towards the protection of the city walls. Judging by Admiral Chang's words spoken aboard the *Wellesley* the day before, he had probably given orders for a token defence only for the sake of his honour (and his head), and wished to save his men's lives. At any rate the British troops landed unopposed and discovered an empty beach with abandoned gun pits littered with dead bodies and discarded weapons and equipment. The British captured ninety-one Chinese cannon.

Next, the British rolled their two 9-pounder naval guns to within 400 yards of the Ting-hai city walls, later adding another brace of 9-pounders, two howitzers and two mortars. But Bremer told the ad hoc battery to hold fire until the following day. The damage that these guns could have done to a crowded city was not lost on the Chinese: they quietly retired and when a British reconnaissance party approached a city gate they found it barricaded with sandbags, though undefended. There was no desire among the British to inflict unnecessary casualties on the Chinese. A company of the 49th Regiment captured the gate and hoisted the Union Jack above it. 'The main street was nearly deserted, except here and there, where the frightened people were performing the kow-tow as we passed,' recalled Viscount Jocelyn. 'On most of the houses was placarded "Spare our lives" and on entering the jos-houses [temples] were seen men, women, and children, on their knees, burning incense to the gods.'[5] Total British casualties amounted to one man wounded.

On 7 July the recently promoted Rear Admiral Elliot aboard HMS *Melville* issued a proclamation that stated that the Chinese on Chusan would continue to be administered under Chinese laws, with ultimate executive authority invested in the British commander-in-chief. Elliot appointed Brigadier General Burrell governor, and interpreter Gutzlaff chief magistrate. Britain now had a safe anchorage off the Chinese mainland for the forthcoming campaign to capture Canton.

Canton was located some miles up the Pearl River, the passage well protected by a series of heavily fortified islands, as well as a myriad of waterways, sand bars and other obstacles to navigation. The British were forced to conduct over a dozen operations to capture or destroy emplaced Chinese forces before they could invest Canton, as well as striking at other places along the Chinese coast. One of the most invaluable weapons at the disposal of the British was the steam-driven warship, which enabled the Royal Navy to operate in Chinese rivers and to manoeuver at will, free of the wind. The Chinese had not seen anything like it before and it was truly a turning point in the history of naval warfare.

The first of these operations came to be called the Battle of the Barrier, and it occurred on the boundary between Portuguese Macau and mainland China on 19 August 1840. A narrow, sandy isthmus separated Macau from the mainland. Facing the border and defending the eastern side of the isthmus were Chinese breastworks that contained about 1,500 troops with emplaced artillery. British warships moved into the shoalwater on the eastern side of the isthmus. The Chinese had positioned eight war junks along the western flank of the isthmus to provide covering fire.

At noon on 19 August, Captain Henry Smith aboard HMS *Hyacinth* prepared to attack. Alongside the *Hyacinth* was HMS *Larne*, a cutter named *Louisa* and the steamboat HMS *Enterprise*. The vessels opened fire at the Chinese positions onshore, which promptly returned that fire, and the junks attempted to join in. 'The junks, which were aground in the inner harbour, were utterly useless, for none of their guns could be brought to bear, though several of the thirty-two pound shots of the ships found their way over the bank, much to the consternation of the occupants of the junks,'[6] recalled Lieutenant John Bingham.

Once the bombardment had done its work, Captain Smith ordered his landing force into action. This consisted of 110 Royal Marines, ninety armed seamen from HMS *Druid* and 180 Bengal Volunteers. Little fighting was encountered and the British suffered only four men wounded. Between 100 and 180 Chinese were killed or injured during this short battle and many cannon captured.

The British now believed that they had some leverage with which to negotiate concessions from the Chinese and perhaps avoid further costly naval operations. In October 1840, the Daoguang Emperor dismissed Commissioner Lin and replaced him with Qi Shan, a 54-year-old Manchu nobleman and former provincial viceroy. Lord Palmerston instructed Elliot to have the ports of Canton, Amoy, Foochow (now Fuzhou), Ningpo (now Ningbo) and Shanghai opened to British trade. London also instructed Elliot to acquire the cession of an island off the Chinese coast, and obtain financial compensation for destroyed opium and attendant naval and military costs. Elliot initially demanded seven million Chinese dollars in compensation to be paid over six years and the surrender of Canton and Amoy as permanent British possessions. Commissioner Qi refused, offering five million over twelve years – the two men eventually agreed upon six million Chinese dollars. Qi refused, however, to countenance any territorial concessions, as the emperor would not stand for it.

Elliot offered to abandon recently captured Chusan Island for another port to be decided later. Again, Qi refused. Exasperated, Elliot warned Qi directly: 'There are very large forces collected here,' he said, referring to the large numbers of British warships and troops at the mouth of the Bocca Tigris. 'Delays must breed amongst them a very great impatience.'

No settlement could be reached for months as the Chinese determined not to permit a permanent British presence in their country. Rumours circulated among the foreigners that the emperor meant for war. Finally, on 5 January 1841, Elliot told Commodore Bremer to prepare for an attack on Canton. He informed Commissioner Qi that unless British demands were met a general assault would be launched in two days time.

When no reply was forthcoming from the Chinese, Elliot gave orders to Bremer to begin the assault. At 9am on 7 January, a large force of British Indian troops (504 Royal Marines, 33 Royal Artillery, 104 men from the 26th and 49th Foot, 76 Bengal Volunteers, 607 of the 37th Madras Native Infantry and 137 sailors) landed from the warships *Wellesley*, *Blenheim* and *Melville* two miles below the Chuenpee batteries. In command ashore was Major Simson Pratt,

26th Foot. The landing was unopposed by some 2,000 Chinese defenders. Accompanying the infantry force was another thirty seamen manhandling a 24-pounder howitzer and two 6-pounder field guns.

The British force advanced two miles inland until they came upon a strong Chinese defensive position: two forts with many dug-in cannon surrounded by a protective ditch and breastworks. When the British approached, Chinese soldiers started cheering and yelling, waving flags and then opening fire with their cannon. The naval artillery had been established on a nearby hill and the seamen opened fire on the forts, the two sides trading shot for perhaps twenty minutes. In the meantime Bremer ordered his ships to move in and bombard the two Chinese forts. A squadron consisting of HMS *Queen* and HMS *Nemesis* under the command of Captain Edward Belcher, poured fire onto the upper fort. He would be the first person to survey Hong Kong Harbour in 1841.

Commanding the second squadron to bombard the lower Chinese fort was Captain Sir Thomas Herbert, a veteran of both the Battle of Trafalgar in 1805 and the War of 1812. Herbert's division consisted of HMS *Calliope*, *Hyacinth* and *Larne*.

The effect of the naval bombardment was devastating and both Chinese forts were silenced in less than an hour. By 10am the upper fort was in British hands while the Royal Marines stormed the lower fort at the point of the bayonet.

In Anson's Bay, fifteen Chinese war junks under Admiral Guan Tianpei attempted to disrupt the British operations. HMS *Nemesis*, a 660-ton iron paddle frigate known to the Chinese as 'the Devil ship' fired a single rocket at one large junk, causing a catastrophic explosion that completely demolished the vessel. 'It blew up with a terrific explosion,' recalled a British witness, 'launching into eternity every soul on board, and pouring forth its blaze like the mighty rush of fire from a volcano.'[7] Dismembered bodies rained down along with masses of debris. In a short space of time, another ten junks were destroyed by accurate British gunnery. The other junks struck their colours by about 11.30am after witnessing this horrifying spectacle.

The next phase of the operation was by this stage fully underway, commanded by 50-year-old Napoleonic Wars and War of 1812-veteran, Captain James Scott, aboard HMS *Samarang*. Scott attacked

Tycocktow Island to the west of Chuenpee Island, aiming to knock out the forts that were armed with 191 cannon. The forts opened fire at 10.20am. The *Samarang* manoeuvered to a position just 200 yards from the main fort, dropped anchor and proceeded to unleash repeated deadly broadsides against the Chinese positions. The *Samarang* was joined by *Modeste, Druid* and *Columbine,* and together they unleashed hell. Within ten minutes the British ships had silenced the Chinese guns, with the exception of one or two, and Scott ordered cutters containing his landing parties to row for the shore and storm the forts. The Chinese remained inside the forts surrounded by smashed cannons and equipment and the British marines and blue-jacketed sailors fought their way in. After taking the forts and 100 prisoners, the Chinese guns were spiked and thrown into the river.

The battle ended with a complete British victory. Between 500 and 600 Chinese had been killed along with 200–300 wounded. The British suffered just thirty-eight men wounded. The forts that defended the entrance to the Bocca Tigris had been captured and the way was open for the next phase of the campaign to capture Canton.

For the Chinese, the battle was an unmitigated disaster with serious political consequences. Why had the British been so easily able to defeat them? The answer may lie in the Chinese administrative system, which was riddled with corruption and self-interest that led to military paralysis when decisive action was called for. Officials have always been masters of self-protection and, in the case of a well armed and aggressive adversary like the British hammering on the national door, Chinese officials fretted about the 'correct' response, hence the token resistance put up by various Chinese admirals and generals during the First Opium War. Chinese officials would order a half-hearted defence largely so that when they lost the battle they could claim that it was not their fault but due to outside factors, notably their opponent's technological advantages. In this way, the officials generally kept their positions and sinecures, and most vitally, their heads. Officials always looked to their superiors for orders, orders that were often not forthcoming or vague when given – the result was passivity when firm action was required. Chinese mandarins, military officers and local officials simply hunkered down and waited for the British storm to pass, made the correct noises and generally survived the typhoon to continue their corrupt and self-serving governance.

The Chinese were prepared to negotiate and horse trade with the British in the hope that a few territorial concessions would satisfy the land-hungry barbarians, and these diplomatic moves were as opaque as everything else in China. The British were exasperated by the long-winded Chinese way of negotiating and this led to more frustration and fighting.

Following the British victory, Admiral Elliot met with Commissioner Qi on 20 January 1841 to sign a convention with regard to Canton. The port city, it was agreed, would be opened for trade by 2 February. This date came and went, and still the Chinese did not open the city. On 11–12 February a further meeting was held at the Bocca Tigris. Elliot gave the Chinese another ten days to open Canton. Commodore Bremer was less than impressed with the Chinese attitude: 'I must confess that from this moment my faith in the Chinese Commissioner was completely destroyed.'[8]

Officers witnessed a build-up of Chinese strength on North Wangtong Island, and on 13 February Bremer dispatched HMS *Nemesis* to Canton where she was ordered to remain until 18 February, awaiting Commissioner Qi's reply to the British terms. On the morning of the 19th the *Nemesis* returned without any reply from the Chinese having materialised. As the vessel passed North Wangtong Island she was fired on. The Lieutenant-Governor of Canton offered 30,000 Chinese dollars for the heads of Elliot and Bremer, or 50,000 dollars if they were taken alive.

In the meantime the Chinese had received some reinforcements. On 21 February, General Xiang and 1,000 regular soldiers from Hunan arrived in Canton followed by General Yang and 1,000 Yunnan troops. Commissioner Qi inspected these new arrivals and their defensive positions on 24–26 February, just as the British were further reducing his defences down river.

Chapter 2

Harrying the Coast

*Finding dead bodies of Tartars in every house we entered,
principally women and children, thrown into wells or otherwise murdered by their own people, I was glad to withdraw the
troops from this frightful scene of destruction.*

Major General Hugh Gough, 1842

Captain Thomas Herbert aboard the devil ship *Nemesis*, accompanied by Admiral Elliot, sailed the back passage past Anunghoy
Island in the Pearl River on 23 February 1841. Herbert, a member
of the Irish landed gentry who had joined the navy in 1803 and had
served worldwide, including fighting pirates off Cuba and Mexico,
had sailed to China via the perilous Cape Horn route in 1840
aboard the *Calliope*.

The *Nemesis* led an assault force that consisted of *Calliope*,
Samarang, *Herald*, and *Alligator*. Without warning the vessels ran
into a masked Chinese battery. The offending battery was quickly
captured after light Chinese resistance. Twenty or thirty Chinese
were killed for no British casualties and eighty cannon captured.

Three days later, the British fleet attacked the forts on Anunghoy
and North Wangtong Islands. Captain Sir Humphrey Senhouse
aboard HMS *Blenheim* commanded the assault on Anunghoy,
assisted by the *Melville*, *Queen* and four rocket boats. 59-year-old
Senhouse, a Trafalgar veteran who had already been in the Navy
for forty-three years, had been mentioned in despatches for his
gallantry during the fighting in America in 1813 and had been
knighted first by Hanover in 1832 and then by Britain two years

later. In 1839 he had been appointed second-in-command of naval forces in China.

The South Anunghoy Fort was reduced first, the *Blenheim* dropping anchor 600 yards distant and firing concentrated broadsides. Five minutes later the *Melville* anchored just 400 yards from the fort and opened fire. The Chinese made a desultory reply and then their gun crews fled. Senhouse immediately landed 300 Royal Marines who quickly overwhelmed the few remaining defenders and captured the fort. Within two hours of the operation starting all of Anunghoy's forts were in British hands.

Admiral Guan Tianpei had been killed in one of the forts along with over 200 of his men. Family members identified his body on 27 February, and HMS *Blenheim* fired a gun salute in Guan's honour as his body was being repatriated. It was an interesting gesture in the midst of a bloody campaign and was indicative of the British attitude towards their adversaries. A British officer wrote of Guan: 'His death excited much sympathy throughout the force, he fell by bayonet wound in his breast, as he was meeting the enemy at the gate of Anunghoy, yielding up his brave spirit willingly to do a soldier's death, when his life could only be preserved through the entertaining of degradation.'[1]

Now it was the turn of the north fort. The warships *Wellesley*, *Samarang*, *Druid*, *Herald*, *Alligator* and *Modeste* bombarded North Wangtong Island into bloody submission. The batteries, manned by over 2,000 Chinese soldiers, were silenced in less than an hour. Major Thomas Pratt led the landing party ashore that consisted of 1,037 troops from the 26th and 49th Foot, 37th Madras Native Infantry, Bengal Volunteers and Royal Marines. During the short fighting that followed the British lost five men wounded while the Chinese suffered 250 killed or wounded and 1,300 taken prisoner. The disparity in casualties was glaring. Pratt's troops captured a staggering 339 Chinese cannon.

Another series of Chinese river defences had been dealt with taking the British a step closer to Canton. On 27 February *Calliope*, *Herald*, *Alligator*, *Sulpher*, *Modeste*, *Madagascar* and *Nemesis* resumed their advance up the Canton River from the Bocca Tigris. The ships passed Tiger Island and Second Bar before they reached First Bar Island at noon. Here the British spotted the 34-gun former East Indiaman *Cambridge* flying the red flag of a Chinese admiral.

Field fortifications mounted forty-seven cannon, and row upon row of white tents in the paddy fields beyond marked the camp of the regular Imperial Chinese reinforcements from Hunan and Yunnan. Upriver loitered over forty war junks. It seemed clear to British officers surveying this array of defences with telescopes, that the Chinese still had plenty of fight left in them.

The Chinese gun positions opened fire and *Modeste* quickly closed to within 300 yards of the shore and returned fire with interest. Rockets from the *Madagascar* and *Nemesis* screamed off in the direction of the Chinese camp, setting much of it on fire. The *Cambridge*, the only modern ship that the Chinese possessed, opened fire, but British warships battered her mercilessly, with most of her crew jumping overboard and swimming for the shore. The war junks wisely stayed well out of range of the British broadsides, their crews watching the seeming inexorable progress of the barbarians up the river with awe, anger and fear.

After an hour of trading fire with the Chinese, Captain Herbert ordered the landings to commence. 'I landed with the seamen and marines,' he wrote, 'and stormed the works, driving before us upwards of two thousand of their best troops, and killing nearly three hundred.'[2] Every Chinese fort was in British hands within thirty minutes of the first landing, an incredible testament to the fighting qualities of the troops involved, and once again a damning indictment of poor Chinese leadership and tactical acumen.

Lieutenant Watson and a party of seamen boarded the battered *Cambridge* and captured the vessel after a short but sharp hand-to-hand fight with the remaining Chinese crew. The ship's magazine was deliberately exploded just after dark. In total, the British lost one man killed and eight wounded during the entire operation. Chinese losses were again astoundingly heavy – General Xiang and about 300 of his men fell, while another 300 were wounded. Another ninety-eight cannon were captured and disposed of by the British. It was fast shaping up into one of the most one-sided wars in history.

On 2 March, Bremer dispatched Captain Belcher and HMS *Sulphur* to reconnoitre the Junk River, one of the many waterways that led into Canton. Lacking an engine, the *Sulphur* was being towed down the river by three ship's boats under the command of Lieutenant Richard Symonds when twenty-five dug-in guns on Whampoa Island (now the Huangpu District of Guangzhou) opened fire. Symonds immediately ordered the towlines cut and then the three cutters pulled hard for the island and landed. The sailors, who were not trained infantrymen, stormed the forts that were defended by 250 Chinese troops, and put them to flight into the nearby jungle where they were harried by cannon fire from the *Sulphur*. The British captured the forts for the loss of only one man, destroyed all of the guns and blew up the magazines. Between fifteen and twenty Chinese were killed.

Major General Hugh Gough arrived at the British fleet aboard HMS *Cruizer* to take over command of all future land operations from Commodore Bremer. Gough was one of the 19th century's most celebrated soldiers who, by the end of his career, had commanded more general actions than any other army officer except the Duke of Wellington. Born into an Anglo-Irish family in 1779, Gough was commissioned in 1794 into the 78th Highlanders with whom he had served in Southern Africa and the West Indies. With the 87th (Royal Irish Fusiliers) he had taken part in the attack on Puerto Rico and later captured Surinam. During the Peninsula War, Gough had served under Wellington and was wounded several times, including at the crucial battle of Talavera. For his services on the Iberian Peninsula, Gough was knighted by King Charles III of Spain and promoted to major general in 1830. He was to prove indispensable during the First Opium War when energetic generalship was required, and was appointed commander-in-chief of British land forces. The Chinese never managed to find their own Gough to rally and lead their own forces with determination and energy. Their system of military patronage simply did not produce such officers at the time.

HMS *Nemesis* and three other vessels under Captain James Scott were sent on a reconnaissance of the Broadway River, another of the Pearl's tributaries, as the British probed for a way into Canton. On 13 March, the British vessels came under fire from Houching Fort and from a collection of war junks. In a short, sharp little fight the fort was first silenced and then stormed, and the junks blasted out of the water. 115 Chinese guns were captured and nine junks sunk. British casualties were again ludicrously small – just three men wounded.

British forces now approached their prize – Canton. The Chinese defences looked formidable, but judging by their previous desultory performances in the battles to defend the Pearl River, the British were not overly worried. Nevertheless, what was to happen at Canton was surprising and historical.

The British assault on Canton began on 18 March 1841 when four divisions of ships approached from the western and southern branches of the river. The British would quickly take the wharf and docks but the rest of Canton was well defended. As usual, the Chinese relied on static forts armed with cannon. A battery of nine guns in a sandbagged position defended the Canton Wharf. The Macao Passage, a waterway leading into the city, contained two large forts. The Lower Battery was armed with twenty-two cannon and the Upper Battery with nine. Western Fort contained ten guns that covered the city suburbs, which stretched from the river to the city walls. The foreigners' trading area, or Canton Factories, was defended by the Red Fort mustering twenty cannon. Another fort named Dutch Folly was mounted with twenty-five guns, while the Chinese Arsenal was covered by another sandbagged position with thirteen cannon. Finally, the Chinese had moored two junks opposite the Admiral's House on the waterfront, armed with fifteen guns.

The British determined to capture the wharf area and the foreign trading buildings, the main target being the two-story Old British Factory. Leading the assault was Captain Bourchier. By noon on 18 March, the British had silenced and then stormed the batteries defending the Macao Channel. HMS *Modeste* was placed 300 yards in front of the principal Chinese battery, while the *Madagascar* quickly joined in the bombardment. HMS *Algerine* and *Starling* passed on ahead, cutting through the other British ships. They engaged the Chinese war junks and destroyed them all. The tenders *Hebe* and *Louisa*, under the cover of the warships' guns, landed Royal Marines who swiftly completed the capture of the Canton Wharf area and the foreign factories despite quite determined Chinese resistance. A general advance soon carried the landing parties to the British Factory, from which the Union Jack was triumphantly hoisted to cheers and much waving of shakos and muskets.

HMS *Herald* had diverted Chinese attention at a critical point during the battle, drawing off some of their fire whilst the landings were underway. Captain Bourchier was the hero of the hour. His quick actions at the conclusion of the fighting undoubtedly saved Canton's suburbs and the hundreds of thousands of Chinese living there from a major disaster. 'I cannot refrain mentioning Bourchier's conspicuous and energetic exertions in towing off the burning junks,' wrote Captain Herbert to Commodore Bremer, 'which were drifting upon the suburbs of Canton, and soon would have evidently set fire to that part of the city, and involved the destruction of the whole.'[3]

The port of Canton, excluding the walled city, was now under British occupation for the cost of only seven wounded. The Chinese had suffered over 400 casualties. The Chinese were not content to let the British control the port, and less than three months later they made a determined effort to drive the invaders back into the river. The British had set up defensive positions and these were unsuccessfully assaulted by thousands of Chinese on 21 May 1841. The British decided that the only way to prevent further attacks was to capture the entire of Canton, meaning the great walled city: an extremely hazardous undertaking.

Canton, a city of one and a half million, was defended by a massive wall thirty feet high. 30–40,000 men garrisoned the wall and several forts that were located outside the city gates. The city was surrounded by flooded paddy fields, forcing an approaching army onto two-foot wide bunds, or mud banks, that meant that only the smallest artillery guns could be dragged forward. The British decided to try and capture the high ground north of the city wall and the banks of the river running along the west side of the city.

Two forces were available to the British. The Royal Navy would land around 1,000 Royal Marines and sailors, while General Gough commanded 2,223 British and Indian soldiers. The 23 May was spent reconnoitering the Chinese positions by land and water, and gathering up local sampans and junks that could be used to land the assault forces. The main landing was scheduled for the morning of the 24th. Two columns would be used, with Gough commanding the right column that included Captain Bourchier and his Naval Brigade. As the 24th was also Queen Victoria's birthday a general gun salute was fired, undoubtedly a mystifying event to the local defenders.

The right column landed safely at noon, piloted through the river by Captain Belcher. A unit of the 49th Foot quickly threw out picquets to protect the landing point. The main column set off on foot the next morning, the Chinese keeping their distance. As the column approached the city walls the men could make out four large forts positioned on the steep northern heights, each fort circular or square in shape and bristling with cannon. The city walls were also lined with guns and gingals, large-calibre two-man Chinese blunderbusses. The 49th Foot swiftly occupied various heights while the 37th Madras Native Infantry was ordered to occupy a height to the left of the outermost fort.

The 18th Royal Irish and the Royal Marines took a height opposite a square tower in the city wall, while the Naval Brigade occupied heights to the right of this position in front of two oblong forts near Canton's mighty North Gate. From these positions the British attempted to storm the forts and walls. Large numbers of Chinese troops crowded the defences, colourful banners flying in the wind. The 49th Foot first entered both of the forts on the left with the 37th Madras close behind. After a few shots were exchanged the Chinese garrisons fled to the city and both forts were swiftly occupied.

'At this moment our situation was not the most secure in face of a force, which by all accounts, must have amounted to 40,000 men,' wrote Captain Humphrey Senhouse. 'We had gained the exterior forts gallantly, but a warm fire soon came from the town walls, and numerous bodies advanced, drew out, and came under the ridges within pistol shot of our gate.' Chinese infantry in formed units attempted to close with the British head-on while another large party tried to cut Gough's communications back to the beach. 'The skirmishers were, however, soon driven back, and in their retreat drawing our troops after them,' noted Senhouse.

'Our men were warmly fired at from the heights, divided from them by a rice field, two narrow paths only led to it, but the Royal Irish led in the most gallant manner by Captains Grattan and Sergeant on one pathway, the former of whom encouraged his grenadiers amidst a heavy fire, preceding them at some distance.'[4] The 18th Royal Irish commanding officer, Lieutenant Colonel

Adams, led a second group along the pathway on the left. They were reinforced by a company of Royal Marines from HMS *Druid* under Lieutenant Maxwell, the Chinese quickly abandoning the height. They also started to leave their tented camp on the reverse slope, this movement rapidly descending into a rout.

In the afternoon the British and Chinese exchanged artillery and rocket fire, British shells setting fire to some sections of Canton. On the morning of the 25th a white flag unexpectedly appeared on the town walls. 'An interpreter was sent to inquire what was wanted,' wrote Senhouse, to whom the Chinese officer stated, 'they would fight no more', and begged to see the general commanding the troops.'[5]

The Chinese were told that they must produce their own General by 3.30pm or the firing would continue, the British insisting that General Gough would only treat with his Chinese counterpart in rank. When the appointed hour came and went and no Chinese general appeared Gough did not order the bombardment to recommence, noting, 'it would have been easy to have burned the town.' Heavy rain started and the troops instead spent their time preparing to assault the massive city walls. The British wanted to avoid unnecessary destruction. 'The General and myself were equally of the opinion that such a measure [a bombardment] should only be resorted to as a last resort,' wrote Senhouse, 'and that the storming of the walls, and the possession of the heights within, would be a sufficient and unquestioned proof of the city being at our mercy.'[6]

On 27 May, the troops were ready to storm the city – Gough and his staff had estimated that it would take two hours to seize the walls. But a dispatch arrived from Rear Admiral Elliot proposing instead that terms be sought with the Chinese and the military operation delayed until noon. In the event, the storming was delayed for far longer.

In the meantime the citizenry of Canton, fed up with the incompetence of the Manchu troops sent to defend them, began to take up arms themselves and formed a citizens army that was soon several thousand strong. Elements of this force began to approach to the north of the main British camp on 30 May. A detachment that consisted of Captain Hatfield and one company of the 37th Madras was sent out to drive them off. But the exceptionally heavy rain meant that the Indian sepoys' flintlock muskets were rendered unusable. When the Chinese realised that the small Indian force had no firepower they quickly closed in with edged weapons 'and came to close quarters with them boldly and bravely.'[7]

The colonial Indian Army was always a step behind the regular British Army technologically and this was cruelly exposed before Canton. The flintlock musket, which had been in service in one form or another since the 1660s, was in the process of being replaced by the new percussion musket in 1839. Rain meant that a flintlock's flashpan powder would become wet, failing to ignite when struck by the weapon's flint. The new percussion cap removed the need for a flint, steel frizzen, and powder pan as the cap was fitted with explosive fulminate of mercury, and though fiddly to fit during combat, made the weapon impervious to weather. The Indian regiments had not been issued with these new weapons.

By nightfall Captain Hatfield and his sepoys were surrounded, but 'they with the great coolness and devotion of their lives, formed into a square, and awaited with perfect sang-froid the endeavour to destroy them by the [Chinese] long-lance over the charged bayonet.'[8] In the centre, a couple of officers had managed to keep their powder dry and they fired an occasional shot at the Chinese. It looked as though the Chinese would overwhelm the small force by sheer weight of numbers 'if a company of the Blenheim's marines, with percussion muskets, under Lieut. Whiting of that Corps, commanded by Captain Duff of the 37th native infantry had not then sent in quest of them,' reported Senhouse. 'A musket fired, was happily answered from the square, three cheers were exchanged, the marines coming up, gave their volley – they re-loaded and fired once more, and the brave Sepoys were liberated.'[9]

The British decided not to attempt to storm the city on 31 May, following a meeting between General Gough and the Chinese Governor. One reason was that the extremely large Chinese citizens' army was a real threat during land operations far from the protection of the fleet's heavy guns, and the British did not have sufficient manpower to engage in a costly house-to-house fight for the city. They also had no desire to raze it to the ground. But they had made their point. On 1 June, the British troops withdrew in good order from the four forts they had occupied and by 8.30pm every man was back aboard the ships. British losses amounted to fifteen killed and 137 wounded, the first serious casualties sustained during the war reflecting the determination of the citizens of Canton to defend their city. Chinese losses were 1,000 killed and over 3,000 wounded.

After a period of rest and reorganisation the British decided to capture some of the ports that the British government had asked the Chinese to open to trade. The first target was Amoy (now Xiamen) in Fujian Province. On 26 August 1841, an invasion force numbering 2,500 troops and fifteen ships appeared off heavily fortified Gulangyu Island opposite the city. The island contained a large Chinese garrison and 500 cannon. Hugh Gough remained in command of the troops while 60-year-old Rear Admiral William Parker led the naval force from the 74-gun *Wellesley*. Parker had been a young officer at the famous Battle of The Glorious First of June, and had later served under Nelson. In 1828 he had commanded King William IV's royal yacht and later the Channel Squadron under Sir Edward Codrington. Now he was commander-in-chief East Indies and China Squadron and would shortly be created a baronet by Queen Victoria.

The British followed the usual pattern of naval bombardment swiftly followed by a landing. The Royal Navy ships battered Gulangyu's defences for four hours, but with little apparent effect. Eventually Parker ordered the troops and marines ashore to take out the well-protected gun batteries. It was a stiflingly hot day and the British forces suffered badly from heat exhaustion and water shortages. Once again, Chinese troops refused to fight for their positions and after a short but desultory resistance the British forces, led by the 18th Royal Irish, captured the defences for the loss of only two men killed and fifteen wounded. Chinese casualties were heavy.

The next day the remaining Chinese garrison of Amoy pulled out without a fight and the British occupied the city. The 18th Royal Irish and HMS *Druid*, *Pylades* and *Algerine* garrisoned and protected the island. Within a short time British and other foreign traders began to arrive, quickly turning Gulangyu Island into a secure little enclave under British protection.

On 29 September, the British fleet returned to Chusan Island, which duly fell to them the following day, 1 October 1841, for a cost of two killed and twenty-seven men wounded. The Chinese casualties were, as usual, horrific, with over 1,500 killed.

Next on the target list was the port city of Ningpo in Fujian Province. However, before moving on the city the British were first compelled to storm and occupy the town of Chinhai (now Zhenhai) which stands on the mouth of the Ningpo (now Yong) River twelve miles northeast of Ningpo. As usual the Chinese had strongly fortified the town's approaches with gun emplacements and a sizeable army that numbered 8–9,000 men. The British landing force, once more under Hugh Gough, consisted of 2,098 soldiers and marines.

The left column, consisting of the 55th Foot and 18th Royal Irish, landed two miles west of Chinhai on the west bank of the river, and crossed a large swamp and two wooden bridges over a canal. The right column, mostly the 49th Foot, landed on a promontory a mile west of Chinhai, advanced inland and linked up with the left column assaulting various Chinese gun emplacements on a line of hills. Ten warships bombarded the Chinese positions. The river was blocked at its mouth by a line of huge iron pikes and sunken junks. Once through the outermost defences the British speedily took the city gates and occupied Chinhai.

On 9 March 1842, a large force of Chinese approached the city's West Gate firing gingals, trying to force it open. A light company of the 55th Foot commanded by Captain Danbeney drove the enemy out into the suburbs beyond the gate. This tiny force of fifty British soldiers took on 1,200 Chinese a mile beyond the gate. 'Danbeney immediately attacked them,' wrote Colonel T.H. Schoedde, Chinhai garrison commandant, 'and put them to flight, pursuing them with as much celerity as he could.'[10] The Chinese disappeared into the maze of alleyways and streets, destroyed several canal bridges as they went, and then vanished. At least two Chinese officers and thirty men were killed.

It was now the turn of the South Gate to be attacked. The guards were overwhelmed by the sheer weight of Chinese numbers and they fell back. Captain McAndrew took a company of the 49th Foot and proceeded down the street that led to the gate. The Chinese had taken the gate and managed to penetrate to the market place in the centre of Chinhai. 'McAndrew instantly commenced street firing, and also made several charges with the bayonet on the head of the enemy's column,' recalled Schoedde, 'and finally succeeded in driving them out of the city with very great loss.'[11]

The Chinese surged back to attack the West Gate again, which was defended by a company of the 10th Royal Irish under Lieutenant Armstrong reinforced by a detachment of the 49th Foot under Lieutenant Grant. Colonel Schoedde rushed up Lieutenant Mitchell and another company of the 49th and followed along himself with a final reinforcement company. The fighting was intense. Without orders a party from the 18th Royal Irish under Lieutenant Murray and a pair of Madras Artillery field guns personally commanded by the 49th Foot's Lieutenant Colonel P. Montgomerie arrived in the nick of time.

Montgomerie and Lieutenant Colonel Armine Mountain, Deputy Adjutant General, and a party from the 26th Cameronians stormed through the West Gate in pursuit of the Chinese. Grant led the charge. 'This officer had made a sally across the bridge. The dead bodies of 10 or 12 of the enemy lying close to the gate and on the bridge sufficiently betoken both the determination of the assailants, and the gallantry of the defence.'[12] Schoedde followed 'and upon reaching the centre of the suburb the carnage was perfectly frightful.'[13]

What had occurred in the suburb was an appallingly bloody close-quarters action in which British fire discipline and modern weaponry had ultimately proved decisive. Only about 100 men under Grant, Montgomerie and Mountain had gone forward. 'At a distance of about half a mile at a turn in the street, we came on the enemy in great force,' recalled Montgomerie, 'the whole street, as far as the eye could reach, was a dense mass; the leading portion (among whom a mounted mandarin was conspicuous) brandished their swords and spears, cheered each other with their voices, and appeared determined to stand their ground, if not rush on us.' Massively outnumbered, the British braced themselves, Montgomerie recalling that had the Chinese charged 'they must have swept our small force before them.'[14]

But it was the British who attacked first. 'We advanced, the head of our column delivering their fire, and the next section taking their place, till within twelve to fifteen paces of the enemy; by this time the howitzer was brought to the front.' The gun was wheeled up to virtually point blank range and fired. 'Three rounds of grape in quick succession told with tremendous effect.'[15] The Chinese fled, their column stretching fully a mile along the canal with the tiny British force in hot pursuit for eight miles, Colonel Schoedde recording that 'in the course of the pursuit [the British] killed considerable numbers.'[16] The British estimated that a Chinese army around 5,000 strong had assaulted Chinhai. The British killed 500–600 and took thirty-nine prisoners. Only three British soldiers were wounded during this epic fight.

With Chinhai secured, and the Chinese army routed, the British also invested the more significant port of Ningpo. The Chinese, under Commissioner Yi Kong, mounted further attempts to re-capture both cities, but British forces left the cities and brought them to battle out in the open, where their disciplined musketry and modern artillery would be most effective.

General Ye Puyun advanced from Tunghwa with an army of 6–7,000 men. Recently promoted Lieutenant General Gough moved out from Ningpo on 13 March with just 600 men to meet this threat. A steamer carrying marines, sailors, and three companies of the 26th Foot flanked the British advance. The Chinese column retreated. Newly knighted Rear Admiral Sir William Parker linked up with Gough, adding two small river steamers and a further 250 Royal Marines to the force.

Gough's target was the coastal city of Tsekee (now Cixi) located just over forty miles from Ningpo. A large Chinese force under four generals garrisoned it. There were two enormous entrenched camps on the Segaon Hills half a mile north of the city walls, with guns on the walls and huge gateways, and large stores. Seven miles to the northeast was another 5–6,000 men under Commissioner Wan in a fortified camp in hills covering the strategic Chang Kee Pass.

On the morning of the 15th, the British force, numbering 865 men, disembarked from the steamers four miles from Tsekee and immediately pushed on to the city. 'Upon our approaching Tse Kee and our occupying a hill which commands the southern face of the walls and the south gate, the Chinese fired all the guns and ginjals they had for the defence of this gate,' wrote Gough, 'but with so little effect, and at so great a distance, that it led me to believe that they ... did not propose to defend the city.'[17] Lieutenant Colonel Montgomerie brought forward two guns, and Gough determined to storm the city at once and also to carry the Chinese encampments on the hills.

The Naval Brigade stormed the city walls, climbed them and formed up on the ramparts. The 18th Royal Irish dispersed the enemy to their front and moved on to the north gate. The 49th Foot and the Naval Brigade then converged on the gate, which was located on the spur of a low hill. The majority of the Chinese positions were dug in on the adjacent rugged hills and appeared formidable.

The 18th, with a company from the 36th Madras, was ordered to move up a ravine and occupy a hill to the left of the position. The Naval Brigade moved under the city walls and occupied two large buildings in front of the right hand Chinese encampment. They were to push forward once the 18th had taken the summit of the hill that they were assaulting, in the process turning the Chinese left flank. The 49th was ordered to attack a large Chinese camp to its front. Gough wanted to cut the Chinese defenders off from Tsekee.

Defending the two camps were some of the best troops that the British had so far encountered, including 500 men of the elite Imperial Guards who Gough called 'remarkably fine men.'[18] There were also Muslim Gansu troops, 'a strong and muscular race', and units from Shaanxi Province.

The steep country slowed the British approach, but when the advance sounded 'the 49th, with their accustomed spirit, rushed up the hill, overcoming all opposition and crowned its height within a few minutes, driving everything before them.'[19] Admiral Parker personally led the Naval Brigade during the assault and they quickly reached the summit of their hill and captured the Chinese works. A large force of Chinese began to ascend the hill's reverse slope, but Gough spotted them and directed the 49th to cut them off. 'The carnage at the foot of this hill was extraordinarily great; the 49th in rear, and the naval brigade in front, almost annihilated this body ... as the whole plain was covered with the dispersed and flying enemy.'[20] The 18th Royal Irish, 36th Madras and 26th Cameronians dashed onto the plains and cut off the Chinese from a safe retreat to the defended pass, killing many. By

8pm the entire British force was safely ensconced in the captured Chinese positions, 'where the men found ample bedding and comforts.'[21]

The fighting at Tsekee had been unusually tough – the Chinese troops were among the best the emperor possessed and a lot of the fighting on the hills had been hand-to-hand, as evidenced by some of the officer casualties in the 49th Foot: 'Capt. Reynolds, (wounded) ... Lieutenant Lane, (whose left arm was amputated on the field); and Lieutenant Montgomery, (severely wounded in the thigh).'[22] Total British casualties amounted to three killed and twenty-two wounded, while the Chinese lost 1,000 killed in action or drowned in the canals whilst retreating across the plains. Gough noted that 'a great proportion of Mandarins fell', indicating that Chinese officers fought and died alongside their men. Two Gansu and an Imperial Guards officer were taken prisoner. The following day Gough ordered the city's grain stores to be opened to the local population – by nightfall they had been stripped bare.

The final part of the operation was the reduction of the Chinese mountain camp protecting the pass seven miles northwest of Tsekee. At 1pm on 16 March the whole force moved out of Tsekee and ascended the mountains. When Gough's force arrived they discovered that the Chinese had pulled out, leaving behind weapons, stores and food that the British gathered together and burned. The British then returned to Ningpo on the 17th, mission accomplished without further loss.

In the months to come reports began to filter in that the Chinese were gathering a large and well-supplied army at the coastal city of Chapoo (now Zhapu) in Zhejiang Province, south of Shanghai. The British determined to prevent such a build-up and to this end dispatched the entire military and naval force from Ningpo north along the coast.

On 16 May HMS *Phlegethon* and *Nemesis* conducted a reconnaissance of Chapoo's defences. Two gun emplacements with seven and five cannon each were located three-quarters of the way up a steep hill and covered a large sandy beach. The city of Chapoo lay two miles from the bay and a range of heights terminated at the beach. The Chinese had fortified the heights and they occupied a strong position, garrisoned by up to 10,000 troops.

On the afternoon of the 17th the 72-gun *Cornwallis* led eleven other assorted warships and transports into Chapoo Bay and anchored. At daybreak on the following day, the ships landed 2,220 soldiers, sailors and marines at the eastern terminus of the heights. HMS *Blonde* and *Cornwallis* attacked the Chinese sea batteries on the hill. A 'joss house', as the British referred to temples, and three masked gun batteries with thirty cannon crowned the top of this hill. The Chinese defences on the heights consisted of large numbers of matchlock muskets and gingals. HMS *Sesostris*, a 4-gun steamer, dispersed these Chinese troops with shells as the British forces advanced, and 'the inhabitants of the suburbs and city were duly warned to retire out of the line of our fire,'[23] noted Rear Admiral Parker.

By 9am all of Gough's troops were ashore. 'The General, with his accustomed energy, immediately pushed forward at their head,' wrote Parker, 'the ships ... opening their fire at the same time on the batteries.'[24]

Except for one celebrated incident, the Chinese defenders largely took to their heels. The Naval Brigade under Captain Bourchier took possession of the batteries before the Chinese could ignite mines that they had placed beneath them. Bourchier's men cut off large numbers of Chinese troops that were trying to reach Chapoo. Most Chinese fled, 'but a body of several hundred Tartar troops, having thrown themselves into a large joss house between the heights and the city, resisted with such desperation that they were not subdued until the buildings fell in ruins over them, and not more than fifty men were brought out alive.'[25] During the fierce fighting to capture this temple the commanding officer of the 18th Royal Irish, Lieutenant Colonel Tomlinson, was killed along with several of his men, and Lieutenant Colonel Mountain, Deputy Adjutant General, was severely wounded. Altogether the British lost eleven killed and fifty-six wounded against probably 1,500 Chinese casualties.

Commander Watson from the *Modeste* took an advance party of seamen in boats and crossed a canal to assault the city of Chapoo. 'The city was escalated, and occupied with very little resistance,'[26] noted Parker. Military stores were destroyed. The local citizenry rampaged through their own city, shocking the British by their behaviour. 'The plunder and devastation committed by the natives, from the moment of our entering the city, has, perhaps, exceeded that of any place we have yet visited.'[27] Many locals believed that the British were about to massacre them, so they murdered their own children and then committed suicide before order could be restored.

The penultimate action of the First Opium War was the neutralisation of the powerful Woosung (now Wusong) forts that guarded the entrance to the Yangtze River. If the British could take the forts the way would be open to capture the walled city of Shanghai and move upriver to the ancient Ming Dynasty capital of Nanking.

The fleet sailed from Chapoo on 28 May 1841 and headed north towards Woosung. The first problem that the British faced was making accurate charts of the Yangtze River estuary, as it was extremely shallow for large ships. Detailed reconnaissance was made until 4 June. Difficult tides, calms, fogs and the necessity to anchor at night meant that it was not until the 8 June that the fleet finally rendezvoused off the Amherst Rocks near the Yangtze's mouth.

The steam vessels *Modeste*, *Nemesis* and *Pluto* were positioned off Woosung to intercept any Chinese communications to the defending forts, while six smaller vessels were placed as beacons at the edge of the shoals on the north side of the channel heading into the Yangtze. This was very important, as no landmarks were visible on the low banks of the river. Despite these precautions HMS *Ariadne* ran into a large unmarked rock and was badly damaged.

The fleet crept thirty miles up to Woosung through shallows that were often only three feet deep. The bank at the river entrance was lined with strong Chinese batteries, 'the western side presenting for three miles an uninterrupted fortified embankment, mounting 134 guns between the city of Paoushan [now Baoshan, a suburb of Shanghai] and the village of Woosung.'[28]

A creek bound Woosung, on the opposite bank of which was a semi-circular battery mounting ten 24-pounders, to flank the entrance to the river. Another fort of twenty-one guns was located at the eastern entrance to Woosung. The river mouth was only 320 yards wide but was covered in total by 175 guns.

Finding a landing place was to prove difficult. The Royal Navy spent more time charting the estuary, marking passages and dropping buoys. It was decided that the sailing warships would be towed up the river by the steam gunboats. *Blonde* and *Cornwallis* would anchor against the heaviest batteries at the entrance on the western side, then the sloops would proceed higher up under the cover of the bigger ships' guns to attack Woosung village and the flanking battery opposite.

'Captain Bourchier led in with his accustomed gallantry and ability, closely followed by the *Cornwallis*, bearing my flag,' noted the promoted Vice Admiral Parker, 'under a heavy fire from the batteries on both sides.'[29] HMS *Algerine* came up astern of the *Cornwallis*, and the *Sesostris* proceeded to take station to enfilade the fort on the eastern side but ran aground. HMS *Tenasserim* attempted to bombard the eastern battery as well, but she also ran aground.

'It is but justice to say, that the Chinese evinced much firmness at their guns,' wrote Parker, 'and kept up a smart fire for a considerable time, although it gradually slackened after the ships opened on them.'[30] By 8pm, the Chinese had abandoned their guns under a terrific bombardment. But large bodies of Chinese troops were observed taking position to resist any British landings. More broadsides dispersed these units, along with a few rockets.

Modeste pushed on to the creek at Woosung village. HMS *Columbine* and *Clio* approached the opposite bank of the semi-circular battery, which the Chinese immediately abandoned. Landings by seamen and marines were affected shortly afterwards and the batteries captured. The eastern battery was abandoned shortly afterwards and seamen and marines from *Sesostris* and *Tenasserim* destroyed the guns and works.

The Chinese attempted to disrupt the British operation by sending thirteen war junks against them, but this move failed miserably when every Chinese vessel was blown to pieces by the steamships *Nemesis* and *Phlegethon*. *Nemesis* then ran aground and was stuck fast for several hours. With the gun batteries neutralised, General Gough landed his troops without incident and captured Baoshan town without a shot being fired. Total British losses for the operation amounted to two killed and twenty-five wounded while the Chinese lost hundreds killed and injured. Britain now controlled access to the Yangtze River, entrance to the rice basket of China.

South of Baoshan on a tributary of the Yangtze named the Whangpoo (now Huangpu) River sat the ancient walled town of Shanghai. General Gough occupied it with virtually no resistance, opening the way for the establishment of a British trading concession that would in time grow into the massive Shanghai metropolis and turn an insignificant water town into China's most important city.

With its simultaneous control of Canton and the Pearl River delta Britain had achieved most of its war aims. One last task remained for the British forces – to seize Nanking (now Nanjing), the former capital city of China that was located about 200 miles up the Yangtze River from Shanghai. It was of enormous political significance to the Chinese and its capture would cut China in half.

On 6 July, the expedition left Woosung. Seventy British ships started up the largely unknown Yangtze River. On the 14th a few shots were fired at the leading ships by some small riverside batteries but hastily landed Royal Marines soon chased off the gunners. Two days later, Admiral Parker and General Gough boarded the steam frigate *Vixen* and conducted a detailed reconnaissance of Chinkiang (now Zhenjiang), a walled town located half a mile from the river and next to the Grand Canal. Hundreds of Chinese civilians lined the banks of the river open mouthed with fascination as the *Vixen* puffed her way ahead, her paddle wheels noisily churning up the brown river water.

On the 20th the British fleet, most of it under sail, reached Chinkiang. Just opposite the town in the river was a small island named Kinshan (now Jinshan), its hill crowned with a seven-storied pagoda. From this vantage point Gough could make out that the north and east faces of the city walls were located near a range of steep hills while the west and south walls faced low ground with the Grand Canal bisecting a suburb. One-and-a-half miles lower down a bluff connected by a narrow ridge with a smaller hill, both capped with temples, commanded the northern angle of the city wall. To the southwest of the town, Gough spied three Chinese encampments on the slope of hills.

On the 21st Gough divided his forces into three infantry brigades and an artillery brigade:

1st Brigade under Major General Lord Saltoun landed below a hill opposite Kinshan Island, occupied it with two companies, and formed in the open space out of sight of the town walls to cover the landing of the artillery. 1st Brigade was then to assault the Chinese encampments.

2nd Brigade under recently promoted Major-General Schoedde was instructed to take and hold two hills that commanded the northern and eastern faces of the town walls.

The 3rd Brigade under Major General Bartley was to attack the west gate and the western face of the town.

Gough landed with the 1st Brigade under Saltoun and sent it forward immediately to destroy the Chinese encampments. Three companies of Bengal Volunteers were sent off to attack the enemy's right flank and found themselves first in action 'when the Chinese very gallantly rushed on them, and were not repulsed until they almost came into actual contact.'[31] Saltoun's forces scattered the Chinese from their camps.

Meanwhile the 18th Royal Irish and the 26th and 49th Foot assaulted the town walls. Four officers bravely swam the Grand Canal under fire to determine whether it was fordable by marching troops, but it was found to be too deep. Gough decided to use the suburbs as cover and approached the west gate.

Under cover of Indian artillery, 'Captain Pears, the commanding Engineer, with great spirit and judgment, placed the powder bags, and effectively blew in the gate,'[32] wrote Gough. Once through the demolished gate the soldiers found themselves in some kind of outer works. At this point they met Captain Richards who had led his Royal Marines from *Cornwallis* up onto the ramparts under fire and converged on the west gate. The men of the 2nd Brigade under General Schoedde had also scaled the walls at the northern angle, then commenced clearing westwards and carried the inner gateway, 'which was obstinately defended.' 'A body of Tartars was driven into the division of the western outwork without a possibility of retreat,' recalled Gough, 'and as they would not surrender, most of them were either shot or destroyed in the burning houses.'[33]

The 3rd Brigade under General Bartley was soon engaged by between 800 and 1,000 Tartar troops who 'opened a destructive fire upon our men.' They were eventually dispersed, 'although some of them fought with great desperation.'[34]

Admiral Parker also joined in the fighting, moving along the great walls with a party of Royal Marines, fighting pockets of Tartar troops. The sun was ferocious and the British troops suffered badly with heat exhaustion – some even died from heat stroke.

At sundown, parties pushed on into the Tartar City, the area of Chinkiang where the Manchu soldiers, officials and their families had lived separately from the local Han Chinese population. 'Finding dead bodies of Tartars in every house we entered, principally women and children, thrown into wells or otherwise murdered by their own people, I was glad to withdraw the troops from this frightful scene of destruction,'[35] recalled Gough.

The exhausted and sunburned British troops bedded down for the night in the principal government offices while burning buildings in the Tartar City lit up the sky. The city soon stank of decaying corpses. 'A great number of those who escaped from our fire committed suicide, after destroying their families; the loss of life has been therefore appalling, and it may be said that the Mantchoo [Manchu] race in this city is extinct.'[36]

The next morning a thorough search was made of the town, weapons gathered and destroyed and $60,000 in silver seized from abandoned offices. Cholera broke out, and there was looting. British casualties amounted to 34 dead, 107 wounded and 3 missing.

The British force continued its relentless advance on Nanking and, at this point, the emperor decided to negotiate. After such a series of military and naval victories it was inevitable that the British would ruthlessly exploit their advantage during the negotiations.

On 29 August 1842, three Qing envoys met with diplomat Sir Henry Pottinger aboard the *Cornwallis*, moored before Nanking, a city now under British guns. A 53-year-old baronet, Pottinger had replaced Charles Elliot as plenipotentiary to China. The Qing representatives were led by Keying, 55-year-old member of the Imperial House of Aisin-Gioro and Viceroy of Liangguang. Two other high Manchu officials, Yilibu and Ninjian, assisted him.

The British dictated the terms of the Treaty of Nanking, and Keying largely acceded to their requests. The alternative was more fighting, and the Chinese knew that they would lose. Better to soothe the barbarians now than have them take everything they wanted by force. The Treaty opened five Chinese ports to British trade: Canton, Amoy, Foochow, Ningpo and Shanghai. It also permitted British consuls to reside in those cities. The Chinese government agreed to pay the British $6 million silver dollars for the opium that they had destroyed in 1839, $3 million dollars in compensation for debts owed to British merchants by Chinese merchants in Canton, and $12 million dollars in war reparations. In total, $21 million silver dollars was to be paid in installments over three years – late payments incurring a 5% interest rate. Finally, Hong Kong Island was ceded to Great Britain in perpetuity, and would become a crown colony. In return the British withdrew their forces from Nanking and the Grand Canal.

The Treaty of Nanking had not settled one very important point, and the original catalyst for war, namely the status of the opium trade in China. In fact, the punitive Treaty really only laid the groundwork for another war over the same issues just fourteen years later. This time the British and their new French and American allies would not find the Chinese to be the military pushovers that they had been in 1839–42.

Chapter 3

The Arrow War

A small and turbulent faction of the population of China cannot be allowed to supersede the engagements of their Emperor to the sovereign of Great Britain.

Sir John Bowring,
HM Plenipotentiary to Hong Kong, 1856

A rumbling like thunder could be heard for miles around as a barbarian fleet ruthlessly destroyed a great Chinese metropolis. Lines of wooden and iron men-of-war, their gunports open, and their great cannon mouthing shell after shell into the dense mass of Chinese houses and temples ashore, lined the river before the great city. Fires raged out of control; dead and wounded civilians lay in the partially collapsed streets and courtyards, while thousands of others, clutching their few belongings, endeavoured to escape the maelstrom of shot and shell that rained down from the furious British. China was feeling the wrath of the world's only superpower, and, once again, her coastal cities were suffering bombardment and invasion. The issue, and the excuse for conflict, was once again 'foreign mud' – China's ruination.

By the mid-1850s, Britain was in direct competition with her greatest imperial foe, France, for the Chinese market. The United States was also trying to muscle in. Britain, desperate to maintain its 'most favoured nation' status with China, demanded that the emperor renegotiate the 1842 Treaty of Nanking. The British had plenty of new demands, among them that every Chinese port be

41

opened to British ships, the opium trade be legalised, British imports be exempted from internal transit duties, piracy along the Chinese coast be suppressed, the coolie trade be regulated, and a British ambassador be installed at the Qing Court in Beijing. The French and the Americans actively supported many of these demands, to increase their own influence and power in China by default.

Judging by the emperor's terse rejection of Britain's demand, the Chinese had not yet absorbed the paramount lesson of the First Opium War; that Britain would use overwhelming military force to get what it wanted if diplomatically rebuffed. Britain's iron fist was currently sheathed in a silken glove but, as in 1839, it only took a small incident for that glove to come off. The Second Opium War was much more an expression of Britain's unrivalled maritime power and of her position as effective ruler of much of the world. British Imperial 'will' would not be ignored by China.

The incident that provided a pretext for Britain to go to war with China again was named the *Arrow* – and she was a Chinese ship. On 8 October 1856, Chinese officials boarded the *Arrow* after suspecting it of piracy and smuggling. Twelve Chinese crewmen were arrested. British officials in Canton immediately demanded the crew's release, stating that the *Arrow* was a British-registered vessel and that Chinese troops had insulted the British flag. This was only partly true. The *Arrow* had been registered in Hong Kong and it had been flying the Union Jack when boarded, but the vessel's registration had actually lapsed and therefore it was illegally displaying the flag. British officials ignored these facts and instead insisted that the *Arrow* was protected under the terms of the Treaty of Nanking. Local Qing officials, anxious to avoid another conflict with the British, released the *Arrow*'s crew on 22 October but by now it was too late. The British government was determined to drag China into another conflict and the *Arrow* incident provided the perfect excuse for the British to expand their influence in China at the muzzle of the gun.

China was in an even less advantageous position than in 1839–42 when it came to fending off the British and her allies. Imperial Chinese forces were fully embroiled in trying to destroy the Taiping Rebellion. This event was amongst the bloodiest conflicts in human history, with 20–30 million people perishing between 1850 and 1864. It had begun in Guizhou Province when Hong Xiuquan, a civil service exam failure, led an anti-Manchu rising amidst famine and widespread dissatisfaction with the central government. Hong crowned himself 'king' of the Taiping Heavenly Kingdom and set about conquering the rest of China. Hong's campaign was brought to a halt by the foreign-officered Ever Victorious Army, whose second commander was Lieutenant General Charles Gordon, later immortalised by his death in the Sudan at the hands of the Mad Mahdi in 1885. The British and French also lent military support to the Manchus as they did not wish to see China under the control of a religious zealot like Hong, who claimed to be the brother of Jesus Christ, among other things. This was the background against which the Qing tried and failed to prevent further foreign intervention into their country.

The military operations conducted by the British and their allies during the Second Opium War were very similar to those of the first conflict. The British Plenipotentiary in Hong Kong, Sir John Bowring, did not mince his words when attempting to justify military action: 'I am of the opinion that everything possible should be done to give effect to Treaties which have been pertinaciously and recklessly violated – a small and turbulent faction of the population of China cannot be allowed to supersede the engagements of their Emperor to the sovereign of Great Britain'.[1] Bowring was referring to the refusal of the Chinese to allow British traders to reside inside Canton proper. The British claimed this as a right under the 1842 Treaty. The problem arose largely through incorrect translation of the original treaty, the Chinese version only permitting foreigners to reside temporarily in the harbours of the newly opened treaty ports. The Viceroy of Liangguang, Ye Mingchen, won temporary fame for managing to keep the barbarians out of Canton and he steadfastly refused to yield to Britain's requests. Ye was known to the Chinese as 'Six Nots', because he would not fight, not make peace and not defend, he would not die, not capitulate and not run away.

The initial British target was Canton, and the Commander-in-Chief East Indies and China Station, 54-year-old Rear Admiral Michael Seymour, launched the first operations in late October 1856. Seymour decided that a show of force would be sufficient to cause the Chinese to cave in to British demands. Accordingly,

Royal Navy warships began bombarding Canton on 23 October. This bombardment would continue until 5 November. 'Your violation of Treaty engagements, your discourtesy and inattention to my demands, that the present unwilling resort to force has been rendered unavoidable,' stated Seymour in a letter to Viceroy Ye. 'Neither is it creditable to your Excellency that, in the employment of force on your part, you should have recourse to measures so opposed to civilised practices, as that of offering a reward for the indiscriminate murder of Englishmen.'[2] Seymour was referring to a proclamation that Ye had allegedly reluctantly issued against foreigners in Canton, as the city was slowly being levelled by Royal Navy cannon fire.

Ye stated the Chinese side of the argument. 'The seizure of some criminals on the part of the Chinese Government [referring to the *Arrow* incident] – a small matter – having been misrepresented as a hauling down of your flag. On the 23rd, 24th, and 25th ultimo, you opened fire on the different forts of the city ... But when, following up this, on the 27th and 28th, you opened a fire on the city, by which numberless houses were consumed, with considerable loss of life, the whole populace, thus subjected to a calamity, gnashed their teeth in anger.' Ye claimed that the British bombardment drove hundreds of thousands of Canton's citizens to appeal to him, 'demanding, why, after all the years that the English had traded at Canton, to their great advantage, without any cause of complaint against them, the people of Canton, they should be subjected to such suffering at the hands of the English.'[3]

Ye, not to be outdone by manufactured British outrage over alleged treaty violations, was in combative mood. 'Let your Excellency well remember,' Ye wrote to Seymour, 'that without any injury done to the English by the people of Canton, your Excellency fired at once into the city, and ask yourself whether this consists with the forms of war, as waged by a great State, or whether this is the practice of civilisation.'[4]

None of this made the slightest difference to the British, who continued to portray Viceroy Ye as a troublemaker and a xenophobe. According to Harry Parkes, British Consul at Canton, Ye 'has laboured to associate the people with him, by representing the English as in league with the [Taiping] rebels and outlaws, and has pushed his hostility to the ferocious length of proclaiming rewards for the lives of English subjects, without distinction.'[5]

On 6 November, Seymour carried out a naval demonstration just off Canton, where many of his ships had been stationed when the conflict began. They again bombarded sections of the city to demonstrate to the Chinese that the Royal Navy could hit anywhere in the city with impunity. These bombardments were primarily attacking innocent civilians. Seymour also wanted to dispose of a group of Chinese war junks that had gathered under the protection of the French Folly Fort. The steam vessels HMS *Barracouta* and *Coromandel* attacked the junks. 'Considerable resistance was offered,' noted Seymour, 'and the fire from the junks and forts, in the early part of the operation, was stoutly maintained.'[6]

Seymour decided to blast a route through the Bocca Tigris defences to permit a larger invasion force access to Canton. He sent a summons to the Chinese commander of the Bogue Forts that stated: 'The British Admiral wishes to spare life, and is not at war with the Chinese, and it is necessary for him to hold possession of the Bogue Forts.' An hour later the Chinese general replied that he could not give up the forts without a fight because he would 'lose his head'.

Six days later, on 12 November, the British struck using the same tactics that had served them so well in 1839–42. A British squadron bombarded two Chinese forts on Wangtung Island that mounted over 200 guns. Royal Marines and soldiers then landed and stormed the forts. The Chinese threw stinkpots (earthen pots filled with gunpowder and liquor which blinded victims with smoke) and kept fighting until the British troops stormed the embrasures, before they fled in boats, the British commander noting that there was 'considerable, though ill-directed,'[7] resistance for about an hour before the fighting ended. One sailor was killed and five wounded when HMS *Nankin* was struck by the fire from Chinese shore batteries.

On 13 November, the British force struck again, capturing the 210-gun Anunghoy Island forts. There was little Chinese resistance and there were no British casualties.

In the meantime, the Americans went into action without British support in one of their nation's earliest foreign interventions. US forces had been tasked with protecting American lives by landing

45

a 150-man detachment of US Marines and sailors in Canton. Under the command of Commodore James Armstrong the Americans met no resistance and carried out their tasks. The USS *San Jacinto* arrived to join the *Portsmouth* and *Levant* and landed further shore parties. On 15 November, the entire force was withdrawn, almost without incident. But during the withdrawal down the Pearl River towards the British area of operations, Commander Andrew Foote of the *Portsmouth*, who was taking a small boat to rejoin his ship, was fired on as he passed the Pearl River Forts.

The next day, the Americans planned to attack Canton's citadels in revenge. A steam frigate and two sloops under Commodore Armstrong opened fire. After a two-hour bombardment the Chinese guns fell silent and the Americans immediately opened negotiations with local officials. These talks did not lead anywhere so Armstrong ordered his vessels to bombard two more Chinese river forts. This time the Chinese fought back, hitting the USS *Levant* twenty-two times. Commander Foote led a 287-man landing force that swiftly captured the first fort. The Americans then turned the fort's forty-three cannon onto the second fort and after a short bombardment, captured that too.

It was becoming clear to both the British and the Americans that the Chinese appeared more inclined to fight than they had during the First Opium War. In late November, the American landing force was counter-attacked by over 3,000 Chinese soldiers and only repulsed with the greatest difficulty on 24 November. The Americans went on to capture two more forts and another 176 guns. The US landing forces suffered ten killed and thirty-two wounded, while aboard the *Levant* one sailor died and six were wounded. American military success led to them signing a separate agreement with the Chinese that would assure American neutrality until 1859.

In Hong Kong in January 1857, a Chinese plot to poison Sir John Bowring and his family with arsenic-laced bread was bungled and they survived. The incident divided the British Parliament and pitted the hawkish Tories, led by Lord Palmerston, against the Whigs. On 3 March, a resolution was passed by 263 votes to 249 against the Government on the grounds that its handling of the *Arrow* affair had been too violent and its attacks on Canton unjustified. In response, Palmerston attacked the patriotism of the Whigs who had sponsored the resolution and parliament was dissolved. Following an election and an increased majority for Palmerston, Whig voices supporting China were crushed. The new parliament decided to seek redress from China over the *Arrow* incident, and Britain also requested France, Russia and the United States join her in an alliance.

France joined as a result of the murder of one of its missionaries in China, Father August Chapdelaine of the Paris Foreign Mission Society. In 1844 the French and Chinese had signed a treaty that stipulated that missionaries were only allowed to preach in the five treaty ports then open to France. Father Chapdelaine had flouted this rule by going deep inland to Guizhou Province, in the process converting hundreds of Chinese. He was finally denounced to a local mandarin named Zhang Mingfeng on 22 February 1856, ironically by the brother of one of his converts. Arrested, Chapdelaine was severely beaten and placed inside a small iron cage that was hung at the gate of the local prison. By the time he was dragged out to be beheaded the priest had died – though his corpse was still decapitated.[8]

Although Mandarin Zhang was later demoted for this act, French treaty renegotiations soon broke down with Viceroy Ye in Canton, and the French used the 'Chapdelaine Affair' as a pretext to join Britain in military action against the Chinese, and to press their own territorial and trade demands.

The United States and Russia both sent envoys to Hong Kong with offers of help for the British and French, but both nations fell short of offering military assistance (the recent American naval activity at Canton a purely US national affair unconnected to Anglo-French operations).

During the summer of 1857 the Royal Navy destroyed several Chinese war junks. But the Indian Mutiny delayed the attack on Canton: British forces were fully occupied containing unrest on the sub-continent. With a successful conclusion to the Mutiny, Canton came back into British military focus. The Earl of Elgin and Kincardine, whose father had famously purchased the Elgin Marbles for the nation some years before, took command in China during the campaign to capture Canton. Elgin was formerly

Governor of Jamaica, and Governor General of Canada, and had established representative government in British North America before coming to China in 1857.

On 22 December 1857, British and French troops reconnoitered Canton; sizing up the city's rebuilt and reinforced defences. Britain's General Sir Charles van Straubenzee, a Crimean War veteran, and France's Admiral Pierre-Louis-Charles de Genouilly, exercised joint command of the military and naval operation.

A naval bombardment was opened on 28 December and Lin's Fort, located one mile inland from the river, was captured. The next day, large numbers of British and French troops landed by boat at Kupar Creek, southeast of the city. Following another bombardment the foreign troops scaled the city's walls meeting little resistance – though they managed to open fire on each other on several occasions. 4,700 British and 950 French troops broke into Canton for the loss of thirteen British and two French killed.

Canton had been badly damaged during the naval bombardments and subsequent fighting, with around 30,000 homes destroyed. Ye Mingchen was arrested by the British and shipped off to Calcutta as a military prisoner where he would die of fasting in 1859. In early January 1858, a joint Anglo-French Military Commission was established to rule Canton following Viceroy Ye's arrest and deportation. The Anglo-French Commission ended up governing the city for almost four years.

Defeat at Canton was not sufficient to force the Xianfeng Emperor to capitulate to British and French demands, so Seymour took his force north to attack the Taku (now Dagu) Forts, an impressive network of well-armed gun batteries protecting the mouth of the Hai River and the route to Peking. If the Anglo-French force seized the Taku Forts the way would be open for a march on the imperial capital, spelling a complete disaster for the Qing Dynasty and their probable overthrow.

The Taku Forts lay forty miles southeast of downtown Tientsin (now Tianjin) on the Hai River estuary. Originally constructed during the Ming Dynasty to protect Tientsin against sea raiders, in 1816 the Manchus had reconstructed the forts, building two on each side of the river as problems began to develop with the Western Powers. By 1841 five big forts, three earthen batteries and thirteen lesser earthworks existed. Ten years later, Imperial

Commissioner Sengge Rinchen fully renovated the defences, constructing six forts: two south of the estuary, three to the north, and a sixth on a small ridge on the north shore. The countryside was extremely flat, but each fort was raised up by between 10 and 15 metres. Each fort contained three large artillery pieces and twenty smaller guns, and was constructed of wood, brick and concrete.

On 20 May 1858, Seymour's force bombarded the Taku Forts, meeting only minimal resistance from the Chinese. His forces then went on to occupy Tientsin, which is Peking's port. At this point the Qing Court became amenable to negotiations, and discussions began which culminated in the Treaty of Tientsin, signed on 26 June 1858. The treaty officially ended the Second Opium War, though the fighting would flare up again soon after its promulgation.

The treaty was explicit on the 'rights' of the foreign powers over the Chinese. Britain, France, Russia and the United States were given the right to establish diplomatic legations in the formerly closed city of Peking. Ten more Chinese ports, including Nanking, were opened to foreign trade. Foreign warships and merchantmen won the right to navigate freely on the Yangtze River, and foreigners could now travel in the internal regions of China. Finally, China was forced to pay Britain and France each an indemnity of eight million in silver taels (a 'tael' weighed about 40 grams).

The Russians made a side agreement known as the Treaty of Aigun on 28 May 1858 that adjusted the Russian-Chinese border in their favour, gaining for the Tsar control of a non-freezing area of the Pacific. The city of Vladivostok was founded in 1860.

Although hostilities had officially ended, the most violent phase of the Second Opium War was about to occur. The focus was to be the Taku Forts, gateway to Peking and the Forbidden City. Here the British were to receive a shock from the Chinese that none of them had foreseen.

The trigger that precipitated more fighting was the slowness of the Chinese in permitting British and French consuls, or 'ministers' in the parlance of the day, to take up their positions in Peking as per the Treaty of Tientsin, and of their refusal to ratify the treaty inside the imperial capital. A British and a French envoy arrived off the mouth of the Hai River, then known as the Pei-ho, in June 1859, and decided that they would proceed up the river to Peking with their military escort. The garrison of the Taku Forts decided otherwise and prevented them from moving. The British noted with disquiet that the Chinese had repaired the forts since their bombardment and capture a year earlier, and that they had also erected strong metal barriers in the river that prevented any large ship from entering the channel.

The British task force commander, Rear-Admiral James Hope, told the Chinese to remove the river barriers. The Chinese replied that they had been installed as protection against 'river pirates' and promised to remove them. Instead, the Chinese continued working on their defences. On 21 June, Admiral Seymour sent Chinese commander General Hong Lu an ultimatum – remove the barriers by the evening of the 24th or face military action. Three days passed and the barriers remained resolutely in place.

For the first time the British faced a problem – their large warships that had normally decided most battles with the Chinese since 1839 were unable to get close to the forts because of the barriers, the tidal shallows and the sandbanks that surrounded them. This meant that the British would be unable to liberally plaster the Taku Forts with shells while the invasion force went in.

Seymour and Hope would rely instead upon a force of eleven small steam-driven gunboats, each crewed by fifty men and armed with four or six guns.[9] In total the British had forty-eight guns against sixty Chinese artillery pieces. The steam gunboats fielded a total of 500 men between them. The larger warships, including the French frigate *Duhalya*, stood off with a landing force of Royal Marines and sailors that numbered between 500 and 600 men. They would be landed by steam launch, ships boats and commandeered junks once the forts had been reduced. The British were facing a Chinese force of 4,000 troops.

What followed was a complete and unmitigated disaster for the British, and a national humiliation. For the first time, the Chinese actually remained in their positions and fought it out, and for the first time, because of the skillfully blocked river that prevented the British from bringing their large warships into action against them, the Chinese had the tactical advantage and they ruthlessly exploited it. The British response to a rapidly deteriorating situation was to resort to the kind of suicidal tactics that would become evident during the Battle of the Somme fifty-seven years later – the frontal assault over open ground against prepared enemy positions.

After dark on 24 June, Admiral Hope sent a small reconnaissance party in three boats up the river led by Captain George Willes. His task was to locate and determine whether the Chinese river defences could be overcome. With muffled oars, the British boats approached the first barrier, the row of iron stakes mounted on tripod bases designed to rip the guts out of any British vessel that attempted to enter the river at high tide. Willes' party carefully passed between the stakes and rowed upriver for a further quarter of a mile until they encountered the second barrier.

The second barrier was formidable. The Chinese had strung a heavy cable of cacao fibre and two iron chain cables twelve feet apart across the river, supported every thirty feet by floating booms. Willes detailed two boats to remain at the second barrier and fix a mine under the second boom. Willes, in the meantime, pushed on in his boat to locate the third barrier – two huge rafts positioned to leave only a very narrow channel between them, this channel also protected by iron stakes. Willes climbed out onto one of the rafts without being spotted by Chinese sentries, and quickly determined that it was too substantial to be rammed by one of the steam gunboats. Willes returned to his boat and rode the current silently down to the second barrier where the mine fuse was lit. The explosion illuminated Willes' little flotilla, attracting some inaccurate cannon fire from the surrounding forts, but the sailors escaped unscathed.

Later, during the early hours of 25 June, Chinese were observed repairing the second barrier. As the sun began to rise on a hot, clear day, Admiral Hope began moving his gunboats into bombardment positions near to the first barrier. Nine gunboats would fire on the forts while two more, HMS *Plover* (carrying Hope) and *Opossum* (commanded by Willes), would try to break through the iron stakes and then clear the second and third barriers.

The British plan went awry almost from the beginning. By 11.30am it was high tide, and the gunboats found it difficult to manoeuvre in the narrow channel that was only 200 yards wide and littered with hidden mud banks and through which a strong current ran. HMS *Banterer* and *Starling* ran aground. Curiously, the Chinese forts remained ominously silent, their gun ports closed. No soldiers were observed on the parapets, just a few black flags snapping out in the sea breeze.

HMS *Plover* closed up to the first barrier with *Opossum* behind. Willes ordered a cable to be attached to one of the spikes and, for thirty minutes, the *Opossum* tugged and pulled at the seemingly immovable object. But suddenly, the spike came free of the river-bed, and *Plover* quickly steamed through the resulting gap.

The two gunboats now approached the second barrier. Suddenly, the South Fort opened an accurate and deadly fire. Within minutes the North Fort joined in, plastering both British warships with shot and shell from 600 yards. The British were stunned – the Chinese gunnery was rapid and accurate and soon began to tell. Hope signalled 'Engage the enemy' from the *Plover*'s masthead, and the little gunboat's armament opened fire on both forts simultaneously.

All of the gunboats joined in the bombardment, but instead of slackening off, the Chinese fire actually increased in intensity, causing some British veterans to later convince themselves that the Chinese had been using European mercenaries to man the forts. In twenty minutes of sustained action the *Plover* was all but wrecked, with thirty-one out of forty crew killed or wounded. Her skipper, Lieutenant Rason, was cut in half by a cannonball, Admiral Hope was wounded in the thigh and a member of his staff, Captain McKenna, was killed as he stood beside him. The few remaining unwounded crew, gallantly assisted by some of the lightly injured, managed to keep two of the *Plover*'s guns going.

An American warship, the USS *Toey-Wan*, arrived off the bar. Its commander, Commodore Josiah Tattnall, a veteran of the War of 1812 against Britain, went to the *Plover* in a launch to offer Hope assistance, making his famous 'blood is thicker than water' remark about the amity between the two navies. The United States was officially neutral, but Tattnall offered to send his vessel's steam launch to evacuate the British dead and wounded, an offer that the wounded Hope readily accepted. As Tattnall stepped back into his launch several of his crew reappeared covered in powder stains, excited faces streaked with sweat. When

Tattnall enquired as to what they had been up to, one replied: 'Beg pardon, sir, but they were a bit short-handed with the bow-gun, and we thought it no harm to give them a hand while we were waiting.'

Hope ordered the wrecked *Plover* to drop down river to safety at 3pm. He transferred his flag to HMS *Opossum*. No sooner had he stepped aboard the second gunboat than three of his ribs were shattered by Chinese round shot. Hope was in considerable pain, but he refused to be evacuated. When the gunboat's stern caught fire, an officer from nearby HMS *Haughty* drew Captain Willes' attention to it, but Willes shouted back: 'Can't help it. Can't spare men to put it out. Have only enough to keep our guns going.'

HMS *Lee* and *Haughty* now took the lead. The Chinese barrage rapidly cut into both ships. *Lee*, holed below the waterline, was in danger of sinking as her pumps were overwhelmed. Her skipper, Lieutenant Jones, declared: 'Well, then, we must sink.' Boatswain Woods bravely went over the side to try and plug some of the holes, and shortly afterwards the shattered vessel ran aground.

HMS *Cormorant* now moved ahead of the *Lee* and *Haughty* to take the lead position. In the meantime, *Plover* sank. Admiral Hope was evacuated to the safety of the big warships beyond the bar for urgent medical treatment. Captain Shadwell took over command of the assault, but still the Chinese guns pummelled the British force relentlessly. HMS *Kestrel* sank at 5.30pm. By now, the British had lost six gunboats sunk, wrecked or otherwise disabled. Following a hurried meeting onboard the *Cormorant*, it was decided to storm the forts using landing parties and decide the matter once and for all.

The target was the South Fort, and the method chosen was a full frontal assault across open ground. This suicidal operation began at 7pm, as the light was beginning to fade. Captain Shadwell was in overall command. Captain Vansittart and Commanders Heath and Commerell led the naval landing parties. Sixty French sailors under Commander Tricault from the French frigate involved in the Taku Forts operation joined them. Colonel Lemon led the Royal Marines and Royal Engineers, the latter carrying scaling ladders to tackle the fort's high walls. The operation smacked of desperation. Never before had the British suffered such a devastating reverse when fighting the Chinese, and clearly the

British commanders had no intention of withdrawing before they had taken their objectives, whatever the cost in human life and military materiel. If the Chinese were to win, the ramifications for the one-sided Sino-British relationship were all too obvious.

The Chinese, probably as astonished as their adversaries at their success, now prepared to meet the landings with the same fortitude that they had shown in defeating the gunboats in the Hai River.

The tide had dropped, leaving the Anglo-French force facing 500 yards of open ground before they would reach the right bastion of the South Fort. The ground consisted of stinking, glutinous and, in many places, deep tidal mud, low scrub and three immense ditches. The Chinese forts had fallen silent, and many of the British hoped that the defenders had taken flight or run out of ammunition. But as soon as the first boats carrying the 1,200-strong landing party began disgorging their occupants at the water's edge, all hell was unleashed. The South and North Forts exploded back into life and the sailors and marines hurried forward into a deluge of cannon, rocket, musket and even arrow fire. One of the first to fall wounded was Captain Shadwell, shortly followed by Commander Vansittart who was shot through the leg. Out of the original assaulting force of 1,200 men, barely 150 made it to the second great ditch that was roughly halfway between the waterline and the South Fort. The rest were pinned down, killed or wounded. Of these, some fifty brave men managed to press on to the third ditch below the fort's rampart. With them they carried one scaling ladder, and an attempt was made to scale the wall by ten men. A volley of Chinese musket fire killed three of the assaulters and wounded five more, and the ladder was thrown down by the defenders and destroyed. The mud-bound Anglo-French force had no choice but to retreat or face annihilation.

During the land assault the British lost sixty-eight killed and over 300 wounded. Including the earlier naval operation British casualties amounted to eighty-one killed and 345 wounded. The British withdrawal was completed during the early hours of 26 June after a party was sent to scuttle or burn the beached British gunboats. For the first time in its history China had defeated the barbarians. But Chinese joy at their unexpected victory was to prove short lived, for the barbarians were determined to avenge their humiliation at the Taku Forts and carry their colours all the way to the Forbidden City.

Almost exactly one year later, in July 1860, a small Anglo-French taskforce arrived once more off the Taku Forts. The official reason was to enforce trade agreements made between the British, French and Chinese at the 1858 Treaty of Tientsin, including regularising the opium trade.

Instead of attempting to force the well-fortified Hai River as they had in 1859 with such disastrous consequences, the Allies decided instead to land a small number of well-trained troops and storm one fort to obtain a lodgement in the Chinese position. The Chinese had greatly expanded the number of forts at Taku, and, by 1860, they numbered twenty-six, armed with forty-five artillery pieces. This was a mistake, for the 5,000-strong Chinese garrison was widely dispersed and each fort was neither strongly garrisoned nor well equipped with guns.

Leading the British force of 200 men was Lieutenant General Sir James Hope Grant, while Lieutenant General Charles Cousin-Montauban commanded the 200 French troops. Grant had distinguished himself in China in 1842 during the First Opium War, particularly at the Battle of Chinkiang. He had later played a leading part in suppressing the Indian Mutiny and was knighted for his services.

Instead of sailors and Royal Marines, the British chose to use regular army formations at Taku drawn from the 31st (Huntingdon-shire) Regiment, The Queen's (Second) Royal Regiment of Foot, and the 44th (East Essex) Regiment of Foot.

On 30 July, Brigadier General Sutton's brigade landed at Pei Tang-lo, close to the Taku Forts. A forward reconnaissance was launched by the Queen's during which two men were wounded by Chinese fire from one of the forts. The main assault was made on 12 August, the assaulting force once again being forced to cross the tidal mud that covered the approaches to the forts. As General Grant remarked, 'It is simply a matter of the degree of filth our men must traverse.'[10]

Very heavy fighting once more erupted as the Anglo-French force crossed the open ground, smashed through Chinese trench lines and spiked bamboo palisades, and eventually closed in on the first fort. An attempt was made to smash in the main door but this proved to be impossible. Two officers and an enlisted man then made a herculean effort to clamber through an open gun embrasure, in the process taking on more than a hundred Chinese soldiers virtually single-handed. Lieutenant Robert Rogers, a 25-year-old from Dublin serving with the 44th Foot, accompanied by Private John McDougall from the same regiment, and Lieutenant Edmund Lenon, 67th Regiment (later The Royal Hampshire Regiment), had swum several ditches under fire before they entered the North Fort, fighting their way over a parapet with sword and bayonet. All three men were awarded the Victoria Cross.

The fort was taken and the Allied troops rested and reorganised themselves within its walls. Over the following two weeks the Anglo-French force went on to capture all twenty-six forts. Compared with the debacle of the previous year, Third Taku Forts was a major Anglo-French victory and indicated that the Chinese might not be militarily capable of repeating their 1859 performance.

British casualties amounted to fourteen killed and forty-eight wounded. French casualties are unknown. The Chinese lost about 100 killed, 300 wounded and 2,100 taken prisoner. The way to Peking was now open.

The Qing Army, led by General Sengge Rinchen, made two final efforts to halt the barbarian army before it reached the Forbidden City. Grant and Cousin-Montauban's army had occupied Tientsin and been reinforced so that it numbered 10,000 men. The force had progressed slowly towards Peking through the horrendously hot summer. On 14 September 1860, General Cousin-Montauban and his deputy, Baron Gros, joined General Grant and the British High Commissioner to China, Lord Elgin, a few dozen miles from Peking. On the 16th, it was agreed that the British and French forces would resume the advance together. Two days later Harry Parkes and Henry Loch, accompanied by a small escort of British, Indian and French troops, preceded the main advance with the intention of opening peace negotiations with the Chinese leadership. They rode under a white flag of truce, but they were captured by Chinese forces near Tongzhou and taken straight to

Peking. Arraigned before the Board of Punishments, the party was imprisoned and tortured. Parkes, Loch and fourteen others were released after the Chinese defeat, but the Chinese had inflicted the torture of 'slow slicing' to twenty of the party, where limbs were amputated and tied off to increase the victim's sufferings. These twenty soldiers died horribly and, when their bodies were discovered, they were virtually unrecognisable. This event was the cause of immense anger among the British and French, for diplomatic envoys travelling under a flag of truce should have been respected, and the incident fuelled strong anti-Chinese sentiment at all levels of the military command and stirred calls for swift and terrible revenge.

A British reconnaissance force that blundered into a huge Chinese army the day after the kidnappings of Parkes and his party was shocked by the fates of their countrymen and by the size of the Chinese forces opposing them. 'We were surprised to see a very large body of Tartar cavalry, numerous guns, and masses of infantry, drawn up as if intending to dispute our further passage,'[11] wrote St. George Foley, Commissioner to the French Headquarters in a letter to British Foreign Secretary Lord John Russell.

On 18 September 1860, General Sengge met the Anglo-French force at the small village of Zhangjiawan, close to the Peking suburb of Tongzhou. Thirty thousand Chinese troops attempted to defeat the Allies, but the modern equipment, superior tactics and better leadership of the Anglo-French force hopelessly outclassed them. The French turned the Chinese left flank, while the British and Indian forces attacked their front. 'The movement succeeded admirably, the Tartars being completely routed, with great loss, the French killing great numbers in the village on the left, the cavalry cutting them up, as they were driven out onto the plain beyond.'[12]

The Chinese army retreated, leaving 1,500 men behind dead on the battlefield. British and French casualties were ludicrously small – just twenty British and fifteen French soldiers had been killed.

The British remained extremely concerned for the safety of the Parkes party. 'Great anxiety prevails respecting the fate of Mr. Parkes, officers, and men, who still remain in the hands of the enemy,' wrote Foley. 'The generals-in-chief have written to threaten the capture of Pekin, should they be murdered or ill-treated.'[13]

Three days later General Sengge tried to stop the Anglo-French force again, this time within Peking at the Palikao (now Baliqiao), or Eight Mile Bridge, that was linked to the famed Summer Palace. The battle was a farce. The cream of the Qing Army, primarily its fabled Mongolian Cavalry, threw themselves in suicidal charges against the French and British lines and they were cut down in huge numbers. 'The enemy met us in the open, their force composed of many thousand cavalry, large masses of infantry, and numerous guns. The Tartar cavalry charged up to within 100 yards of the [British] guns and infantry, the fire from which drove them back. On the French left, the [British] King's Dragoon Guards arrived just in time to charge and cut up a great number of them. The enemy, after much resistance, was gradually driven back to the canal, our artillery causing them great loss.'[14]

The Chinese last stand was at Palikao Bridge, after 'having ten guns placed there. The French 12lb. guns soon silenced them, and the whole Tartar army retired towards Pekin, leaving their camps in our possession.' Grant's British troops were heavily engaged on the left 'and succeeded in inflicting great loss upon the enemy.'[15]

Swords and lances were no match for rifles and modern artillery. The Chinese lost over 1,200 men before breaking and fleeing into Peking. Allied casualties amounted to just two British killed and twenty-nine wounded, while the French lost three killed and eighteen wounded.

Tongzhou is only twelve miles from the Forbidden City. Chinese resistance was at an end, but what followed was one of the greatest acts of cultural vandalism in modern history and the shameful denouement to a shameful war.

On 22 September, the Anglo-French commanders received letters from the Chinese authorities suggesting a parley. Peking lay at the Allies' mercy. On 6 October, British and French troops began entering the Imperial capital. The Xianfeng Emperor fled from the Forbidden City leaving his younger brother, Prince Gong, to negotiate with the barbarians. Large scale looting by Allied soldiers broke out almost immediately as the Summer Palace and Old Summer Palace were each occupied.

The Summer Palace, an Imperial playground closed to ordinary Chinese, consisted of a complex of buildings, gardens and lakes around the 200-foot high Longevity Hill. The Old Summer Palace, or Gardens of Perfect Brightness, was an ancient 860-acre private sanctuary containing many masterpieces of Chinese art. On 18 October, Lord Elgin, infuriated by the Chinese torture and murder of members of Harry Parkes's truce party, ordered that the Old Summer Palace be razed to the ground in revenge. Elgin believed that destroying one of the Imperial family's more significant cultural artifacts would serve as a warning to the Chinese to desist from using kidnapping as a bargaining tool. It was an immense job, and it took 3,500 British and Indian troops three days to destroy the complex, and still thirteen royal buildings survived.

The destruction was by no means popular among the troops who were ordered to carry it out, for the palace complex was exquisite. Twenty-seven-year-old Captain Charles Gordon of the Royal Engineers, who would go on to become one of the British Empire's greatest heroes, was sickened by the destruction. 'We went out, and, after pillaging it, burned the whole place, destroying in a vandal-like manner most valuable property which [could] not be replaced for four millions. We got upward of £48 apiece prize money. The [local] people are very civil, but I think the grandees hate us, as they must after what we did to the Palace,' wrote Gordon. 'You can scarcely imagine the beauty and magnificence of the places we burnt. It made one's heart sore to burn them; in fact, these places were so large, and we were so pressed for time, that we could not plunder them carefully. Quantities of gold ornaments were burnt, considered as brass. It was wretchedly demoralising work for an army.' The contents of the Old Summer Palace today grace many private homes and national museums in Britain and France, and the Chinese were able to save many important artifacts overlooked by the foreign troops. Unfortunately, although some of the Old Summer Palace escaped the flames in 1860 the rest was to be thoroughly destroyed in 1900 following the conclusion of the Boxer Rebellion. Today only scattered ruins and a few small pavilions remain to remind the Chinese of their second terrible defeat at the hands of the barbarians. Elgin had considered destroying the Forbidden City but had chosen the Old Summer Palace as the 'least objectionable' monument to be flattened. In this, the Russian and French diplomats Count Ignatiev and Baron Gros supported Elgin.

The Emperor's brother, Prince Gong, signed the Convention of Peking on 18 October 1860. Among its many stipulations the Convention granted Britain, France and Russia the right to establish embassies (known as 'legations') in Peking, in an area adjacent to the Forbidden City that soon became known as the Legation Quarter. The Chinese were forced to pay Britain and France an indemnity of 8 million silver taels, and Britain was handed the town of Kowloon, opposite Hong Kong Island, in perpetuity. The opium trade was legalised, and Christians were granted freedom of worship, the right to own property and the right to evangelise in China. Tientsin was also opened to foreign trade. The Emperor died soon after and the Qing Dynasty was on its knees – humiliated by a tiny force of barbarian soldiers. This would have great ramifications for the ruling dynasty in the eyes of its people and lead to the Self-Strengthening Movement, when China attempted with mixed results to modernise its economy and armed forces to avoid further humiliations at the hands of the Great Powers.

China had once been the greatest empire on earth. Now her trade was virtually under the control of foreigners and her great port cities governed by them. Foreign warships patrolled even her rivers. It was perhaps inevitable that before long fresh conflicts would arise with the barbarians, and old mistakes would be repeated with devastating consequences for both rulers and ruled.

The British were the greatest winners from the two drugs wars that they had fought against China. By 1860, Britain controlled Hong Kong and Kowloon and maintained 'concessions', little slices of trading territory ruled over by British officials and protected by British armed forces, in Shanghai, Amoy, Nanking, Canton, Tientsin and many other Chinese cities, both big and small. Protecting these privileged trading enclaves became the primary responsibility of the British armed forces, necessitating the stationing of garrison troops all along the China coast, and the maintenance of a fleet of warships that could be sent to any trouble spot at a moment's notice. But the problem for Britain was the wide dispersal of her armed forces in China, owing to the large number of concessions and the size of the country. This would be cruelly exposed four decades after Prince Gong signed the Convention of Peking when a new, and altogether more frightening, storm blew up in the north of China that threatened all that the British and the other Great Powers had spent so many years carefully constructing. And this time the threat came initially not from China's ruling class, but from the poorest sections of Chinese society, from among the peasant farmers and coolies who had nothing to lose by forcing a fight with their European overlords. They took the name 'Fists of Righteous Harmony', and they intended to drive a fist into the face of every white man in China.

Chapter 4

'Destroy the Foreigners'

If we just fold our arms and yield to them, I would have no face to see our ancestors after death. If we must perish, why not fight to the death?

Empress Dowager Cixi, Peking, 1900

Dense ranks of Boxers advanced towards the Royal Marines who were manning a series of sandbagged positions on the barricades, their Lee Metford rifles tipped with long bayonets. Sweat poured down the young marines' faces as the sun beat mercilessly upon their tropical service helmets, their white tunics stained with blood, dirt and sweat. The Boxers chanted as they came on, louder and louder. The chant was '*Sha, sha, sha!*' – kill, kill, kill. The Boxer's great swords and pikes glinted in the sun, hundreds and hundreds of young Chinese fanatics pushing ever closer to the British lines, their eyes wild with fervour, baring teeth and shaking their weapons at the hated foreigners. A young officer shouted commands above the din: 'At 100 yards, volley fire – present!' – the marines' rifles were instantly levelled, each man carefully selecting a target. A pause, fingers touching triggers, eyes squinting along rifles at the bobbing figures that were approaching – 'Fire!' With a deafening crash the first volley smashed into the front of the Boxer column. Many fell, their places instantly taken by more pressing forward from behind. 'Reload', yelled the officer. 'Fire!' – another dozen were dropped. 'Independent – fire at will!' Frantically working their rifle bolts, the marines fired as fast as they could, a hail of lead tearing great holes in the Boxer lines. But still they came on, running across the open killing ground waving their blades, screaming like madmen until felled by a bullet, or impaled on a British bayonet as they tried to scramble over the barricades. Then, as suddenly as it had begun, the Boxers retreated and the officer ordered 'Cease firing!' They would be back, and perhaps the next time they would get through the thin line of exhausted and grimy marines – if that happened a massacre would follow.

The Boxer Rebellion was the point at which Britain's relations with Qing Dynasty China went critical. It was China's last, and most determined, attempt to turn back the clock on foreign influence, but it ultimately led to the further weakening of the ruling dynasty and its eventual downfall.

The Fists of Righteous Harmony, or Boxers, so named for the callisthenic exercises that they practised, originated in the northern province of Shandong in the last decade of the 19th century. The increasing influence of foreign technology in China, particularly the construction of railways, had robbed many Chinese of their traditional occupations as boatmen and carters. Natural disasters had caused widespread suffering among rural peasants, with tens of thousands surging into cities in search of work and food. The spread of Christianity inside China, a direct result of the 'unequal treaties' that had been foisted upon the nation in the mid-nineteenth century, was deeply resented and many peasants believed that foreign missionaries disturbed the ancient spirits and caused their crops to fail. A common belief among peasants was that foreign priests and nuns used menstrual blood during their ceremonies and sacrificed Chinese children on their altars. Added to these factors was an overall feeling of impotence, from the highest officials down to the lowest farmer, a feeling that China was humiliated, unfairly treated and unable to assert its sovereignty in the face of the overwhelming powers of the Western nations. There was a widespread belief that something had to change – that the Chinese had to throw off the Western imperialists before their nation was reduced to a series of colonies.

The Boxers represented hope. They were a millenarian movement, much like the Sioux Ghost Dance in the United States in 1890, which arose when traditional society was under stress, and like the Native Americans, the Boxers believed that spirituality would defeat the white devils' bullets. Through their training, diet, martial arts and prayers, the Boxers believed that they were immune to Western firearms – some even claimed to be able to fly. Ludicrous though it sounds today, this strange mixture of spirituality and desperation struck a nerve with the dispossessed Chinese masses. It appeared a simple proposition: rid the country of foreigners and all would be well again. Unfortunately for the various Boxer sects, ridding China of the Western Powers would prove to be an extremely challenging enterprise, and one that would require official help.

By 1898, groups of Boxers had already begun attacking and murdering Chinese Christian converts in northern China. They burned churches and even killed foreigners. In October 1898 the infamous Boxer slogan first appeared – 'Support the Qing, destroy the foreigners.'

The Boxer Rebellion coincided with a tumultuous period in Chinese history. Empress Dowager Cixi (pronounced 'Sir Shi') had ruled China off and on for several decades. She had been the favourite concubine of the Emperor Xianfeng at the time of the Second Opium War. She had borne him a son who became emperor on his father's death in 1861, but the boy had died three years later. Through her influence, Cixi was able to have herself declared regent over her young nephew, Emperor Guangxu, until he came of age in 1889. In September 1898 Cixi moved against Guangxu, had him placed under house arrest and took power for herself. The emperor's life was only spared at the intervention of the foreign ambassadors in Peking, but he was finished as a ruler.

In January 1900, with Qing power crumbling, Cixi decided not to officially suppress the Boxers, who were causing considerable mayhem in the country around the capital. The Great Powers protested but 'Old Buddha', as Cixi was nicknamed, ignored them. By the spring, Edwin Conger, the American Minister, reported to Washington DC that 'the whole country is swarming with hungry, discontented, hopeless idlers.' On 30 May, the British Minister, Sir Claude MacDonald, led the foreign powers' diplomatic efforts in demanding that foreign troops be dispatched to Peking at once in order to protect the eight legations.

Limited by the Chinese authorities to just 400 men, the legation guards had little apart from rifles and revolvers with which to defend the Quarter. The Royal Marines had a single four-barrel Nordenfeldt machine gun that was prone to jamming; the Austrians a little 1-pounder field gun with only 120 shells, and the Russians brought boxes of 9-pounder shells with them but stupidly left the actual firing piece on the Tientsin railway station platform. It was also necessary to defend the Roman Catholic Beitang Cathedral on the other side of Peking, which was threatened by the Boxers. Thousands of terrified Chinese converts and the religious staff had sought refuge behind its high perimeter wall. Thirty-one French and twelve Italian marines were dispatched to the Beitang.

The Legation Quarter in Peking, a mixture of Western-style architecture and traditional Chinese buildings and gardens, measured about 1,500 square yards and was located between the massive walls of the Imperial and Forbidden Cities. A foul-smelling canal ran north to south, bisecting the Quarter. The enormous 40-foot high Tartar Wall towered over one section of the Quarter and this would prove to be the most important line of defence. It had to be denied to the Chinese at all costs.

On 5 June, the Boxers tore up sections of the railway that linked Peking with its port Tientsin. Four days later Sir Claude MacDonald cabled the British Commander-in-Chief, China Station, Vice Admiral Sir Edward Seymour, stating that the situation in Peking 'was hourly becoming more serious,' and that 'troops should be landed and all arrangements made for an advance to Peking at once.' As a much younger officer, Seymour had served in his grandfather's fleet in China in 1857–60. He had seen with his own eyes the military failings and hesitancy of the Chinese when faced with well-trained Western troops armed with modern weaponry.

Although the British and Americans were all for pushing straight on to Peking, the other Powers wanted to await more reinforcements and attempted to prevaricate. Tough talking US Navy Captain Bowman McCalla stood up and declared: 'I don't care what the rest of you do. I have 112 men here, and I'm going tomorrow morning to the rescue of my own flesh and blood in Peking. I'll be damned if I sit here 90 miles away and just wait.'[1]

McCalla's strong words galvanised the Allies into action. Admiral Seymour did not hesitate and, within twenty-four hours, he had assembled a relief force consisting of over 2,000 sailors and marines (916 British, 455 Germans, 326 Russians, 158 French, 112 Americans, 54 Japanese, 41 Italians and 26 Austrians). Seymour's chief of staff for the expedition was Captain John Jellicoe, while Captain McCalla went as the senior American officer. The force was anticipated to arrive in Peking on 11 June, but this date came and went and no sign of the relief was seen.

The distance from Tientsin to Peking by rail was seventy-five miles, and Seymour believed that he could simply load his men aboard commandeered trains and steam into Peking a day later. In fact, although the expedition departed Tientsin on 10 June, they had grossly underestimated the determination of the Boxers, as well as elements at the Imperial Court, to stop them in their tracks. Taking just three days rations and with a machine gun mounted atop the first engine, they chugged off with few worries.

But Allied overconfidence played well for the Chinese, as Seymour arrogantly walked into a trap.

On 10 June, Seymour's force advanced twenty-five miles without incident. When they arrived at the Hai River bridge at Yangcun they discovered thousands of Imperial troops were camped nearby. These were under the command of 64-year-old General Nie Shicheng, who had previously fought the French in Taiwan in 1885 and the Japanese in 1894. He was a subordinate of General Ronglu, Cixi's cousin and a grandson of the Xuantong Emperor. Ronglu issued contradictory orders to General Nie. Nie was confused, did nothing, and waited.

As Seymour's trains puffed on across the boiling hot landscape they stopped frequently while engineers and troops got down to repair damaged or missing sections of the track. On 11 June, they passed the smouldering ruins of Langfang Station, recently torched by the Boxers. The first assault came when Boxers came screaming across the plain heading directly for the trains. 'Not more than a couple of hundred, armed with swords, spears, gingals and rifles, many of them being quite boys,' noted Captain McCalla. 'There was no sign of fear or hesitation, and these were not fanatical braves, or the trained soldiers of the Empress, but the quiet peace loving peasantry – the countryside in arms against the foreigner.'[2]

They were met with disciplined rifle and machine gun fire from the Western troops, and Seymour's men eventually won through. But it was an unnerving experience. Many Western sailors and marines noted that it usually took more than one rifle shot to immobilise a charging Boxer, for they seemed almost not to feel the bullets, nor to desist from attacking even when faced with certain death.

While Seymour's relief column slowly made its way towards the capital, the situation in the Legations was rapidly deteriorating. On 13 June, a Japanese diplomat, Akira Sugiyama, was brutally murdered in the street by Imperial troops belonging to radical conservative General Dong Fuxiang. He was a Han Chinese in charge of Muslim Gansu troops, 10,000 of whom had been sent to Peking and named the Wuwei Rear Troop.

Sugiyama had foolishly left his legation and was heading to the railway station expecting to meet Seymour's trains. On the same day the first Boxers, dressed in their distinctive red clothes and sashes, were seen for the first time actually within the Legation Quarter. The situation deteriorated quite rapidly there-after, especially since the German Minister, Klemens, Baron von Ketteler, along with some German legation guards, captured an innocent Chinese boy and beat him to death. This incident seemed to provide the Boxers with the excuse that they needed to assault Peking in huge numbers.

The Boxers set fire to every Chinese shop that did business with foreigners on 15 June. Widespread fighting ensued as the desperately outnumbered Legation guards and volunteers sallied forth from the hasty defences to rescue trapped Chinese Christians. Barricades had been erected, built from carts, barrels and sand-bags, loopholed for riflemen. The Westerners all knew that the price of defeat would be torture and murder. One of their number, Professor James, had already been seized and brutally murdered by the Boxers – his severed head had been mounted on a pole within sight of the defences, and it served as a gruesome warning of the fate that awaited them all should the Boxers have breached the defences.

Initially, the Imperial Court informed the foreign diplomats that they regretted these incidents, and were dispersing the trouble-makers – but this was a bare-faced lie. The Imperial Court was openly siding with the Boxers, contradicting Cixi's own orders to protect Foreign Legations. Boxers and General Dong's Gansu troops slaughtered Chinese Christians throughout Peking.

The Imperial Army consisted of three main elements. Firstly there was the so-called Manchu Bannermen. Numbering 460,000, the Bannermen were the hereditary descendents of the tribes that had put the Qing Dynasty into power in the early seventeenth century. Any member between the ages of 16 and 60 was able to draw rations from his Banner. Their reliability as soldiers was varied, but they were completely politically reliable, as they owed their continued wages to the survival of the Qing Dynasty. They were armed in a rather haphazard fashion and often indifferently led. Most of the Imperial troops encountered by the Great Powers during the Boxer Rebellion were Bannermen, such as the army of General Ronglu in Peking.

The second type of unit was the Green Flag Regiments, half a million strong, raised in the provinces. But these were really the private armies of the regional governors, and they rarely left their home bases. They played little or no part in the Boxer Rebellion.

The third, and some might argue most effective, force was the Gansu Fighting Braves: 30,000 Muslim tribesmen from the Far West of China. Fanatical, tough and used by the regime to enforce its will, they were more of a gendarmerie than an army, though they would take part in much fighting in 1900 under General Dong Fuxiang, who brought a third of the force to Peking in 1898.

In the Legation Quarter in Peking, each nation was responsible for defending a particular sector. The British and French guarded their respective legations with the Austrians providing a mobile reserve. The Americans, Germans and Russians also defended their own legations as well as a long section of the vital Tartar Wall. The Japanese and Italians, less the marines at the Beitang Cathedral, defended the abandoned Fu Palace complex lying adjacent to the British Legation compound. The Austrian, Belgian,

Dutch and Italian legations had all been abandoned because they were indefensible.

Among the civilian men trapped in the Legation Quarter, 125 volunteered as riflemen, many of them former servicemen. Other civilian men were drafted onto committees, as the foreigners tried to organise themselves properly for a potentially long siege. There were committees for rations, fuel, water, sanitation, fire, and Chinese labour. The women created a nursing service and sewed sandbags for the defences. There was plenty of food and water – though the 2,700 Chinese Christians squatting in the Fu Palace were not fed from the Westerners' food store. They had to make do with vermin, dogs, cats and roots, or work as labourers to receive rations. This reflected the ingrained racial hierarchy of the era, and was perhaps not the Western Powers' finest tale to emerge from an otherwise heroic story.

Sir Claude MacDonald, British Minister and a former army officer who had seen action in Egypt in 1882, was elected Commander-in-Chief of the Peking defences. 'MacDonald exercised command with tact and understanding, appreciating that his own experience counted for little in the sort of brutal, bloody street fighting that was taking place, yet offering the moral support of an older soldier to the permanently tired junior officers and NCOs who commanded detachments around the perimeter.'[3]

At Tientsin, the situation was fast becoming extremely perilous for the city's 700 foreign inhabitants. Tientsin in 1900 was actually two cities – a two square mile Chinese walled city, and two miles away the foreign settlements along the Hai River that had been established following the Second Opium War. Around one million Chinese inhabited both cities. Two thousand four hundred troops had been dispatched from the Allied fleet to protect the foreign settlements from attack.

On 15 June, the Boxers attacked the walled Chinese city, burst inside and ran amok, burning churches and brutally murdering Christian converts. The next day a mob of Boxers attempted to storm the foreign settlements but the troops' disciplined volleys soon dissuaded them. Close by, the large Imperial army commanded by General Nie, as before, did nothing – Nie had still not received any orders to either attack the foreigners or to protect them.

The Chinese government was split between reactionary conservatives who wanted to use the Boxers to rid China of foreigners; and moderates, who favoured diplomacy in dealing with the Great Powers. On the 16 or 17 June, Empress Dowager Cixi held a mass audience with the members of her Grand Council, and other interested parties, to try and gauge which way the wind was blowing concerning the Boxers. When one high mandarin doubted the Boxers' claims to magical protection, Cixi replied: 'Perhaps their magic is not to be relied upon; but can we not rely on the hearts and minds of the people? Today China is extremely weak. We have only the people's hearts and minds to depend upon. If we cast them aside and lose the people's hearts, what can we use to sustain the country?'

Cixi's position remained for a time unclear. Believing it was right to protect the Legations, she initially made contradictory statements that led to confusion among both her subordinates and Legation diplomats. But eventually her attitude hardened into support for the Boxers. When the Great Powers demanded control over China's defences and economy, Cixi stated to the Grand Council: 'Now they have started the aggression, and the extinction of our nation is imminent. If we just fold our arms and yield to them, I would have no face to see our ancestors after death. If we must perish, why not fight to the death?'

With Cixi's new resolve guiding her wavering generals, the Peking field army began to blockade the Legations. 'I have always been of the opinion, that the allied armies had been permitted to escape too easily in 1860,' said Cixi. 'Only a united effort was then necessary to have given China the victory. Today, at last, the opportunity for revenge has come.'[4]

For the fourth time in modern Chinese history, the Taku Forts, scene of ferocious battles in the First and Second Opium Wars, were at the forefront of the conflict. A great fleet of foreign warships lay off Tientsin in the Bohai Sea. On 16 June, a meeting of the naval commanders from the different powers decided that capturing the Taku Forts at the entrance to the Hai River was vitally important, and the key to maintaining a foreign foothold in northern China.

The Allies faced the same problems as when they last attacked the forts in the Second Opium War. The sand bars and narrow 200-yard channel at the mouth of the river prevented large warships from directly assaulting the forts. Smaller and more vulnerable gunboats and torpedo boat destroyers would have to be used instead. These vessels, with their shorter-range armaments, were easier targets for Chinese gunners, as the events of 1858 had demonstrated.

In 1900 the Taku Forts were well armed with modern artillery and manned by 2,000 Chinese troops. The Chinese also had four modern German-built torpedo boats tied up at Taku, and if properly handled these formidable vessels had the potential to seriously disrupt Allied naval operations. The Allies would deploy ten smaller vessels and just 900 men to assault and storm the forts.

Imperial Russian Navy Vice Admiral Hildebrandt sent a message to the forts' Chinese commander informing him that the Allies would occupy the position 'by consent or by force,' and demanding that he surrender by 2am on 17 June. The Chinese disregarded this missive, and instead they opened fire on the Allied gunboats at 12.45am. The Russian gunboat *Koreetz* was very badly damaged. Another Russian gunboat, *Giliak*, ran aground while the British vessels HMS *Whiting* and *Lion* and the Russian *Iltis* were all hit multiple times.

Fortunately for all concerned the Chinese did not send their brand new torpedo boats to sea, leaving them inexplicably tied up. The *Whiting* under Lieutenant Colin Mackenzie, and HMS *Fame* under Lieutenant Roger Keyes, each destroyer towing a whaler containing a ten-man boarding party, came alongside and after a brief fight they seized them intact.

Artillery exchanges continued until nearly dawn. It was decided to disembark the sailors and marines from the gunboats preparatory to launching a ground assault against the Northwest Fort. Led by 200 Russians and Austrians, followed by 380 British and Italians, with 300 Japanese closely behind, a powder magazine was detonated in the fort shortly before the Allied forces arrived, a lucky shot from one of the gunboats killing or wounding many of the Chinese defenders. The Japanese were given the honour of storming the fort, which they did so with their customary suicidal bravery and lack of concern for casualties. British and Italian sailors and marines led the assault on the North Fort and it was quickly captured.

That left the two intact forts on the south bank of the Hai River. The Allies cleverly decided to use the guns that they had captured in the two northern forts, bringing them to bear on the southern emplacements along with the guns of the Western warships lying off the river mouth. The two southern forts were subjected to a short but very intensive barrage, during which another magazine was blown up. Chinese troops were then observed running away, and the Allied forces crossed the river and took possession of both forts by 6.30am. Total Allied casualties were 172 killed and wounded. Chinese casualties were unknown.

The Allied assault on the Taku Forts erased any lingering doubts in Empress Dowager Cixi's mind that complete support for the Boxers was both necessary, and desirable.

On 19 June, in response to the attack on the Taku Forts, Cixi ordered that all foreigners should leave Peking within twenty-four hours – they were promised an escort from the Imperial Army to assure their safety through Boxer lines. The next day the German Minister, Baron von Ketteler, was murdered in the street by a Manchu captain, prompting the not unreasonable assumption by Sir Claude MacDonald and the other diplomats, that to leave the Legation Quarter would be tantamount to a death sentence.

The Empress Dowager declared war on the Great Powers on 21 June 1900. However, many of her regional governors actually refused to support the war and maintained a neutral stance, including Li Hongzhang in Canton, Yuan Shikai in Shandong and Zhang Zhidong in Wuhan. General Yuan actually suppressed the Boxers in his province. All of this meant that the 'war' was limited to Peking and Tientsin, and the country in between, rather than being a national war of liberation as envisioned by the Imperial Court.

Tientsin was in extreme danger following the battle at the Taku Forts. Cixi ordered General Nie to cooperate with the Boxers and to destroy the foreign settlements. Approximately 13,000 Imperial troops and Boxers set about this task with alacrity, bringing up modern artillery and opening a fearsome bombardment upon the thinly held defence lines. Nie's guns would mouth a total of over 60,000 shells into foreign Tientsin during the course of the siege, but fortunately for the defenders, poor quality controls and corruption at Chinese armaments factories meant that a high proportion of those shells were duds.

An attempt was made to reinforce Tientsin's small garrison with fresh troops from the fleet. 440 Russians, and 131 US Marines under the command of Captain Littleton Waller, travelled the thirty miles from the coast along the railway but they were ambushed by at least 2,000 dug in Chinese troops just two miles from the foreign settlements and forced to retire. The Americans lost three men killed and thirteen wounded.

A much more serious assault was mounted by the Chinese against Admiral Seymour's relief column on 18 June, when Generals Ma Fuxiang and Ma Fulu's mixed Gansu and Boxer forces attempted an encirclement. The Chinese force included 5,000 Muslim cavalry armed with modern rifles. The Allies managed to fight them off with great difficulty, as the trains were assaulted from multiple points. Seymour lost seven men killed and fifty-seven wounded while 200 Gansu Braves fell alongside a hundred Boxers.

Seymour's force was now threatened by professional troops commanded by General Dong. His subordinates, General Ma Fuxiang and General Ma Fulu, commanded two separate forces that were each several thousand strong. Inconclusive clashes between Seymour's column, Boxers and Gansu troops left five Italian marines dead while the Chinese lost at least 102 killed. Wounded Boxers often feigned death, only to jump up and resume the attack when Seymour's troops came near to them.

Seymour's advance could go no further. The Chinese had successfully stopped the Allies in their tracks. Seymour was encumbered with multiple wounded, his supplies were insufficient for a protracted battle through to Peking, and more large-scale Chinese attacks were expected. Seymour decided to retire to Tientsin, get more men and supplies and try again to get through to the besieged Legation Quarter before it was too late. But soon, going back by rail also became impossible.

For Admiral Seymour, getting back safely to Tientsin soon proved to be as difficult as advancing to Peking. Seymour managed to turn his trains around and started back. Everything went well until he arrived at the bridge over the Hai River at Yangcun. The bridge had been severely damaged, burned by Boxers or Imperial troops. The force was left with two choices. They could cross the river, and march 18 miles to Tientsin down the railway line, or they could collect small boats and row thirty miles along the Hai River to safety. Unsurprisingly, the mostly naval force under Seymour's command chose to stick to the water. But traversing the Hai was to prove far from easy, for at every village along the river Boxers lay in wait. Fighting would be continuous, causing numerous casualties, including Seymour's chief of staff, Captain Jellicoe, who was shot in the head and nearly killed.

Seymour's bedraggled and exhausted men managed to row three miles down the river on the first day, fighting all the way. The men were on quarter rations, and most had less than ten rounds per rifle. The Americans were the exception: they were well supplied with cartridges, but because of the international nature of the relief force, equipped with a variety of different rifles of different calibres, this ammunition could not be shared out. Though they faced an uncertain fate there was a determination among the men not to be captured. 'There was no thought of surrender,' recalled US Navy Lieutenant Wurtzbaugh. 'The intention was to fight to the last with the bayonet.'

By 23 June, Seymour's force was just six miles from Tientsin but nearing the end of its collective tether. But then an opportunity suddenly presented itself. Out on the plain near the river was the large Xigu Arsenal; a giant store for Imperial weapons and supplies, and the Chinese had foolishly left the place virtually unguarded. Allied troops quickly captured the Arsenal, and found it packed to the rafters with modern weapons, ammunition and food. When the Chinese realised their error, they launched a strong attack against the Arsenal in an attempt to recapture it but, Seymour's men, resupplied and refreshed, beat them off. However, they remained besieged.

James Watts, an extremely brave young British civilian from Tientsin who had accompanied the Seymour expedition, volunteered to ride through the Chinese lines to Taku to bring word of their plight. Watts set off with an escort of three Russian Cossacks and managed to get through to Taku. A telegram was immediately sent to Tientsin apprising the garrison of Seymour's location, and the dire straits that his expedition was in.

On receipt of the message from Taku, a relief force of over 2,000 men marched out on 25 June and relieved the Arsenal the same day. The next morning the exhausted survivors trekked back into Tientsin. 'I shall never forget to my dying day, the long string of dusty travel-worn soldiers, who for a fortnight had been living on quarter rations, and fighting every day,' recalled a British missionary. 'The men were met by kind ladies with pails of tea which the poor fellows drank as they had never drunk before – some bursting into tears.'

Admiral Seymour's expedition had been a costly and embarrassing failure. Sixty-two of his men had been killed and 232 wounded, with the survivors sent packing the way they had come by superior Chinese forces. It was a humiliation that the Western Powers would not take lying down.

In Peking, the 23–25 June witnessed the fiercest fighting so far as Boxers and Imperial troops tried to overwhelm the defences with mass assaults. The desperate defenders shot down their attackers in droves, and eventually the Chinese tired of the slaughter and resorted to different tactics. They began constructing mobile barricades that they used to slowly tighten the perimeter around the Legation Quarter, building more solid defences behind them.

On 23 June, the Chinese tried to burn the British out of their legation but instead they burned down the Han-lin Library, a priceless repository of Chinese literature. Many sinologists amongst the foreign defenders were heartbroken to watch such treasures go up in smoke – many salvaged what they could from the ruins, and some volumes can today be found in the British Library, Bodleian and other repositories and collections around the world.

The defenders decided to counter-attack the Chinese on 24 June and push them back. An American bayonet charge west along the top of the Tartar Wall pushed the Boxers back half a mile. To the east, the Germans also went in with the bayonet, killing dozens of Boxers in brutal hand-to-hand combat. In the Fu Palace, the defending Japanese and Italians feigned a retreat, leading the

Boxers into a trap. The Japanese and Italians suddenly turned about, and opened devastating volleys upon their exposed foes.

A seven-strong party of Royal Marines led by Captain Lewis Halliday made a sortie from the British Legation to try and deal with Boxers attacking the legation's wall. In an alley, five Boxers armed with rifles confronted them. In the ensuing melee one marine was fatally wounded and Halliday himself was shot through the left shoulder and lung at close range. Disregarding his wounds 'he responded by shooting four of his opponents with his revolver, the fifth escaping round a corner when the weapon misfired.'[5] Halliday led another sortie later that day against a small building that the Boxers were using as a firing point, demolished it and cleared the line of fire from the legation wall. Captain Halliday was awarded the Victoria Cross for these two very gallant actions and spent the remainder of the siege in hospital.

On 29 June, a last message was received in Tientsin from the Legations: 'Situation desperate – Make Haste!'[6] The situation in the Legation Quarter was indeed becoming desperate. On 1 July a surprise attack forced the Germans off the vital Tartar Wall, and the Americans were taken in the rear and forced to join the German retreat. The US Marine Corps commander Captain Myers personally led a counter-attack consisting of his own men, supported by Royal Marines and Russian troops. At the same time, the French were forced out of their legation but they quickly counter-attacked and retook their former positions. An Italian sortie into the Fu to try and capture a Chinese artillery gun failed with some loss of life.

At the western end of the Tartar Wall the Chinese were observed busily constructing a wooden tower that, when completed, would allow them to fire down into the American defence zone. Captain Myers once more led an assault force of his own men and some Royal Marines to capture the tower, which they did during the early hours of 3 July. The tower was burned but Myers was badly wounded and taken to hospital.

On 7 July, the defenders had a stroke of good fortune when Chinese Christians discovered a buried cannon when they were digging a trench. It dated from the Second Opium War, and was cleaned and restored by British and American naval personnel. It was discovered that with some small modifications the Russian's 9-pounder shells fitted the muzzle-loader and could be safely fired. The cannon was mounted on an Italian gun carriage and known variously as 'Old Betsy', 'The Dowager Empress', and 'The International Gun'. The gun soon proved its worth when it successfully destroyed a Chinese artillery position close to the perimeter.

The Chinese virtually abandoned costly frontal assaults and instead settled into lobbing shells into the Legation Quarter and sniping. They also started underground mining. On 13 July an enormous mine was exploded beneath the French Legation. It started a massive fire, but killed only two sailors.

Admiral Seymour, in order to open the road to Peking, planned an assault on the Chinese walled city at Tientsin. He knew that he must relieve the Legations as speedily as possible, and after the false start of the previous two weeks, time was running out. On 13 July, an assault force of 6,900 men was ready. This consisted of 2,500 Russians, 2,000 Japanese, 900 Americans, 800 British, 600 French and 100 Germans and Austrians. The Chinese defences were formidable, consisting of a curtain wall 20 feet high and 16 feet thick, with massive stone gates on four sides, the walls lined with 12,000 riflemen, machine guns and a few modern artillery pieces. It was probably the most formidable objective that any Western army had faced in China since 1839.

The terrain that the Allied army had to cross was also a considerable challenge. Between their start line and the objective was one mile of largely open, flat and treeless farmland and swamp, intersected by canals and earthen bunds. The only redeeming features were numerous Chinese burial mounds, and the canal banks. 'The country was a flat level one with grave mounds and dikes in great numbers and these already dug trenches were of very considerable help to us in such an open, fire-swept plain we would have had difficulty advancing,' wrote Colonel Meade. 'The fire of the Chinese both in artillery and infantry was fearfully accurate.'[7]

The attackers would be at a major disadvantage. The plan was for the city to be simultaneously stormed on two sides. The British, Americans, Japanese and French would try and smash their way in through the South Gate, while the Russians and Germans attacked the East Gate. Tientsin civil engineer Herbert Hoover, later President of the United States, guided the force towards their objective.

In the early hours of 13 July, Hoover and a party of US Marines guided three columns of British, American, Japanese and French troops to the South Gate approaches. Firing erupted from the high walls and gatehouse. It was so severe and accurate that the regiments were forced to lie down in the mud. The 9th US Infantry Regiment lost their commanding officer, Colonel Emerson Liscum, within minutes of arriving. The 2nd Battalion, Royal Welch Fusiliers was similarly pinned down. Its soldiers, dressed in khaki Boer War uniforms, white webbing and khaki-covered pith helmets, desperately fired their Lee Metford rifles as bullets whipped past their heads or stitched across the mud all around them. Their officers lay alongside them, grasping their drawn swords and service revolvers. Several 12-pounder naval guns that had been laboriously hauled ashore from HMS *Terrible* provided fire support. These same guns had been used earlier in the year to relieve Ladysmith in South Africa.

The Japanese commander, Major General Yasumasa Fukushima, had previously fought the Chinese in 1898 and he warned the British field commander, Major General Dorwood, that, if trapped, the Chinese would fight to the death, but if left an escape route they would retire. The Japanese tried several times to blow in the South Gate, but each attempt was shot down with heavy casualties, or the Chinese cut the fuses. The attacks were cancelled. The Americans alone had taken over 140 casualties during the day's fighting.

At 3.30am on 14 June, a Japanese volunteer went on a suicide mission to the South Gate. Lighting a very short fuse he was killed in the resulting explosion, but the South Gate was successfully blown in. The Japanese charged inside with American and British troops hot on their heels. The Russians now attacked the East Gate again and also broke it. This provided the Chinese with an egress, and most of the defenders now fled Tientsin. What followed was a shocking display of barbarity on the part of the Russians and Germans, who started looting houses and raping Chinese women, many of whom were bayoneted to death immediately afterwards.

American and British troops tried to intervene, resulting in some fighting between the Allies. The Japanese did nothing – they were, at the time, shocked by the atrocities and by the behaviour of their Western allies.

Casualties for the operation had been heavy. The Japanese lost 320 killed and wounded, the Russians and Germans 140. The Americans suffered 25 killed and 98 wounded, the British 17 killed and 87 wounded, and the French 13 killed and 50 wounded. The strength of the Chinese defence and the numbers of casualties concerned the new overall commander deeply.

54-year-old Major General Sir Alfred Gaselee wanted to push on to Peking with a reinforced army, and the Americans supported him. Gaselee was a highly experienced soldier with over thirty years of campaigning behind him, mostly in India. A former commanding officer of the 5th Gurkha Rifles, Gaselee stepped into the post of relief force commander when the actual appointee, German Field Marshal Count von Waldersee, had not arrived in China in time. The other Allies had favoured waiting until they had assembled an army of at least 50,000 men, which would have taken many weeks. Gaselee and his American counterpart knew that such a delay would probably mean the deaths of their compatriots in Peking, rendering the entire operation pointless, so they decided to press on with less than half that number.

The Peking casualties continued to mount. The commander of the Royal Marines detachment, Captain B.M. Strouts, was killed helping to relieve exhausted Japanese troops in the Fu on 16 July.

The Chinese government's attitude suddenly began to shift with news that General Gaselee was preparing to march from Tientsin. MacDonald received conciliatory notes from the Imperial Foreign Ministry and a ceasefire was adopted. News arrived in the Legation Quarter from a Japanese agent that the Allies had taken the walled city of Tientsin and a column was marching to their relief. But the attitude of the Chinese government soon began to harden again when no relief column appeared. Ceasefire violations increased, and the behaviour of Chinese officialdom became increasingly odd. 'The Imperial Government, for example, having learned of the death of the then Duke of Edinburgh, sent

MacDonald its formal note of condolence; barely had he finished reading this when his bedroom was wrecked by the explosion of a Chinese shell.'[8]

On 4 August 1900, Gaselee led his new 18,800-man army out from Tientsin towards Peking. The force consisted of 8,000 Japanese, 3,000 British, 4,500 Russians, 2,500 Americans and 800 French. The Germans had decided not to join in.

The following day, the relief ran into determined Chinese resistance at Beicang, only six miles from Tientsin, where 8–12,000 Chinese troops and 26 guns were dug in on both banks of the Hai River. In Peking, some pro-ceasefire officials were beheaded and full-scale attacks launched once more upon the Legation Quarter.

The British force in China was mostly formed from Indian Army units, as it was both quicker and more effective from a health and acclimatisation angle to send in native troops partly led by British officers (see endnote for list of Indian Army units involved).[9]

The Americans, British and Japanese advanced up the west bank of the Hai River while the Russians and French went up the east side. The plan was for the Japanese, with British and American support, to turn the extreme right flank of the Chinese lines while the Russians and French turned the left flank on the opposite bank.

At 3am on 5 August, the Japanese captured the Chinese artillery battery on the extreme right of the line, and then pushed around on the flank. A half hour artillery duel commenced between the Chinese and Japanese during which a Japanese infantry regiment crept forward and launched a direct assault on the Chinese positions by the river. The Japanese advanced in close order through corn and millet field under a storm of fire. The Japanese had requested cavalry support from Britain's Bengal Lancers, but this failed to materialise. The Japanese, with their usual disregard for casualties, pushed on anyway and took the Chinese trenches at the point of the bayonet.

Flooding halted the joint Franco-Russian advance. The Chinese suddenly started limbering up their guns and towing them off the battlefield. Then their infantry broke contact, retreated, and cut through riverbanks to flood the fields behind them. The Allied force did not pursue and instead bivouacked in the abandoned Chinese positions, waiting for their supply train to come up from Tientsin. The Japanese had lost 60 killed and 140 wounded. The British lost one man dead and 25 injured by artillery fire, and the Russians 6 wounded. The Chinese casualties amounted to over 50 dead.

The next day the Allies' advance continued to Yangcun, twelve miles from Beicang. Here, the 10,000-strong Chinese army had dug in again on the east bank of the Hai River, incorporating a 30-foot high railway embankment into their defences. The country consisted of corn and millet fields. The heat was tremendous, with temperatures of 104 degrees Fahrenheit that caused twenty per cent of the Allied troops to fall out of the line with heat exhaustion that in some cases proved fatal. Water was soon exhausted, adding considerably to their suffering.

The Allies deployed 5,000 yards from the Chinese positions. From left to right: the Russians, British Indian, and US Army supported by the US Marines, with the Bengal Lancers anchoring the right flank.[10] The American and Sikh battalions, supported by British and Russian artillery, deployed into dense skirmish lines and advanced. They were subjected to intense, though largely inaccurate, rifle and artillery fire as they approached their first objective, a small village with a bridge beyond. When 150 yards from the objective, the American and Indian troops took cover beyond the 30-foot tall railway embankment and prepared to attack.

Following their officers, who went over the top with their swords drawn, the American and Indian troops charged over the embankment and rushed the village. Faced with such a determined bayonet attack the Chinese defenders broke and fled. At this point communications broke down, with the British and Russian artillery continuing to fire into the village, resulting in a friendly fire incident. Several Americans were killed and wounded before the guns fell silent. Altogether the US forces suffered eight killed and 57 wounded.

Indian cavalry scouting hamlets east of the bridge and Yangcun reported to the American commander, Brigadier General Adna Chaffee, that these locations were strongly held. Chaffee sent in the 9th and 14th Infantry Regiments to clear them. The heat was appalling, Colonel Daggett of the 14th Infantry remarking that the sun in China 'had more power to prostrate men than I had witnessed in our Southern States or Cuba or the Philippines.'[11] Britain's reliance on Indian troops paid off in conditions like these. Fortunately, the Chinese defenders fled.

Over the next seven days, the Allied army slowly and agonisingly marched towards Peking, following the Hai River. The weather continued to cause great suffering, particularly among the European and American troops. 'No shade, not a drop of rain, nor a breath of air,' recorded Lieutenant Smedley Butler. 'The cavalry and artillery kicked up clouds of dust which beat back in our faces. The blistering heat burned our lungs. Nearly half our men fell behind during the day, overcome by the sun.'[12]

The battle of Yangcun resulted in six British killed in action, 38 wounded and one dead of heatstroke. The Americans lost 24 killed or died from wounds, 2 dead from sunstroke and 49 wounded, with Russian casualties of 7 killed and 20 wounded.

By the time Gaselee's army approached the walls of Peking on 13 August 1900, hundreds of men had fallen out due to sunstroke and exhaustion, reducing the force to about 10,000 men. The thought uppermost in everyone's mind was whether they were too late, and all they would find would be the butchered bodies of their countrymen. As the army closed to within five miles of Peking, the sounds of artillery and machine guns from within the city were clearly heard – people were still evidently resisting.

After a day's delay caused by the Russians reorganising themselves, a plan was made. General Gaselee had received a map drawn by MacDonald from one of his agents that detailed the Legation Quarter's defences and also the best routes into the city. Gaselee chose not to share the last part of this information with his allies. Peking's defences consisted of several walls, with cities within cities like a Russian doll. The outermost defence was the city wall that ran twenty miles around Peking. It was studded with sixteen huge gates. Inside this was the Tartar Wall enclosing the Imperial City – 40 feet high and 40 feet wide at the top, and already the scene of much fighting during the siege. The Legations nestled between the Tartar Wall and the wall of the Forbidden City, the 'Great Within'.

The Allies decided to split up and smash their way into the city through four of the outermost gates located on the east side. The Russians would assault the most northern of those gates called the Dongzhi-men; the Japanese would take the next gate south, the Chaoyang-men; the Americans the next one, the Dongbei-men and finally the British Indian forces, the most southerly one called the Guangqui-men. The entire assault was treated as a race – whichever national contingent relieved the Legations first would win immortality.

The Russians decided that they needed a head start, so ignoring the agreed plan they assaulted the American target gate, the Dongbei-men, at 3.30am on 14 August, killing thirty Chinese soldiers outside the fortification before blowing in the great red doors with an artillery gun. Russian troops poured in only to find themselves stuck between the outer gate and another, inner gate. The Chinese poured fire down onto the Russians, and the Russians were pinned down for hours. Twenty-six Russians died at this gate and a further 102 were wounded.

With the Russians having seized the Americans' target gate, the US troops moved 200 yards south along the enormous wall. Trumpeter Calvin Titus bravely volunteered to scale the wall. He made it unscathed and several other American soldiers clambered up the 40-foot face. At 11.03am, the Stars and Stripes was flying from atop the Outer City Wall, accompanied by much cheering and whooping from below. Under fire, American troops clambered down the other side of the wall and headed west towards the Legations.

The Japanese met stiff resistance at their gate, including coming under Chinese artillery fire. The British knew of a better way into the Imperial City. Once over the Outer City Wall the British, led by a returned businessman, wended their way through the warren of streets in the Chinese City to the great Tartar Wall. British troops also saw a Royal Navy sailor standing atop a huge wall in the far distance signalling to them using semaphore flags: 'Come in by the water gate.' MacDonald had already informed Gaselee that the quickest way through would be via the Water Gate, a drainage canal leading under the enormous wall. Seventy Indian sepoys of the 7th Duke of Connaught's Own Rajput Regiment followed their British officers, including General Gaselee who led very much from the front, through the sewage, mud and stinking sludge in the canal, despite coming under sporadic rifle fire from the Hata-men to their right, and arrived inside the Imperial City unscathed. They moved quickly into the Legation Quarter and promptly lifted the 55-day siege at 2.30pm, being greeted by hysterically happy civilians and legation guards. A few shots were fired at them by Gansu troops, who then fled. British casualties amounted to one man dead from sunstroke.

The Americans arrived at 4.30pm after skirmishing with various Chinese strongpoints during their drive through to the Legation Quarter. One man had been killed and nine wounded. The Japanese and Russians were relieved later in the day. The following day, Japanese and French troops relieved the stubborn defenders of the Beitang Cathedral.

The defence of the legations and Beitang Cathedral had cost the legation guards 64 killed and 156 wounded. Foreign civilian casualties were 12 dead and 23 wounded. About 1,000 Chinese Christians had also perished during the siege.

If the victorious Allies thought that they would have an opportunity to punish the Dowager Empress they were to be disappointed. She, along with the Emperor, and a select few of her court, slipped out of the Forbidden City disguised as peasants in three wooden wagons on the morning of the next day, the 15th. Cixi had fled to Shanxi for what remaining Chinese officials euphemistically labelled a 'tour of inspection.' General Ronglu was left behind to negotiate the peace terms with Gaselee and the Allied Powers.

In the meantime, Peking was thoroughly looted by the victorious Western troops. Palaces were stripped of their valuables, public auctions were held, and a steady and profitable business done in jade, ceramics, jewellery, and art works, a good proportion ending up in famous Western museums where it remains on display to this day, much to China's chagrin. One journalist described the Allied army as 'the biggest looting expedition since Pizarro.' Peking, like Berlin forty-five years later, was an occupied city divided into national sectors.

A Peace agreement, known as the 'Boxer Protocols', was signed on 7 September 1901. China was forced to pay an indemnity to the eight Great Powers amounting to $335 million, plus interest, over a thirty-nine year period. The Protocols stipulated that all officials who had supported the Boxers be executed or exiled (one high ranking victim was General Dong Fuxiang who was sent into exile), and China's northern fortifications pulled down.

With peace terms agreed, and the palaces stripped of their valuables, a victory parade was held in the Forbidden City just to make the point before the Imperial Court. Then, on 17 September 1901, the Allied army left Peking, except for legation guard units, and returned to the coast. The Boxer's legacy was British guard battalions at Tientsin and Shanghai, plus a reinforced company at Peking until 1940. The US followed suit by stationing the North China Marines permanently at Tientsin and Peking. The gunboats of the Great Powers regularly patrolled the Yangtze River until 1941.

The Qing Dynasty had been fatally weakened by its support for the Boxers and entered a rapid decline over the coming years. Dowager Empress Cixi returned from exile on 7 January 1902 to live in the Forbidden City. She died there in 1908 – the same day the imprisoned emperor, her nephew Guangxu, also died in mysterious circumstances. China's new 'Son of Heaven' was a 3-year-old named Pu Yi. In 1911, a revolution transformed China from a feudal absolute monarchy into a republic and Pu Yi, by then aged 6, abdicated the following year. The Last Emperor was allowed to live in the Forbidden City until 1924, a monarch without a country, until rudely ejected by a warlord who had taken control of Peking. So the Qing Dynasty passed into history, replaced by warlordism, dictatorship and eventually foreign invasion and civil war. A major contributory factor in its demise was Cixi's support for the Boxers.

Sir Claude MacDonald's inspirational leadership during the siege won him promotion to ambassador to Japan, and he died there in 1915. General Gaselee was promoted and appointed Knight Grand Commander of the Order of the Indian Empire in 1901. He died in England in 1918. Captain Halliday, who had won a VC in a Peking back alley during the most desperate moments of the siege, ended his career as a full general. Sir Edward Seymour, far from suffering for the mistakes made on his first relief expedition, ended up as an Admiral of the Fleet. John Jellicoe,

Seymour's able subordinate, who had been shot in the head during the relief, went on to command the Fleet at the Battle of Jutland in 1916. Lieutenant Roger Keyes, who commanded HMS *Fame* during the boarding of the Chinese destroyers at the Taku Forts, would later become Chief of Combined Operations during the Second World War.

The Relief of Peking was one of the first examples of a multi-national military expedition, and although there were internal differences and rivalries, the alliance held and the army achieved its objectives. Much of the reason for the operation's success can be attributed to the strong and diplomatic leadership displayed by General Gaselee. Unfortunately, within thirteen years, many of the allies who saved the Peking Legations would find themselves on opposite sides during the First World War.

Chapter 5

Slaughter in Shangri-La

I got so sick of the slaughter that I ceased fire, though the general's order was to make as big a bag as possible.

Lieutenant Arthur Hadow,
Norfolk Regiment, Tibet, 1904

Tibet – the name conjures up images of Mount Everest, Buddhist monasteries perched atop snowy precipices, the rhythmic chanting of saffron-robed monks, a mysterious Shangri-La hidden at the top of the earth, inaccessible, unknowable and elusive. Tibet – nation or province? It is the perennial question that occupies the Chinese government today. China claims Tibet as a vassal state (or in modern communist parlance 'autonomous region'), citing evidence that the successive religious rulers, the Dalai Lamas, had been vassals of the Qing Dynasty emperors for centuries. When Mao Zedong's People's Liberation Army bloodily occupied Tibet in 1950, 'The Great Helmsman' could argue that he was merely confirming and formalising this ancient relationship with China. The question of Tibet's status, like that of Taiwan, remains a taboo subject in China today, and few Chinese question the legitimacy of China's claim to the country. Surprisingly, British interference in Tibet in the early twentieth century was an important contributing factor to the current situation.

Just two years after the successful conclusion of the campaign to eradicate the Boxers, Britain found herself at war once again in China. But this war was to be unlike all the other wars Britain had waged against the Celestial Empire, for this conflict was fought on the periphery of the Qing Empire in a country that even today has the power to divide political opinion, and to cause deep controversy. It was also a war that was fought not for opium or, indeed, for any kind of trade or territorial benefit, but to keep another powerful empire out of the British sphere of influence. The campaign was led by one of the British Empire's greatest explorers who took British and Indian troops to the highest land-mass on earth – the Himalayas.

The Chinese had first gained control of large areas of what is now modern Tibet between 1724 and 1728. The Qing Dynasty established a resident commissioner, or *Amban*, at Lhasa and in 1750 had ruthlessly crushed a Tibetan rebellion. The *Amban* closely advised the religious ruler of Tibet, the Dalai Lama. In 1792 the Chinese successfully ejected a Nepalese invasion of Tibet and afterwards established garrisons along the border with Tibet's Himalayan neighbour. Tibet was not, however, made a province of China. In 1834, the mighty Sikh Empire invaded and annexed the Kingdom of Ladakh, a culturally Tibetan region that adjoins Tibet. Then, in 1841, the Sikhs invaded Tibet proper but a joint Chinese-Tibetan army threw them out. As the 19th century pro-gressed, the Qing Dynasty became progressively weaker, and her control over Tibet weakened until it became virtually symbolic.

Britain's most geographically extreme war was an extension of the 'Great Game', the diplomatic and espionage tug-of-war between London and St. Petersburg. Here it would be played out in the high Himalayas. The British administration in India rightly feared Russian expansion south. China, and by default Tibet, was one area where such an expansion of Tsarism appeared probable by the early 20th century.

Rumours abounded in India that the Chinese were planning to gift Tibet to Russia as part of a strategic realignment. If this were to happen, one of the buffer states that kept the Russians out of India (the others being Afghanistan, Nepal, Sikkim and Bhutan) would be eliminated. Many British colonial administrators felt that the close relations enjoyed by Tsar Nicholas II's representa-tive and the 13th Dalai Lama at the Potala Palace in Lhasa had lent credence to their hypothesis. Also a Russian explorer had actually been the first European to live in Lhasa in 1900.

In 1903, the Viceroy of India, Lord Curzon, keen to extend British influence into Tibet, proposed to the Chinese and Tibetan authorities that their envoys should meet with British representatives at Khampa Dzong, a village just north of the Sikkim border, to discuss 'trade'. The Chinese ordered the Dalai Lama to attend, but he refused and also refused to provide porters and transport to move the Chinese *Amban* to the meeting place. Curzon instructed Major Francis Younghusband to lead an expedition to Khampa Dzong.

Younghusband was born to a British military family in India in 1863. After Sandhurst, he was commissioned into the 1st King's Dragoon Guards in 1882. His first Asian expedition was made in 1886–87 when he was on leave from his regiment in India. Younghusband explored Manchuria's Changbai Mountains, crossed the Gobi Desert to Chinese Turkestan (now Xinjiang Province, China), and charted a route from Kashgar to India. These formidable achievements led to his election as the youngest member of the Royal Geographical Society and the award of the Society's Gold Medal. As a captain in 1889, Younghusband, with a small escort of Gurkhas, had charted Ladakh, the territory that bordered Tibet, and the Karakorum. In 1890, Major Younghusband was seconded from the army to the Indian Civil Service as a political officer.

In July 1903, Younghusband arrived at Gangtok, Sikkim. British policy had shifted from trying to entice the Tibetans into trade to attempting to provoke a war that would lead to a British victory, and the right to establish diplomatic and trade missions in Lhasa (and end once and for all Russian influence in the country). Younghusband and the expedition's military commander, Lieutenant Colonel Herbert Brander, searched for a pretext to enter Tibet, and discovered one when some Tibetan yaks drifted over the border. Younghusband branded the yak invasion 'Tibetan hostility' and, in August 1903, crossed the border in force.

Based at Khampa Dzong ('dzong' meaning fort), Younghusband's force consisted of 3,000 fighting men plus over 10,000 Sherpas, porters and camp followers. Younghusband assumed the post of 'British Commissioner to Tibet' while Brigadier General James MacDonald was to lead the enlarged military expedition. Under his command, MacDonald had the best high altitude troops that the British Indian Army could provide, as well as considerable modern firepower that was to be used to lethal effect. For the invasion of Tibet, Younghusband and MacDonald took with them 1,150 men consisting of eight companies of the 23rd Sikh Pioneers and a half company of the Madras Sappers and Miners. There were six companies of the 8th Gurkha Rifles. A Maxim gun detachment from the Norfolk Regiment provided support along with two 7-pounder guns manned by Gurkhas and two 10-pounder guns of the 7th Mountain Battery, Royal Garrison Artillery.

The Tibetans were keen to avoid a war with the world's largest superpower. Their own armed forces consisted of a mediaeval army, armed with swords, spears and ancient matchlock muskets. Its soldiers were brave, but no match for machine guns, modern rifles and artillery. The Tibetan general commanding forces at Yadong sent a message to MacDonald stating that he would not attack the British if they did not attack him. Younghusband replied on 6 December 1903: 'We are not at war with Tibet and that, unless we our ourselves attacked, we shall not attack the Tibetans.' But, although Younghusband's army had been encamped at Khampa Dzong for months, no Tibetan officials had come to talk. Sitting still for several months at such an altitude and under extreme weather conditions inevitably cost lives. 'We had twelve cases of pneumonia among the sepoys,' wrote Younghusband of his mostly Indian force, 'eleven of which, from the altitude, proved fatal. And one poor young fellow in the postal department, Mr. Lewis, had to have both his feet amputated for frost-bite, and eventually died of the effects.'[1] But in true imperial style, the mission to Lhasa was not only a military one; it was also one of exploration and discovery. 'Captain Ryder would go off surveying,' recalled Younghusband, 'Mr. Hayden would make geologising expeditions; Captain Walton would collect every living animal of any size and description he would detect; Captain O'Connor would always be surrounded by Tibetans, of every degree of dirt.' Younghusband was in his element, commenting that 'the natural scenery was an unfailing pleasure.'[2]

Tibet was an extraordinarily beautiful place that deeply affected many of the British officers who were sent to campaign there. Their memoirs are full of vivid descriptions of the landscape and its people. 'Daybreak on the Thibetan [sic] frontier,' wrote Colonel H.C. Wylly in 1904, 'but a few moments ago it was still quite dark,

Battle of Shajiao Battery, Pearl River Estuary, Canton, 7 January 1841. The 37th Madras Native Infantry storms Chinese positions.

Battle damage on the walls of Chapoo Fort (Zhapu) caused by Royal Navy bombardment, 1842.

Lovell Pattern 1839 Infantry Musket, 0.75-calibre with socket bayonet, standard British weapon during the First Opium War.

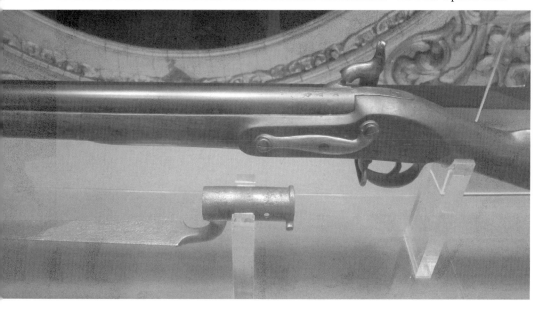

(*Above*) Major Francis Younghusband pictured in Tibet in 1903.

(*Left*) British troops storming the Taku Forts, Second Opium War, 1860.

Interior of one of the Taku Forts following British bombardment and storming, Boxer Rebellion, 1900.

Indian troops parade inside the Summer Palace, Peking, 1902.

HMS *Tamar*, headquarters ship of the China Squadron, Hong Kong, 1905.

'A' (British) Company, Shanghai Volunteer Corps at their annual inspection parade, 1912.

British infantry parading on the Bund, Shanghai, 1927.

Shanghai Volunteer Corps armoured car and infantry guarding the northern end of the International Settlement, 1937.

Shanghai Volunteer Corps machine gun post, 1937.

Shanghai Volunteer Corps soldiers playing mahjong, 1937.

Japanese heavy cruiser *Izumo*, which attacked HMS *Peterel* in Shanghai, 8 December 1941.

Japanese prisoner being searched by a British officer during the liberation of Hong Kong, September 1945.

HMS *Amethyst* and
Able Seacat Simon, 1949.

Damage to
HMS *Amethyst*
caused by Chinese
artillery, 1949.

HMS *Consort*, 1949.

2nd King Edward VII's Own
Gurkha Rifles (The Sirmoor Rifles),
Hong Kong, early 1970s.

Bicycle patrol from 6th Queen
Elizabeth's Own Gurkha Rifles
apprehends an 'illegal' on the
Hong Kong border, 1985.

British naval traditions linger post-Handover: Hong Kong Sea Cadet Corps parade, 2010.

British hardware still displayed outside Gun Club Hill Barracks, Kowloon, 2013. This former British barracks is now used by the People's Liberation Army, though the name remains unchanged.

British Army traditions post-Handover: Hong Kong Adventure Corps mount guard at Sai Wan Military Ceremony, November 2012.

and then a greyness came stealing down the pass; the snow-capped hills around us take on a pearl-coloured and then a soft pink hue, rocks with the snow lying in their fissures are drawn sharp against the sky.'[3]

In April 1904, Younghusband decided to advance his force fifty miles to Tuna, knowing full well that the Tibetans would have no choice but to resist. 'We moved along as rapidly as possible at those high altitudes and encumbered with heavy clothing,' noted Younghusband. The cold was intense. On 4 April, the Tibetans made their first attempt to stop the British advance on Lhasa at Chumik Shenko with catastrophic results.

'A short way out we were met by a messenger from the Tibetan General, urging us to go back to India. I told the messenger to gallop back at once and tell the Lhasa General that we were on our way to Gyantse, and were going as far as Guru, ten miles distant, that day. I said that we did not want a fight, and would not unless we were opposed, but that the road must be left clear for us, and the Tibetans must withdraw from their positions across it.'[4] The British force advanced across a gravelly plain and halted 1,000 yards from the Tibetan defences. Facing Younghusband and MacDonald at the high Himalayan pass at Chumik Shenko were 3,000 Tibetan troops who were dug in behind a 5-foot high rock wall. On the scree slope behind and above the wall were eight stone bunkers, or sangars. The Tibetan general rode out to meet the British force having first ordered his men to extinguish their musket fuses – lighting them again would be a laborious and time-consuming process. The Tibetan's apparently peaceful gesture effectively rendered his men's firearms useless at the critical moment. 'They rode up briskly with a little cavalcade,' recalled Younghusband, 'and we all dismounted, set out rugs and coats on the ground, and sat down for the final discussion.'[5]

Younghusband reiterated his previous arguments but the Tibetan general virtually ordered the British to return to Khampa Dzong, and to negotiate from there. 'There was no possible reasoning with such people,' wrote Younghusband. 'They had such over-weening confidence in their Lama's powers. How *could* anyone dare to resist the orders of the Great Lama? Surely lightning would descend from heaven or the earth open up and destroy anyone who had such temerity?'[6] Younghusband explained that he had waited for Tibetan envoys for eight months, to no avail, and all of his letters had gone unanswered so that he was under orders to advance to Gyantse. The Tibetans were given fifteen minutes to decide whether or not to resist the British advance. Younghusband was deeply frustrated by the Tibetan's strong belief in the Dalai Lama, and in their religious charms. 'We might just as well have spoken to a stone wall. Not the very slightest effect was produced,' he recalled. 'After all, our numbers were not very overwhelming. The Tibetans had charms against our bullets, and the supernatural powers of the Great Lama in the background.'[7]

The British officers noticed that the Tibetans had failed to fortify the western side of the great mountain pass, leaving them exposed to a flanking move. Younghusband was later at pains to state that he and MacDonald flew in the face of military logic and gave the Tibetans repeated chances to back down, knowing full well that the British could have destroyed the Tibetan forces at any time. Instead, Younghusband risked his men's lives by ordering them to approach the Tibetan positions across completely open ground and 'shoulder' the Tibetans out of those positions without opening fire. 'The Tibetans on their side showed great indecision. They also had apparently received orders not to fire first, and the whole affair seemed likely to end in comedy rather than in the tragedy which actually followed.'[8]

After the Indian troops had removed most of the Tibetans from their positions a change of heart occurred. The Tibetans began returning to their positions and they would not leave the wall. They were huddled together 'like a flock of sheep behind the wall,' noted Younghusband. 'Our infantry were in position on the hillside only 20 yards above them on the one side; on the other our Maxims and guns were trained upon them at not 200 yards' distance. Our mounted infantry were in readiness in the plain a quarter of a mile away.'[9] The Tibetan general and his staff remained on the British side of the wall, mingled in with the sepoys.

Younghusband and General MacDonald conferred, and decided to order the disarming of the Tibetan soldiers. 'I sent Captain O'Connor to announce to him [the Tibetan general] that General Macdonald and I had decided that his men must be disarmed,' recalled Younghusband, 'but he remained sullen and did nothing.'[10]

Younghusband forcefully maintained that it was the Tibetan general who fired first. 'After a pause, the disarmament was actually commenced, he [the Tibetan general] threw himself upon a sepoy, drew a revolver, and shot the sepoy in the jaw.' All hell now broke loose. 'Not, I think, with any deliberate intention, but from sheer insanity, the signal had now been given,' wrote Younghusband. 'Other Tibetan shots immediately followed. Simultaneous volleys from our own troops rang out; the guns and Maxims commenced to fire.'[11]

The fighting was at very close quarters for the first few minutes. 'Tibetan swordsmen made a rush upon any within reach, and the plucky and enterprising Edmund Candler, the very able correspondent of the *Daily Mail*, received more than a dozen wounds, while Major Wallace Dunlop, one of the best officers in the force, was severely handled.'[12] When the fighting broke out the Tibetans, with their greater numbers, posed a serious threat to the British troops. 'For just one single instant the Tibetans, by a concerted and concentrated rush, might have broken our own thin line, and have carried the Mission and the military staff,' recalled Younghusband. 'But that instant passed in a flash. Before a few seconds were over, rifles and guns were dealing the deadliest destruction on them in their huddled masses.'[13]

The Tibetan general was among the first to die. Rifle fire crackled along the British front ranks, while the Norfolk's Maxim guns hammered out lines of bullets that cut down hundreds. The Tibetans bravely refused to run away and instead they retreated slowly back down the pass with their fronts to the British, huge numbers of their men falling dead and wounded as they went. When the British sent in a cavalry troop, the Tibetans fixed bayonets and bravely repulsed them before they reached shelter half a mile from the wall. 'I got so sick of the slaughter that I ceased fire, though the general's order was to make as big a bag as possible,' wrote Lieutenant Arthur Hadow, commanding MacDonald's machine gun detachment. 'I hope I shall never have to shoot down men walking away,'[14] he added in disgust. 'The plain was strewn with dead Tibetans, and our troops instantly and without direct orders ceased firing – though, in fact, they had only fired thirteen rounds per man,' wrote Younghusband.

Tibetan casualties amounted to between 600 and 700 dead, with 168 wounded. British casualties echoed the one-sided victories of the Opium Wars in China – just twelve wounded. 'After the action, General Macdonald ordered the whole of the medical staff to attend the wounded Tibetans. Everything that with our limited means we could do for them was done. Captains Davies, Walton, Baird, Franklin and Kelly, devoted themselves to their care. A rough hospital was made at Tuna.'[15]

'It was a terrible and ghastly business,' said Younghusband, 'but it was not fair for an English statesman to call it a massacre of "unarmed men", for photographs testify that the Tibetans were all armed: and, looking back now, I do not see how it could possibly have been avoided.'[16] Younghusband placed the blame for the high death toll squarely on the Dalai Lama: 'Ignorant and arrogant, this priest herded the superstitious peasantry to destruction.'[17]

Younghusband felt that the slaughter, though a terrible thing, would serve a useful purpose in convincing the Dalai Lama to submit to negotiations. Writing to Lord Curzon in India, Younghusband stated: 'I trust the tremendous punishment they have received will prevent further fighting, and induce them at last to negotiate.' In this Younghusband was to be sorely disabused, for although profoundly shocked by the events of 4 April, the Dalai Lama did not immediately order peace envoys to be sent out. 'Tibetan politics were those of drift,' wrote Younghusband, 'that Chinese officials were too engrossed in self-seeking, and hence the Tibetans shirked action.'[18] The day after the fighting a 2,000-man Tibetan force retreated without engaging the British and Younghusband resumed his march to Gyantse.

The fort at Gyantse was one of the most astounding sights in all Tibet. 'Gyantse ... has two principle features,' wrote Younghusband, 'the jong [Dzong] and the monastery, called Palkhor Choide. The jong is a really imposing structure built of strong, solid masonry, and rising in tiers of walls up a rocky eminence springing abruptly out of the plain to a height of 400 or 500 feet. It has the most commanding and dominant look.' The fort was originally constructed in 1390; its lofty position completely dominated the surrounding area and the route to Lhasa. 'The monastery immediately adjoining it at a part of the base of the hill is also impressive from the height and solidity of the walls with which it is surrounded, and by the massiveness of the buildings within the walls.'[19]

Some important buildings near the Dzong were taken by British troops, and a defensive posture maintained, though the mighty Dzong itself remained unconquered.

'The demeanour of the inhabitants was respectful,' noted Young-husband of the citizens of Gyantse town. 'The people said they had not the slightest wish to fight us, and only desired to escape being commandeered by the Lhasa authorities.'[20] But the Tibetans' dilatory tactics continued to irritate Younghusband. On 22 April, he sent a message to India suggesting that the best remedy for such tactics was to move the Mission to Lhasa and carry on negotiations directly with the Dalai Lama in the capital, and not from halfway at Gyantse. 'Our prestige, I urged, was then at its height, Nepal and Bhutan were with us, the people were not against us, the Tibetan soldiers did not care to fight, the Lamas were stunned. By a decisive move a permanent settlement could be procured.'[21]

However, just two days after Younghusband had sent this message to Lord Curzon, rumours arrived in Gyantse that the Tibetans were gathering military forces again, that they were building defensive walls across the road at Karo-la Pass blocking the way to Lhasa, and had established camps containing between 700 and 800 soldiers there. Lieutenant Colonel Brander, in com-mand of the Mission escort, with 500 men, two artillery guns, two Maxims and some mounted infantry, left on 28 April to find out if the rumours were true.

One company of mounted infantry under the command of Captain Hodgson was sent to reconnoitre the 16,000 feet Karo-la Pass. On 1 May, Hodgson sent word that three miles beyond the pass he had encountered a wall stretching for 600 yards across the valley. This obstacle was defended by 1,000–1,500 heavily armed Tibetans who opened a strong fire the moment Hodgson's company approached them. After returning fire, Hodgson retired to Gyantse. Further reports reached Younghusband that Tibetan troops were assembling in the Rong Valley and at Shigatse. It seemed clear that the Dalai Lama was not prepared to allow the British to enter Lhasa easily.

Brander asked permission to attack the Tibetans before things came to a head. 'He had much frontier experience, and I also had some, and we both of us knew that when such gatherings take place it is a pretty sound general principle to take the initiative, and hit hard at them before they have time to accumulate over-whelming strength.'[22] Brander would take with him two-thirds of the British force leaving Major Murray, 8th Gurkha Rifles, in command of the remaining third at Gyantse. Karo-la Pass was forty-five miles from Gyantse. If Gyantse was attacked in force there were doubts that the small number of troops remaining could hold it; and if it fell, Brander's force would be trapped between enemy forces with his supply lines cut. But Young-husband and the other officers knew that they could not leave the Tibetans in control of Karo-la and nearby Kangma as they threatened the British lines of communication. Younghusband informed Lord Curzon of the expedition and also sent a message to the Chinese and Tibetans that the British were there to negotiate, and not to fight.

'There could be no question, then that we meant to negotiate and not to fight,' wrote Younghusband, 'yet they still neither sent a negotiator, nor said they had any intention to negotiate, instead they massed troops to attack us.'[23] Brander's assault was given the green light to proceed.

Brander left Gyantse on 3 May with three companies from the 32nd Sikh Pioneers, one company from the 8th Gurkhas, two 7-pounder field guns and two Maxim machine guns. The next day wounded Tibetans who were being treated at Gyantse warned the British that some form of attack was likely (many Tibetans were not loyal to the Lamas, who had ordered them to fight the British). Major Murray dispatched a mounted patrol to reconnoiter the land around Gyantse but he found nothing.

'At dawn the next morning the storm burst,' recalled Young-husband. 'I was suddenly awakened by shots and loud booing close by my tent. I dashed out, and there were Tibetans firing through our own loopholes only a few yards off.'[24] Eight hundred Tibetans had marched through the night from Shigatse and assaulted the British position at 4.30am, just as dawn broke. They attempted to rush the British post, 'a substantial house with a garden at one side, the wall of which we had loopholed.'[25] The Tibetan attack was almost successful. 'They as nearly as possible forced an entrance, but were stoutly held at bay by two gallant little Gurkha sentries till our men turned out.' Younghusband, still clad in his pyjamas and half asleep, rushed to the citadel, the place from which the British had decided to make a last stand, though he later felt rather ashamed. 'Personally, I did not deserve to get through the attack unscathed ... the first thought that struck me was to go to the rendezvous, agreed upon beforehand, in what we called the citadel. But I ought, as I did on other occasions – and as I think always should be done in cases of any sudden attack – to have made straight for the wall with whatever weapon came to hand, and joined in repelling the attack during the first crucial moments.'[26]

The British quickly turned the tables against the large Tibetan force. 'As at Guru, once the single favourable moment had flashed by, nothing but disaster lay before them.' The battle ended at 6.30am, and approximately 250 Tibetans were killed or wounded. Major Murray immediately pursued the retiring Tibetans two miles down the road to Shigatse before another large body of enemy troops fired on his party. Murray and Younghusband realised that Gyantse was besieged.

Murray, with the assistance of the sapper officer Captain Ryder, reinforced the British position during the day. The British garrison amounted to only 170 men. Night-time attacks were expected; for the British lost the advantage that their long-range modern rifles gave them once darkness had fallen. 'They fired a good deal during this and the following nights,' recorded Younghusband, 'but we kept a good watch, and we heard afterwards that the Lamas tried to organise a second attack on us, but the men refused to turn out.'[27]

On 6 May, Colonel Brander had successfully cleared Karo-la Pass, but the battle had hung in the balance for a few minutes. The Tibetans were armed with locally made and foreign rifles and they were concentrated behind the loop holed stonewall that they had constructed across the Pass. Word had reached Brander that Gyantse was under attack. 'To attack such a position at a height of over 16,000 feet above sea-level, surrounded with glaciers, with only a sixth of the numbers opposed to him, and with his communications not over safe behind, Colonel Brander had in truth to set his teeth and steel his nerves.'[28] In the history of the British Empire such intestinal fortitude as displayed by Brander and his men when faced by overwhelming enemy forces often was the magic element that led to ultimate victory.

Major Row and his Gurkhas were ordered to scale the steep hillsides of the gorge and drive the Tibetan defenders, who were dug in on the cliffs, from their lofty positions and then attack the wall defenders from above. Unfortunately, the weather turned against the British as a howling snow blizzard reduced visibility to just a few feet. Captain Bethune led a frontal assault on the wall, which failed disastrously. 'Poor Bethune,' wrote Younghusband, 'a typically steady, reliable and lion-hearted officer was killed. The guns proved absolutely ineffective. Ammunition was none too plentiful.'[29]

The Gurkhas saved the day. Suddenly they emerged above the wall at 18,000 feet (2,000 feet higher than the summit of Mont Blanc). The blizzard blew itself out and the Nepalese riflemen opened fire down into the packed ranks of enemy soldiers who were holding the wall. The Tibetans panicked and began to run away until the entire position gave way and the great mass of Tibetan troops fled. Captain Ottley and a company of mounted infantry chased them halfway to Lhasa, killing many.

On 7 May, Major Murray was relieved when Brander's force arrived back at Gyantse. Soon, his mounted infantry would be proving their worth against the Tibetans. A party of Tibetan horsemen was spotted sauntering unsupported along the valley out of reach of the British rifles. Twenty mounted infantry under Captain Ottley dashed out in pursuit. Another body of Tibetan horsemen descended and attempted to cut Ottley off. 'But Captain Ottley was not to be so easily caught. He suddenly wheeled on to some rising ground, dismounted his men as quick as lightning, and was blazing away at *both* parties before they could realise what had happened. In a moment several Tibetans dropped, and the remainder scuttled away as fast as they could.'[30]

Colonel Brander judged the Dzong too difficult to capture with his available artillery and troops. Instead, he harried the surrounding area, clearing villages, demolishing strong points and maintaining a supply service to the rear.

On 14 May, the British Government, communicating through the Viceroy in India, concluded that recent events made a British advance to Lhasa inevitable. Younghusband was told to inform the Chinese *Amban* that he would give the Dalai Lama another month to send someone to open negotiations at Gyantse, after which he would resume his advance on Lhasa.

General MacDonald at Chumbi prepared to support the mission. On 24 May, strong reinforcements reached Gyantse consisting of two powerful 10-pounder mountain guns commanded by Lieutenant Easton, a company of Indian sappers and miners, fifty Sikhs and twenty mounted infantry. One much appreciated arrival was Captain Sheppard of the Royal Engineers, a brave, resourceful and well-known officer from whom much was expected.

On 26 May, the command assaulted the strongly built village of Palla, 1,100-yards from the British position. It was well defended, and the British launched a night assault. 'A few sharp rifle cracks rang out, and soon from the jong and from the Palla village there was a continuous crackle, with sharp spouts of flame lighting the darkness,' recalled Younghusband. Captain Sheppard dashed up to the wall of a solidly defended house in the village, shot three Tibetans with his revolver, placed a charge of gun cotton, lit the fuse and dashed for cover. 'Soon after a great explosion was heard, followed by a deadly silence.'[31] A breach had been made. Captain O'Connor did the same at another house. Lieutenants Garstin and Walker tried the same tactic against another well-defended property, but the fuse failed and Garstin was killed. A further eleven Indian soldiers were also wounded. Major Peterson of the Sikh Pioneers then stormed the village house by house with artillery support.

On 5 June, the government in India ordered Younghusband to proceed to Chumbi, with an escort of forty mounted infantry under Major Murray, to meet with General MacDonald. At Kangma, a fortified position held by the British, Younghusband met the garrison that consisted of Captain Pearson and 100 men from the 23rd Sikh Pioneers.

The next morning Younghusband found himself under attack. 'I had risen at 4.30am ... to make an early start, and was just dressed when I heard that peculiar jackal-like yell which the Tibetans had used when they made their attacks on Gyantse. I instantly dashed on to the roof, and there, sure enough, was a mob of about 300 of them weighing down upon the post, and before our men were out they were right up to the walls, hurling stones and firing at me up on the roof.'[32]

'We all, dressed or undressed, dashed to the walls, seizing the first rifles we could find, and firing away as hard as we could,' recalled Younghusband. 'As before ... they suffered terribly for their want of military acumen. Sixty or seventy were killed.'[33] The rest were driven off.

Strong reinforcements arrived from India consisting of the rest of the mountain battery under Major Fuller, a wing of the Royal Fusiliers, who were regular British troops, the 40th Pathans and 29th Punjabis. On 26 June, the reinforcements reached Gyantse after defeating 800 Tibetans at the village and monastery of Niani.

MacDonald now had to break up the Tibetan forces that were investing Gyantse. He began by attacking a strong position on a ridge topped by the Tse-Chen Monastery and several fortified towers and sangars on 28 May. The battle took most of the day. At 5.30pm, the 8th Gurkha Rifles and 40th Pathans stormed the position, well supported by the artillery. One British officer, Captain Gaster, was killed and three others wounded during the assault.

Peace feelers were once again extended to the Tibetans. The important Te Lama came to talk to Younghusband from Shigatse. He was in favour of peace but wanted the advice of other more senior lamas. The Tongsen Penlop from Bhutan was closely involved in these negotiations, urging the lamas to stop fighting and come to an understanding with the British. A durbar was organised under tents, but talks soon broke down.

The British now determined to assault and capture the mighty Gyantse Dzong. 'It was built of solid masonry on a precipitous rock rising sheer out of the plain. It was held by at least double, and possibly treble, our own force, and they were armed, many hundreds of them, with Lhasa-made rifles, which carried over a thousand yards.'[34]

At 1.45pm on 5 July 1904, MacDonald opened brisk rifle fire on the Dzong. At 3.30pm two guns, six companies of infantry and one mounted infantry company were sent to make a feint on the northern side of the Dzong. This succeeded in getting the Tibetans to reinforce that side. After dark, the British column was quietly withdrawn. Just after midnight twelve guns, twelve infantry companies and one of mounted infantry with a half company of sappers moved out into two columns to a position southeast of the Dzong. The attack commenced with 'the whole jong lighting up with the flashes of rifle and jingal [sic] fire, and down below our own fire getting hotter and hotter.'[35]

The British forces reorganised, with Colonel Campbell and the 40th Pathans on the right, and Major Murray and the 8th Gurkhas on the left. The Royal Fusiliers supported. Captain Sheppard succeeded in setting a charge under the walls of the strongest held house in the fortress, opening a breach. On his left, Lieutenants Gurdon and Burney also blew breaches in houses, Gurdon being killed in the process.

At 3pm, MacDonald ordered four companies in reserve, and the 10-pounder guns to commence firing on the portion of the wall to be breached for the main assault. Bit by bit the great wall tumbled under a storm of shells until, by 4pm, a big enough opening had been created. 'Rapid firing' was ordered and the infantry and Maxim guns showered the fortress's upper floors with fire to cover the assault force as it slowly climbed up to the breach. 'Very, very gradually ... the Gurkhas, under Lieutenant [John] Grant, made their upward way. First a few arrived just under the breach, then more and more.'[36] Supported by the Royal Fusiliers, the Gurkhas soon found themselves in a bottleneck before the breach and under intense enemy rifle fire. Grant and Havildar Karbir Pun broke through alone, and despite being wounded, the two men carried the attack into the Dzong. Grant was later awarded the Victoria Cross and Pun the Indian Order of Merit First Class, a glowing citation appearing in *The London Gazette*:

... on emerging from the cover of the village [they] had to advance up a bare, almost precipitous rock face with little or no cover and under heavy fire. Showers of rocks and stones were at the time being hurled down the hillside by the enemy. Lt Grant followed by Havildar Karbir Pun at once attempted to scale it but on reaching the top he was wounded and hurled back as was the havildar who fell down the rock some 30 feet. Regardless of their injuries, they again attempted to scale the breach and covered by the fire of men below were successful ... the havildar shooting one Tibetan on gaining the top.[37]

The Gurkhas and Royal Fusiliers charged through the breach, fighting tier to tier until the Union Jack was at last unfurled atop the fort's highest pinnacle.

On 14 July, the British began their advance on Lhasa un-opposed, the capture of Gyantse Dzong appearing to have destroyed Tibetan morale to resist. Once again, Younghusband sent letters ahead to both the Dalai Lama and the Chinese *Amban* asking for negotiations. But just when it seemed that Tibetan resolve to stop the British had cracked, a fresh block on the expedition was imposed at Karo-la Pass, where the British had already fought. The wall across the 16,600-foot pass had been repaired and extended, buttressing against the surrounding mountains that reached up to 24,000 feet high and were topped with snow. Behind the wall the Tibetans had constructed a line of rock sangars. About 1,500 Tibetans garrisoned the position.

A 7am on 18 July 1904, the attack began when the Royal Fusiliers attacked in the centre and the 8th Gurkhas and 40th Pathans sent parties out onto each flank. The artillery had a field day, firing from several hundred feet above the Tibetan position, the high altitude making the shells travel faster and longer. The Gurkhas and Pathans struggled up to 18,000 feet, turned the Tibetan flanks and then the artillery pursued the fleeing enemy with shrapnel shells.

Following the breaching of the Karo-la Pass position, the first signs that the Tibetans wished to negotiate reached Major Younghusband. A deputation of high lamas from Lhasa met Younghusband at Nagartse, a few miles on from Karo-la Pass. The war-fighting phase was now well and truly over after one of the most extraordinary campaigns in British military history, fought 'on the roof of the world'. Younghusband now assumed command from General MacDonald who, with the exception of 2,000 troops, marched back to Sikkim.

Younghusband reached Lhasa on 4 August 1904 only to discover that the Potala Palace was empty – the 13th Dalai Lama had fled to Outer Mongolia, fearing British retribution. The Chinese *Amban's* troops escorted Younghusband into the city where he spent some weeks intimidating the Regent, Gandon Tri Rimpoche, and an *ad hoc* Tibetan government, into signing the so-called 'Anglo-Tibetan Agreement'.

Younghusband's self-drafted agreement allowed for Anglo-Tibetan trade at Yadong, Gyantse and Gartok, and forced the Tibetans to pay an indemnity of 500,000 pounds (later reduced). The Chumbi Valley would be ceded to Britain until the indemnity was paid, and the Tibet-Sikkim border recognised. Tibet was forced to promise that it would have no relations with any other foreign power, making Tibet a British Protectorate. Naturally, the Chinese immediately rejected this last part of the treaty and Britain actually backed down – formally accepting Chinese claims over Tibet.

Acting Viceroy Lord Ampthill later reduced the indemnity by two thirds and a revised agreement, the Anglo-Chinese Convention of 1906, agreed to recognise China's rights over Tibet in return for a sizeable 'bribe' from the Qing Court. Britain also agreed not to annex Tibetan territory or to interfere in the administration of Tibet by China.

The British returned to India, and peace returned to Tibet. But that nation's status continued to provide conflict and diplomatic uncertainty for generations to come. In 1910, the dying Qing Dynasty made one last attempt to re-establish its authority over Tibet when it sent General Zhao Erfeng and an army to depose the Dalai Lama and introduce direct rule from Peking. The Dalai Lama fled south, this time to British India. Zhao was deeply unpopular with the Tibetans, who resented his harsh policies and his disrespecting of local culture. Two years later the Qing Dynasty was finished. Imperial troops were escorted from Tibet and the Dalai Lama returned to rule what was, in effect, a sovereign nation.

For thirty-six years, the 13th Dalai Lama, and the regents who succeeded him, ruled Tibet without interference, even fighting Chinese warlords for control of ethnically Tibetan regions of the Chinese provinces of Xikang and Qinghai. In 1914, Tibet signed the Simla Accord with Britain and ceded a region known as South Tibet to India – the Chinese denouncing this agreement as illegal.

Francis Younghusband was made a Knight Commander of the Order of the Indian Empire in 1904. He was British Commissioner in Kashmir in 1906 and promoted to lieutenant colonel two years later. In 1917 he was honoured again, this time being appointed a Knight Commander of the Order of the Star of India, made President of the Royal Geographical Society in 1919 and was Chairman of the Mount Everest Committee, encouraging George Mallory and others in their attempts to climb the highest mountain in the world. He died of a stroke in Dorset in July 1942.

By the 1930s and 1940s, a negligent Tibetan government was taken advantage of by the Chinese Nationalists, who sought to regain influence in Lhasa. Once the People's Republic of China was established, Mao Zedong concluded an agreement with the present 14th Dalai Lama that gave China complete control over the nation. The Dalai Lama and his government fled to India in 1959 when the rest of the nation rose up in rebellion against communist Chinese rule. Tibet suffered harshly under communist rule throughout the great unheavals and movements of the 1950s and 1960s. Between 200,000 and 1,000,000 Tibetans died during the Great Leap Forward and the Red Guards destroyed 6,000 monasteries during the Cultural Revolution. Huge numbers of Han Chinese have displaced Tibetans in Lhasa and the other major cities, dominating government and business. Dissatisfaction came to a head in 2008, with widespread protests against Chinese rule, but these were crushed by Chinese troops. Tibet remains as important in international relations today, as when Francis Younghusband led his march to Lhasa in 1904, and as mysterious.

Chapter 6

Showing the Flag

We lived like little tin gods, mostly prostrate on our beds …
while our man – an ever-smiling Chinese gentleman – bustled
about the room and generally helped us to stave off exhaustion.

Private Ralph Shaw, Royal Army Ordnance Corps,
Shanghai, 1937

The 1st Battalion, The Queen's Royal Regiment (West Surrey)[1] was
a typical British infantry battalion, the backbone of the Empire.
With a regimental history stretching back to 1661, the Queen's
was the senior English line infantry regiment and one of dozens of
regionally-recruited battalions that acted as policemen throughout Britain's far-flung colonies. The story of its tour of duty in
China between 1930 and 1934 is typical of the experiences of
British soldiers between the wars, and stands as a fascinating case
study of the lives and duties of British troops in Northern China
before the Second World War.

The Queen's were bound for Tientsin, the great port city close
to Peking, where Britain had maintained a trade concession since
the Second Opium War. Since the disaster of the Boxer Rebellion
in 1900, Britain had maintained an infantry battalion in Tientsin,
plus ancillary units, as well as a detached company that served as
the British Legation Guard in Peking.

The Queen's were already serving abroad in 1930 when the order
came to move to China. Based at St. George's Barracks in Malta, a
strategically vital British naval base in the central Mediterranean,
the battalion boarded the troopship HMT *Neuralia*, an old coal-

burning steamer, on the morning of 8 October 1930. 'As the strains of Auld Lang Syne faded away [the ship] made for the open sea and the long journey to China. There was a certain amount of regret in leaving Malta,' recorded the regimental history. 'It had been a station that had everything in one place – wonderful facilities for sport, racing and fishing. It was a nice climate for the families, with friendly locals and the Royal Navy to work and play alongside.'[2]

With an almost festive air, the Queen's and their families steamed east. 'The entertainment committee was soon at work. Boxing, Tug-of-War and obstacle races were organised. There was dancing since the band was on board, concerts ... There were children's sports and parties and the inevitable singsongs after dark.'[3] Although aboard ship, the battalion, under Lieutenant Colonel H.C. Ponsonby DSO MC continued with a training programme, especially weapon training. 'The officers had to study for promotion exams and war games ensued with a lot of argument!' A daily sweepstake was also run on the ship's mileage and a prize collected from the Orderly Room. 'Troops were required for sentry duties, galley duties, messroom and general cleaning duties and of course spud bashing. All accommodation had to be clean and ready for inspection by the Captain at 1100 hours.'[4] With each passing day, the Queen's drew closer to China, and its unique military challenges.

Private Ralph Shaw had been sent to Shanghai in 1937 at the commencement of the Sino-Japanese War. He would find China much changed compared with the peaceful tour made by the Queen's in 1930–34. Shaw, who was serving as a clerk in the Royal Army Service Corps, travelled directly from Britain. 'I got fitted out with tropical kit: pith helmet, khaki drill tunic, shorts, stockings and, after leave ... reported at Southampton docks where the *Dilwara*, eternally spick and span, waited for me.'[5] The troopship was given the usual send-off. 'A band played on the quay as we boarded, were shown our quarters and where to stow our kit bags. Going with me to Shanghai were the 1st Battalion, Durham Light Infantry, some reservists of the Royal Army Medical Corps, who had rejoined after a workless existence in a country gripped by terrible depression, other odds and sods from the Royal Engineers and some sailors who would be manning the Yangtze river gun-boats.'[6] The voyage would take the *Dilwara* via Malta, the Suez Canal and India. 'All aboard. A long blast from the *Dilwara's* siren. Ropes cast off and we are slowly swinging away from the quay. The band plays "Auld Lang Syne" and a lump comes to my throat, my eyes are wet. I look down at the people waving goodbye ... For the first time in my life I am leaving dear old England. "Goodbye Blighty." After all, it won't be long before I'm back – three years.'[7]

When the Queen's shipped out from Malta, officers and married men received cabins for the voyage, but the ordinary squaddie 'had to use his allotted space, often well below the water line, for living, eating by day and for slinging hammocks by night. Fresh air was at a premium and was obtained from large canvas funnels which stretched high above the upper deck where they caught the wind as the ship made way.' Once clear of the Suez Canal, the *Neuralia* entered the calm and boiling hot Red Sea, 'so hot that the ship had to turn around and steam into the wind to get a little air into the ship. Sleep was very difficult.'[8]

The first port of call was Bombay in British India. 'When the ship was berthed all troops went for a short route march and it was a joy to stretch one's legs. Colombo was reached in the evening in pouring rain which obscured the pleasant view of green trees and sandy beaches.' The tip of Ceylon was the last land the Queen's saw until the Malay Straits. The ship did not stop at Singapore but arrived at Hong Kong just before sunset on 5 November 1930 after several days of rough weather. After a short route march to give the men some exercise, the *Neuralia* slipped her anchor and headed north up the Chinese coast. 'The lights on the Peak and the network of lights disappearing over the stern made a fine sight as the ship headed up the coast for Shanghai.'[9]

For Private Shaw, travelling out to Shanghai in 1937, life aboard ship was no bed of roses. 'Getting into a hammock needed con-siderable agility. Staying in it in the Bay of Biscay needed great physical power.'[10] Ordinary soldiers were billeted well below deck, their quarters serving as both sleeping accommodation and dining room. 'After stowing hammocks we lowered from hooks in the ceiling great long tables which we fixed to the deck. We hauled in benches and then ate our grub.'[11] The soldiers were kept very busy during the voyage. 'After breakfast out with the buckets and swabs to sweep waves of sea-water from hose-pipes across the deck and into the scuppers.' A soldier's lot was not a happy one. 'In other "dungeons" below deck, the Durhams and the remainder of the human cargo were similarly keeping their quarters "all shipshape and Bristol fashion" and mightily cursing the fate that had befallen them,'[12] wrote Shaw.

Every port that Shaw's ship stopped at was a part of the British Empire. 'We were a proud lot, bred on a liberal diet of Empire-worship, of our superiority over other less favoured races. We were exports from a country which owned most of the world.'[13] The impression was given that the sun never set on the British Empire, and this was borne out by the reality of travelling by ship in the 1930s. 'We passed Gibraltar and saluted the Union Jack there. We dropped in at Malta and saw it again. At Port Said it was in evidence everywhere. In the morning we marched behind the Durhams band through the town and were watched by large crowds of "Gippos",' wrote Shaw. 'On the banks we saw British troops who shouted that we were going the wrong way. We waved at them. They waved back. We saw them ordering the natives around and our hearts glowed with pride that we were Britons, that we should never be slaves as the "Gippos" were.'[14] And so the voyage through the outposts of Empire continued. 'At Port Sudan we marched again and saw the "fuzzy-wuzzies" pushing railway trucks at the behest of sun-tanned Englishmen.' After further stops at Aden, Bombay, Colombo, Penang, Singapore and Hong Kong, the *Dilwara* finally approached the entrance to the Whangpoo River, and Shanghai. 'We entered the estuary of the river and made for the Woosung forts where we dropped anchor prior to picking up one of the British Whangpoo river pilots who would guide us to our Shanghai anchorage.'[15] Unlike the Queen's seven years before, they were entering a war zone.

The Queen's spent only a day in wet Shanghai in 1930 before leaving in the early morning on the final stretch of their journey.

'The temperature slowly dropped and the deck sentries were withdrawn to warmer regions below. The last night at sea, November 10th, the temperature dropped thirty degrees in two hours and the problem was how to keep warm.'[16]

The following day was Armistice Day and 'the Two Minutes Silence was a chilly affair standing on a frosty deck in a stiff icy breeze.' At 1pm, Mainland China was finally sighted. The ship docked at the small town of Ching Wang Tao (now Qinhuangdao) in northeast Hebei Province over 200 miles east of Peking on the Bohai Sea. The town contained only eight white inhabitants at that time. Half the battalion boarded a heated train for the journey to Tientsin on 13 November, while the other half and the soldiers' families remained on the ship until sent on by train on the 15th. D Company and the Machine Gun Platoon were detached and sent to Peking where they would be based for six months as the British Legation Guard, protecting the British Minister and his diplomatic staff just a stone's throw from the now empty Forbidden City.

For the remainder of the battalion, Tientsin was to be their home for the next two years. 'The accommodation in Tientsin was very good. The barracks and offices were single storeyed with a cook-house, dining hall and bath house, all being centrally heated. There was a good size gymnasium and drill square. The officers' quarters consisted of three small two storey buildings in which each bachelor had a bed sitting room; their mess was in the British Concession about 200 yards away. Married officers had quite nice houses.'[17] As well as a single infantry battalion, the Tientsin Garrison consisted of the Tientsin Signal Section from the Royal Corps of Signals, and a detachment from the Royal Engineers. The locally raised Tientsin British Volunteer Corps, consisting of local white businessmen and settlers, was designed to augment the regulars in times of emergency. The Garrison maintained a small Brigade Headquarters to manage all of these units effectively.

In Peking, the officers' mess and the barracks for the British Legation Guard was inside the Legation compound. They consisted of substantial brick-built two-storey structures with proper baths and hot, running water. 'Each officer had a Chinese servant instead of a batman, and they were excellent. A Chinese Head Boy ran the officers' mess with Chinese staff under the Mess Sergeant. The system was that the Head Boy obtained the staff and dealt with their wages. While they were employed they had to give so much each week to The Head Boy. If they were sacked and therefore unemployed the Head Boy had to keep them. This meant the Head Boy only employed the best.'[18]

British soldiers were very pleased to be based in Tientsin and Peking. 'These two cities were the best stations in the world for our troops as living was so cheap and there were so many facilities. There were plenty of bars and White Russian girls to entertain both our men and those of all the other nations,' noted the regimental historian. 'Mrs Veasey, a Queen's wife, remembers her hairdresser was one of these girls driven to flee from Russia after the Revolution. One of our officers became fluent in Russian, which stood him in good stead while working with the Russians in Berlin many years later.' As well as British troops, Tientsin and Beijing contained soldiers and sailors from the United States, France, Italy and Japan, 'as each nation had its own Concession with Chinese civil police.'[19]

The climate of North China did take some getting used to. 'Tientsin is located in a flat barren plain and in those days was quite the ugliest place imaginable! When the Battalion arrived the temperature registered about 15 degrees [Fahrenheit] of frost by day and about 20 degrees at night. The cold was bearable except when accompanied by wind, then life became uncomfortable! North China is very cold and dry in the winter and very hot and dry in the summer. If the wind was off the Gobi Desert, sand storms were likely to take place.' Still a constant problem today in this region of China, 'the sky would become yellow with sand and the light poor until the wind dropped, then the sand would fall like rain and covered everything.'[20]

Uniform regulations took the extremes of temperature into consideration. In winter men on sentry duty wore a long leather fur lined coat called a 'poshteen', with long leather fur lined Gilgit boots, and leather fur lined gloves. All members of the Battalion were issued with greatcoats and leather jerkins and a fur cap with the regimental cap badge worn in the centre. In summer, the headdress was the solar topee, more commonly known as the pith helmet.

The primary purpose of stationing an infantry battalion in Tientsin and Peking was to 'show the flag'. An endless round of parades were organised in order to do this. This meant excellent turnout, and a lot of spit and polish. Every Sunday there was a church parade in Tientsin, with the Battalion marching behind its band to the church, the streets lined with onlookers. Guards of honour were constantly requested, and often accompanied by the regimental Colour Party. Various British and foreign dignitaries and senior military officers were impressed by the high standard of drill and turnout managed by the Queen's. Armistice Day parades were held annually in Tientsin and in Peking, a march past being organised in both cities that was joined by many former British soldiers who were living locally.

Tensions were such that the Battalion paraded with each man carrying 20 rounds of live ammunition for their Lee-Enfield rifles, China at the time being in the grip of warlordism and a weak central administration. The King's birthday was marked with yet another parade that culminated in the firing of a *feu de joie*, which required a lot of practice beforehand. On St. George's Day 1934, the Queen's trooped their colour on the Ming Yuan sports ground in Tientsin before a large international audience, and the British Consul General took the salute. After the battalion had marched off, the Corps of Drums Beat Retreat. The Queen's even staged a military tattoo towards the end of their tour directed by Regimental Sergeant Major G. Osborne MM, that included a recreation of a battle that occurred in September 1897. The 'enemy' was provided by the Royal Corps of Signals, who were suitably kitted out with turbans and blacked-up faces who 'much enjoyed the experience of brandishing swords and yelling their heads off whilst making all sorts of queer noises.'[21]

In Shanghai, the British maintained a sizeable garrison built around two infantry battalions. Supporting the infantry was the Shanghai Signal Section, Royal Corps of Signals, and detachments from the Royal Engineers, Royal Army Service Corps, Royal Army Ordnance Corps and Royal Army Pay Corps. The Royal Military Police maintained discipline. The city also boasted the Shanghai Volunteer Corps, which by 1932 included several hundred Britons serving in particular SVC companies, the most colourful probably being the Shanghai Scottish.

111

Every six months, a fresh company from the battalion at Tientsin replaced the company and platoon stationed in Peking. One of the strangest duties undertaken by the Peking detachment was to man two howitzers that stood guard alongside the stone Chinese lions at the entrance to the British Legation. The infantrymen thus received training as gunners. The detachment also had twenty pack mules that were taken care of by Chinese stable boys.

Recreation opportunities were numerous. 'During the hot weather the companies and the families went to the seaside at Shan Hai Kuan (now Shan Hai Guan) on the coast, adjacent to the small port where the Battalion had landed and where the Great Wall reaches the sea. The French, Italians and Japanese had summer camps there too, but the Americans went further down the coast.'[22] During the hottest part of the year the Royal Navy moved from Shanghai to the coastal port of Weihai with their families. There was a lot of socialising between the navy and the army. Platoons were marched into the hills near the Great Wall for field training, sleeping out for up to a week. The families went with them and moved into bungalows on the beach.

While the Battalion was encamped at Shan Hai Kuan village the Japanese occupied Manchuria after engineering a crisis known as the Mukden Incident. This was the start of Japan's efforts to dominate Manchuria, and then Eastern China that eventually culminated in a full-blown invasion in 1937. Japanese troops came right up to the British camp boundary. 'They seized the Chinese parade ground and barracks and flew the new Manchurian flag. This was too much for one of our junior officers, and next morning a replacement flag was in position – a white flag with a red chamber-pot in the centre! Luckily the Chinese were the suspects and the Japanese wrath fell on them, saving an international incident.'[23]

The social life of the Battalion continued unabated. 'There was time for beach parties, riding Mongolian ponies inland, picnics of every description and boat trips. The Japanese did not interfere if such parties strayed into their new territory. The Sergeants had their Mess in a tin hut, where whist drives and dances were run.'

At the Legation in Peking a 'talking machine', or film projector, arrived and films were shown six times a week in the NAAFI. The soldiers also built a swimming pool. The Japanese conquest of Manchuria barely registered. Colonel Ponsonby handed over command to Lieutenant Colonel J.D. Boyd DSO in 1932. 'China was a very lively station for all ranks, with parties taking place in all the messes. At Christmas a special tea party was held for the children of the Regiment.'[24]

The one thing the British and the Chinese had in common was a love of the sport of kings. Wherever the British went in the world a racetrack soon followed. In Shanghai, the racecourse was one of the very first things that was constructed after the First Opium War. The Queen's organised regimental race meetings for the officers and men who rode. One story concerns Lieutenant Monty Sydenham-Clarke. A keen racer, Sydenham-Clarke won a race in Tientsin and was presented with an inscribed watch as a prize. Many years later in 1941, when the Battalion was serving in the Western Desert, Sydenham-Clarke was reported missing in action. Sadly, his body was not found for several weeks, and was identified solely by the watch that had been presented to him by the Tientsin Race Club.

The British are renowned for their love of sport, and in China the Queen's enjoyed cricket, hockey, rugby, soccer, ice hockey, ice yachting, skating and polo. At Peking there were clay tennis courts, and at Tientsin a drag hunt was organised. International boxing competitions were a favourite of the Battalion. A healthy body did not necessarily mean a healthy mind, and the soldiers followed the time-honoured pastimes of all military men when off duty of drinking and seeking female company. 'The rate of exchange may have been in my favour,' noted one soldier, 'but I was still broke on Saturday night.'[25]

Because China was a family posting, the wives formed an important part of the social life of the Battalion. 'The ladies were frequently entertained in the Sergeants' Mess, and the Corporals' Mess ran a ball in Peking. Life was very social with the facilities of the local clubs available and with the hospitality of the foreign military units. The Royal Navy, in particular, gave some wonderful parties.'[26] And a young wife with children did not need to be tied to the kitchen sink. Cheap local labour, then as now, meant that children could be left with *amahs*, who would also do all the washing and mending. According to the regimental historian, the average English family employed a No. 1 Boy (head servant), a No. 2 boy, a cook familiar with English cuisine, a rickshaw boy, and a groom to take care of the ponies. China and Hong Kong remained extremely desirable postings right up until the Handover in 1997, not least for the social life and the ready availability of domestic servants. The British garrison in Tientsin surprisingly lacked a school for the soldiers' children, although one did exist in Peking. It is presumed that in Tientsin the army hired a schoolmistress.

Tension between foreigners in China and the aggressive Japanese increased when the Queen's was stationed in Tientsin. The Japanese deliberately tried to make life difficult for other foreigners, including setting up checkpoints and roadblocks, but generally they refrained from any overt acts at this stage – that would only come from 1937 onwards, when the Japanese launched a full-scale invasion.

In mid-1934 the Queen's received orders to move to a new posting in Quetta, India. On 2 November, the Battalion was given a huge send-off by crowds of friends and well wishers before boarding a train at Tientsin Station. 'The voyage to India was uneventful and drafts were left at Hong Kong and Karachi to return to the UK. India was not home, but it was much nearer home than China!'[27]

War came to foreign Shanghai on 12 August 1937 when in response to the arrival of Japanese troops to take over the Chinese Municipality, and fearful of being overwhelmed by Chinese refugees, the Shanghai Municipal Council ordered the mobilisation of the Shanghai Volunteer Corps. Quickly the part-time soldiers threw a defensive cordon around the International Settlement, setting up sandbagged machine gun emplacements and roadblocks on all the major routes into the city from Chinese Shanghai and the French Concession. The next day the shooting war began. At 9am on 13 August, the Chinese Peace Preservation Corps exchanged small arms fire with Japanese troops in the Chapei, Wusong and Kiangwan districts of the city. At 3pm, Japanese troops crossed a bridge into Chapei and assaulted various targets. The Chinese 88th Division responded with mortar fire. An hour later and the Japanese ordered warships of their Third Fleet, anchored on the

Yangtze and Whangpoo Rivers, to bombard Chinese positions in Shanghai.

Chiang Kai-shek, the Chinese leader, ordered General Zhang Zhizhang to attack the next day, 14 August. The Chinese outnumbered the Japanese forces, and the idea was for the Chinese divisions to push the Japanese into the Whangpoo River and also blockade the coast to prevent the Japanese from landing reinforcements. The 88th Division attacked the Japanese Army headquarters in Chapei, while the 87th Division assaulted the Kung-ta Textile Mill, home of the Japanese Special Naval Landing Force. The Chinese also decided to use air power during the assault. The heavy cruiser *Izumo*, headquarters vessel for the Imperial Japanese Navy in Shanghai, was permanently moored at the north end of the Bund. It looked like a perfect target for the Republic of China Air Force. Unfortunately, the *Izumo* was very close to the neutral International Settlement, and the Chinese pilots lacked the training and skills to hit her. This did not prevent them from trying. 'Saturday [14 August] will live forever in the minds of all who were in Shanghai that day,' recalled Canadian missionary Margaret Brown. 'I was at the office when the first big Chinese air raid took place and saw the second bomb fall, just missing the Izumo by fifty feet.'[28] Japanese anti-aircraft guns banged away from several areas of downtown Shanghai, including heavy machine guns dug in behind sandbagged emplacements on the roofs of two Japanese banks on the Bund, in blatant violation of the Settlement's neutrality. Two bombs missed the *Izumo* and landed on Nanking Road, then as now the metropolis's overcrowded main shopping street. The bombs struck close to the Cathay and Palace Hotels (now the Peace Hotel). Two more bombs landed outside the Great World amusement centre near the Race Track (now People's Square). The carnage was appalling, with perhaps 2,000 people in total killed and thousands more wounded. 'We saw the bursts of shrapnel very close. There were 1,400 casualties from that one bomb and several were personally known to me,'[29] recorded Margaret Brown, whose office was close to the Cathay Hotel.

The Chinese attacked on a broad front through densely populated city districts until the fighting was lapping against the International Settlement and the French Concession. The problem the Chinese faced was the carefully constructed gun and machine gun emplacements that the Japanese had built, many made from concrete. The Chinese lacked the necessary weapons to reduce them, but they developed instead a strategy of flowing around them, like water around rocks, to encircle and isolate the bunkers and continue the advance towards the Whangpoo River. Initially, this strategy worked. Once encircled the emplacements were assaulted by infantry and destroyed using hand grenades or satchel charges, but the Chinese suffered heavy casualties charging machine gun bunkers with excellent fields of fire. The battle started to swing in the favour of the Japanese when the latter deployed tanks in the city. The Chinese had nothing effective to knock out the tanks with, and Chinese units were mown down, or encircled and gradually destroyed. On 18 August, General Zhang cancelled the offensive.

Later on the 18th the Chinese tried again. A fresh Chinese formation, 36th Division, assaulted the Hueishan docks complex located on the north side of the Whangpoo River. The 87th Division broke through Japanese lines at Yangshupu and managed to link up with the 86th. The Chinese deployed tanks, but unlike the Japanese they were not well trained in infantry-tank cooperation. The infantry could not keep pace with the advance of the armour, and the Chinese tanks began to fall victim to Japanese anti-tank guns. As a result, the exposed Chinese infantry suffered very heavy casualties.

On 22 August 1937 the Japanese 3rd, 8th and 11th Infantry Divisions landed at the coastal towns of Chuanshakou, Shizilin and Baoshan located about thirty miles northeast of Shanghai. The Chinese front had to be lengthened considerably. In downtown Shanghai the fighting atrophied into a bloody stalemate, with both sides reeling from heavy losses. The Chinese managed to hold on to the Chapei and Kiangwan districts for three more months.

Private Ralph Shaw's troop transport, the *Dilwara*, steamed into the International Settlement during the ferocious battle for the city. 'As we sailed up the Whangpoo we saw a veritable armada of Japanese shipping and the havoc caused by war on both banks of the muddy water,' he wrote. 'The Chinese were putting up a good fight but they were retreating inland. In the ruins of villages, of farmhouses, of barns, we saw squat Japanese soldiery, steel-helmeted, grim of visage. They stood and watched us glide past. We waved at them. They did not return the compliment.'[30]

The *Dilwara* tied up at Holt's Wharf. 'We saw khaki-uniformed British police officers, turbanned Sikh constables, Chinese policemen. They all carried revolvers in holsters,' noted Shaw. 'The wharf coolies, thin and ragged, heaved ropes around the bollards. Long-gowned Chinese gentlemen, ledgers in hand, gazed up at us.'[31] The scenes that confronted the newly arrived British soldiers were many and ominous. 'Red-capped military policemen waited to board the ship. A posse of officers stood tapping swagger sticks against their legs. On the river side we could see long lines of Japanese warships tied up in midstream. Above them, White Ensign flying at the stern, was a British cruiser. Further upstream was an American cruiser.'[32] It was quite evident that Shaw and his comrades had entered a war zone. 'Ominously, in the distance, we could hear the sound of gunfire. As we looked across the river we could see palls of smoke rising. Overhead Japanese planes returned from bombing missions. The rumble of artillery was clearly audible.'[33] But for Shaw and his travelling companions, the sounds of conflict were not unwelcome. 'For most of us this was our first sight of a real war. We had never fired shots in anger. We were excited, happy to be at the scene of hostilities which were earning world-wide prominence in newspaper headlines and in cinema newsreels.'[34]

' "Welcome to Shanghai," shouted a burly British police officer from the dock. "I'm a Geordie, too." There were cheers from the Durhams. We were all raring to go.'[35] Life for a British squaddie in pre-war Shanghai was even more languorous than that experienced by the line regiments like the Queen's in Tientsin and Peking. Shaw was RASC, meaning that he was spared a lot of the soldiering required of infantrymen. 'Shanghai was a cushy berth – dead easy compared with Aldershot or Bulford,' recalled Shaw. 'For the first time in my life I had a manservant or, rather, I shared his services with others who lived with me in a barrack room at the British Military Hospital in downtown Shanghai, only a few hundred yards from the Bund waterfront.'[36] At this time the Shanghai Garrison was under the command of Major General Arthur Bartholomew, who was based in Hong Kong in his capacity as Commander British Troops in China. 'The "room-boy" took over the chores that we did ourselves back in Blighty – making the beds, "bumping" the floor, polishing our buttons, cap badges, blancoing our belts, cleaning our boots and so on.' China was a legendary posting for the average soldier. 'So we lived like little tin gods, mostly prostrate on our beds … while our man – an ever-smiling Chinese gentleman – bustled about the room and generally helped us to stave off exhaustion.'[37]

Private Shaw was assigned to the garrison intelligence section that was located inside the Shanghai Municipal Council building. The intelligence section was headed by Major Timothy Gwynnes of the Punjabis, with Captain Davidson-Houston, Royal Engineers, as second-in-command. Their job was to meet with various agents and informers, collect material, and draw up intelligence reports primarily on the Japanese that were then passed on to London. The fighting between the Chinese and Japanese meant that the small intelligence section was very busy. On his first day Shaw was confronted by the sight of a corporal, named Mann, 'busy making a line drawing of a medium-sized Japanese shell picked up, unexploded, in the Chapei district …'[38] Mann and Staff Sergeant Carver would amuse themselves by kicking the live shell backwards and forwards to one another in the office, much to the anxiety of Shaw. Each day, various people visited the office, speaking English with a variety of exotic accents. 'Real cloak-and-dagger stuff it appeared to be when papers were burned daily in a metal dust-pan and I, on joining the office, took an oath of secrecy in the presence of the two officers.'[39]

Shanghai at this time was a hotbed of competing intelligence outfits. The German Gestapo and Abwehr maintained many agents throughout the city. The Japanese *Kempeitai* military police was already looking to the time when Japan would take over foreign Shanghai as well as the Chinese sections of the city. Always suspicious, the Japanese knew that world opinion, and therefore the sympathy of foreigners in Shanghai, was with the Chinese. The Chinese were already receiving unofficial help from Western nations, one of the more prominent examples being the 'Flying Tigers' or the American Volunteer Group of fighter pilots who were taking on the Japanese over China. The Chinese also received advisors and materiel support from Stalin's Soviet Union, heightening tensions along the Manchurian border with Mongolia that would eventually erupt into full-scale battle in 1939.

But, in the run-up to the Second World War, little changed for the British garrisons in China. Hong Kong, Shanghai, Tientsin and Peking all remained plum postings. No one could foresee the horrors to come.

Chapter 7

Christmas in Hell

*Everyday that you are able to maintain your resistance, you
help the Allied cause all over the world.*

Prime Minister Winston Churchill,
20 December 1941

'Obviously, there is nothing you can do with the forces at your
disposal. I would suggest that you strike your colours,' was the
last communication Lieutenant Stephen Polkinghorn had with
the British Embassy in Shanghai. Polkinghorn replaced the receiver
in its cradle, his lip curling in disgust. He had just been advised
to surrender to the Japanese HMS *Peterel*, the Royal Navy's last
remaining Yangtze River gunboat in Mainland China. She sat
moored on the Whangpoo River opposite the Bund, Shanghai's
glittering neoclassical 'Million Dollar Mile'. It was just before
4am, 8 December 1941, and the word 'surrender' was not in
Polkinghorn's vocabulary. A Japanese gunboat moved in the
distance, a signal lamp sending coded Morse to the riverbank,
and a curl of smoke rose from the funnel of the huge Japanese
cruiser *Izumo* moored close by.

The *Peterel* had been protecting British trade on China's rivers
since 1927, but now she had been reduced to a floating communications station on the Whangpoo, organising supplies to the
Chinese Army. Her two 3-inch guns had been mothballed and her
crew reduced from fifty-five to just twenty men. Moored close by
was an American gunboat, the USS *Wake*, also stripped of defensive
weapons and most of her crew. Lieutenant Polkinghorn, the ship's

Royal Naval Reserve skipper, was below when he had received the final phone call from the embassy. The voice at the other end was terse and to the point: 'The Japanese have bombed Pearl Harbor in Hawaii, and Britain is consequently at war with Japan!' Polkinghorn was not surprised. 'You can expect a visit from the Japanese at any time,' continued the measured tones of the diplomat. His vessel represented the last regular British armed forces in Shanghai, and naval honour dictated that he could not surrender his ship without a gesture of defiance.[1]

Polkinghorn ordered: 'Action stations!' when a Japanese launch was seen approaching his vessel. Steel helmets were donned and two Lewis machine guns were loaded, their circular ammo pans smacked into place and the weapons cocked with a solid click. It was 4am, and close by, the *Wake* was being boarded by the Japanese – her skipper, Lieutenant Commander Columbus Smith, was still at his apartment ashore when his ship was captured.[2]

Apart from the *Peterel* and the *Wake* there was precious little else with which to defend foreign Shanghai from the Japanese. The Royal Navy had long since withdrawn its cruisers to fight in the Atlantic and Mediterranean. The multi-national Shanghai Volunteer Corps (SVC) was told to stand down on 8 December 1941. Shanghai itself was really three cities within one. The International Settlement, dominated by the British and American concessions occupied the heart of the city and, although not technically a colony of any nation, was firmly ruled by the Anglo-American municipal council. To the south of the Settlement was the French Concession, ruled directly from Hanoi in Indochina. Surrounding these two conjoined entities was the Chinese Municipality, governed at different times by warlords or the central government in Nanking. The Japanese, whose own concession consisted of the Hongkew District just north of the Bund, had occupied all of Chinese Shanghai in 1937 as they brutally gobbled up eastern China piece by piece. It was only a matter of time before they swallowed up the sweet prize of foreign Shanghai as well.

The British Government had declared the Settlement indefensible in 1940 and had withdrawn the two regular infantry battalions that formed the garrison to Hong Kong. The Americans had followed suit shortly after. Over 8,000 virtually defenceless British citizens continued to live and work in Shanghai, alongside nearly 2,000 Americans and the citizens of many other nations. There were also thousands of stateless White Russians who had fled the Russian Civil War as well as over 20,000 Jews who had escaped Nazi persecution to the only free port left open to them.[3]

The British military presence in China was all but snuffed out over the period of a couple of disastrous weeks in early December 1941. It was almost 100 years since British soldiers had first stepped onto Chinese soil, but this particular centenary would go unmarked. Britain would instead fight one of its most desperate battles of the Second World War in Hong Kong, the great First Opium War prize, and be ejected from Shanghai once and for all. In Hong Kong it was called 'Black Christmas' by the Chinese – which turned out to be a very appropriate title.

The major problem for the British military in China was the indefensible nature of its territories. Foreign Shanghai was, by late 1941, a small island surrounded by hostile Japanese forces. Hong Kong could not hope to hold out for long without the kind of massive reinforcement that neither London, nor Far Eastern Command, was prepared to provide. The best that could be hoped was that its defenders would fight a long and protracted battle for the New Territories and Hong Kong Island before surrendering, buying time for Churchill's main strategic focus in the Far East – Malaya, and the giant naval base at Singapore.

The disparity between the forces available at each location are the best indicator of Britain's intentions – Singapore in 1941 was defended by thirty-eight infantry battalions, Hong Kong by six and Shanghai and Tientsin by just a single volunteer reserve unit each. Hong Kong and its under-strength garrison were to be sacrificed by Churchill to buy time to rush more reinforcements to Singapore. A defence of Shanghai or Tientsin would have been suicide for the part-time troops involved – any idea of that was quickly shelved (although it would not stop the members of the Shanghai Volunteer Corps from being rounded up by the Japanese and sent to prisoner of war camps).

Onboard the *Peterel*, a small group of Japanese army officers, *samurai* swords at their sides, climbed the ladder onto the quarterdeck and stiffly saluted. Lieutenant Polkinghorn listened impatiently to their interpreter as the Japanese ordered the New Zealander to immediately surrender his ship or face the consequences. Polkinghorn drew himself up to his full height, stuck out his chin and hissed 'Get off my bloody ship!' The astonished Japanese officers silently filed back into their launch, dumbfounded at the young officer's suicidal boldness.

Polkinghorn's two dozen ratings took cover behind sand bags piled in the gangways, the men manning the machine guns staring intently at the grey bulk of the *Izumo* as the booming report of its massive guns echoed across a city that was just coming to life in the early morning, rattling windows throughout the International Settlement.

The *Peterel* was already rigged with scuttling charges, and Polkinghorn's decision to put up a fight was also necessary to buy enough time to send his ship to the bottom of the river. Polkinghorn cupped his hands to his mouth and yelled 'Open fire!' The chattering of the machine guns, as they blasted long lines of bullets at the monolithic structure of the Japanese cruiser, wounding several Japanese, was drowned out by the whoosh of shells that threw up giant geysers of dirty river water all around the tiny British ship. With a blinding flash and a deafening concussion the *Peterel* was struck, the ship heaving over hard against her cables, flames shooting into the air. Within minutes the whole superstructure was on fire, bodies littered deck, blood flowed, and the cacophony of battle clashed with the high-pitched screaming of the wounded. The *Peterel* lurched again and began to take on a startling list. 'Abandon ship, abandon ship!' yelled Polkinghorn as the vessel threatened to capsize. Men plunged into the brown river, casting away their tin helmets as they dived in. Polkinghorn wrenched off his binoculars and dived in after them.

Apart from this one small battle, the Japanese takeover of Shanghai was remarkably bloodless and terrifyingly quick. The British lost five killed, and fourteen taken prisoner. One man escaped. Petty Officer James Cuming, a radio operator, was ashore when the Japanese attacked, and he joined the Chinese resistance. For three-and-a-half years, Cuming, using the alias 'Mr. Trees', played a cat-and-mouse game with Japanese intelligence, but he was never caught. Lieutenant Polkinghorn was awarded the Distinguished Service Cross after the war.

At the north end of the Bund the British-built Garden Bridge spans Suzhou Creek with the imposing edifice of Shanghai Mansions towering behind. Across the iron bridge, where since 1937 Japanese sentries had controlled access to the Settlement from Hongkew, Japanese Type 95 *Ha-Go* light tanks and Vickers-Crossley armoured cars (ironically British-built) trundled noisily across, followed by trucks flying the Rising Sun flag. Loaded aboard were the men of the 746-strong Shanghai Special Naval Landing Force, Japanese marines. The tanks and trucks moved along the Bund, while others drove up Nanking Road, Shanghai's main shopping thorough-fare, dominated by the tallest building in Shanghai, the dark-brown Park Hotel. Chinese rickshaw pullers and coolies scattered at the approach of the 'shrimp barbarians', as the Chinese called the Japanese. Wearing blue landing rig with army helmets and webbing, the Japanese troops toted long Arisaka rifles with fixed bayonets. Several parties of Japanese marines on foot, accom-panied by Japanese civilians wearing white rising sun armbands, entered the many foreign-owned banks and insurance buildings that lined the Bund and the streets behind, some plastering notices onto their elaborate wrought-iron gates proclaiming that these premises were now under Japanese military control.

British Shanghai had been swept away in one day, but Hong Kong would prove to be a much tougher nut for the Japanese to crack, but the colony soon found itself in the vice-like grip of the immensely powerful Japanese military in China, until its defences were crushed and eventually completely extinguished.

The British commander in Hong Kong, 50-year-old Major General Christopher Maltby, was handed an almost impossible task when his superior, Air Chief Marshal Sir Robert Brooke-Popham, who was responsible for all British forces in the Far East, ordered him to stand firm against a Japanese invasion. Maltby could draw upon a mere handful of regular troops to carry out his task – a mixture of British, Indian and Canadian battalions, with some local volunteer and Chinese units thrown in. Maltby had arrived in Hong Kong in 1940 fresh from commanding a brigade in India, and his posting had coincided with the British decision to wind up North China Command, withdrawing the three battalions from Shanghai and Tientsin, and effectively abandoning the International Settlement to its fate. Press reports noted that Maltby was known to be 'always cool and completely unruffled, and has a quiet sense of humor and tremendous powers of endurance.'[4] These qualities would be extremely useful over the coming weeks.

Maltby had nowhere near enough experienced soldiers and equipment to make a stand in Hong Kong militarily viable. Those in London were fully aware of his predicament and were, as yet, undecided on how to help him. The fact that Maltby had any forces at all with which to defend Hong Kong was only because of a dramatic government U-turn in Whitehall that occurred after considerable wrangling and argument. With the disbandment of North China Command in late 1940, the government also decided to reduce the troop levels that made up the Hong Kong Garrison to just two British infantry battalions, whose roles were to be guarding the border with China and working with the Hong Kong Police in the maintenance of internal order. If, or rather when, the Japanese attack came these two battalions could not have done much except surrender. It was the direct intervention of Air Chief Marshal Brooke-Popham that caused a change in British policy. Brooke-Popham argued that a *limited* reinforcement of Hong Kong would allow Maltby and the garrison to delay any Japanese attack, gaining time for the British to be reinforced elsewhere in Asia. A limited reinforcement would prevent Maltby from being forced into an early and humiliating capitulation that would damage Imperial prestige at home and abroad.

To mount a proper defence of Hong Kong, the army suggested that at least six full infantry brigades would have been required, equating to eighteen infantry battalions. This was immediately rejected. Instead, Brooke-Popham believed that two brigades totalling six battalions could impose a sufficient delay on the Japanese to fulfill his strategic plans for the region. Maltby was told in no uncertain terms by London to fight on for as long as possible before surrendering, and to expect no relief. It was to be a last stand, with no hope of escape.

Maltby attacked the problem of how to complete his almost suicidal instructions with a dogged determination. He would make the Japanese pay for every inch of the colony before raising a white flag. He had two regular, though under-strength, British battalions that had recently been withdrawn from Shanghai: the 2nd Battalion, Royal Scots and 1st Battalion, Middlesex Regiment, the latter re-roled as a machine gun battalion. Canada had rushed two completely inexperienced infantry battalions to Hong Kong as their imperial contribution to the Far Eastern war; 1st Battalion, Winnipeg Grenadiers and the 1st Battalion, Royal Rifles of Canada. These men were completely unprepared for the horrors to come. 'How innocent of combat we were, how naïve of the horrors of war,' recalled Private Phil Doddridge of the Royal Rifles of Canada. 'How far removed from the comforts of home and the good order of Canada.'[5] There were also two Indian Army battalions stationed in the city (mainly composed of reservists); 5/7th Rajput Regiment and 2/14th Punjabis. The British also had several artillery and engineer units along with the usual supporting and ancillary services.

Aiding the regulars were other colonial and volunteer formations consisting of the locally-raised one-battalion-strong Hong Kong Chinese Regiment, two mountain batteries and three medium batteries of the mostly Indian-manned Hong Kong & Singapore Royal Artillery (HK&SRA) and the Hong Kong Volunteer Defence Corps (HKVDC), an infantry unit that amounted to a battalion group made up of bankers, merchants and businessmen of British origin who were living in the colony.[6] These volunteers would fight like lions alongside the regulars and suffer huge casualties in the process.

In total, Maltby had about 14,000 troops. Opposing him would be Major General Takashi Sakai's Japanese 38th Infantry Division that numbered 50,000 battle-hardened troops, the main assault force consisting of three regiments (a Japanese regiment being roughly equivalent to a British brigade) that were poised along the Sham Chun River, the border between Mainland China and Hong Kong's New Territories (a large area of land leased from Qing Dynasty China in 1898 for ninety-nine years).

Famous British battalions like the 2nd Royal Scots had deteriorated after a long period of inaction stationed in the Far East. Because of the exigencies of the European War, many of its best and most experienced NCOs, the backbone of the battalion, had been recalled to Britain to provide cadres for new emergency battalions. When the Japanese attacked, the battalion was both under strength and experiencing discipline problems. Those military forces that did remain in the colony were not on top form, as the debilitating effects of a tropical climate and an active social scene had sapped the strength of the men. At the time, Hong Kong boasted ten thousand prostitutes who worked the hundreds of bars, dancehalls and brothels busily frequented by the local garrison. The 2nd Battalion, Royal Scots had not seen Britain in seven years, one soldier recalling a dance hall that had been renamed the 'gonorrhoea racetrack' by its patrons.[7] Probably Maltby's best unit was the 1st Middlesex Regiment, which was in top fighting condition but had been re-roled as a machine gun battalion rather than remaining as conventional line infantry.

The British plan of defence was to slow down the Japanese advance from the border by staging a series of holding actions behind Kowloon in the mountainous New Territories. Extensive fortifications from which to mount a static defence already existed, and two infantry brigades were created to man them. The eleven-mile long Gin Drinkers Line of redoubts and trench systems was the showcase British defensive position, a Far Eastern Maginot Line. Constructed in 1936–38, the Gin Drinkers Line was not a continuous fortification but a series of strongpoints and bunker systems linked together by paths. The Mount Davis Battery and Stonecutters Island Fort provided artillery support.

The new Mainland Brigade under eye-patch wearing Brigadier Cedric Wallis would hold the Gin Drinkers Line and it was hoped that the position, particularly the impressive Shing Mun Redoubt, would check the Japanese for at least three weeks. 2nd Royal Scots held the west of the Line, including the Shing Mun Redoubt, which also housed the Command Headquarters. The Shing Mun Redoubt consisted of four pillboxes mounted with Vickers and Bren machine guns, interlinked with five-foot deep defensive channels or trenches named after London roads. The Redoubt had space for 128 soldiers, but when the Japanese assault occurred less than half that number were present – a disastrous mistake. The 2/4th Punjabis held the centre of the Gin Drinkers Line and the 5/7th Rajputs the east. The Shing Mun Redoubt was manned by forty-three soldiers drawn from the Headquarters of 'A' Company,

2 Royal Scots, along with the battalion's 8 Platoon supported by elements of 1 Mountain Battery, HK&SRA, all under the command of Captain 'Potato' Jones.

The press was led to believe that Hong Kong was virtually impregnable, a Canadian reporter calling the colony 'the rocky Far Eastern stronghold ... [that] may develop into a Tobruk of the Pacific,'[8] referring to the stand of the 14,000 men of 9th Division under Australian Lieutenant General Leslie Morshead in holding the port fortress city of Tobruk in Libya, a battle that was still ongoing when the Japanese invaded Hong Kong.

Although the press coverage exaggerated Hong Kong's defences, the Gin Drinkers Line, if it had been properly manned by experienced troops, would have posed a serious threat to the Japanese and may well have stopped their advance dead. Japanese generals were so concerned about the position that they expected their attack to be held up for at least a month, and even began to divert reinforcements from their war in China to replace the expected heavy casualties.

Hong Kong Island would be defended by the three battalion Island Brigades consisting of the 1st Winnipeg Grenadiers, 1st Royal Rifles of Canada, and 1st Middlesex Regiment with the HKVDC and HK&SRA in support, all under the command of another experienced British officer, newly-promoted Brigadier John Lawson. The brigade was ordered to man and hold a series of hastily constructed pillboxes and gun batteries situated around the perimeter of the island.

At 8am on 8 December 1941, the Japanese 21st, 23rd and 38th Infantry Regiments stormed across the Sham Chun River using temporary bridges. The British did not attempt to hold the Japanese at the border, but the Royal Engineers did their utmost to impede the Japanese advance between the border and the river, blowing bridges and culverts until forced to retire under the covering fire of 'C' Company, 2/14th Punjabis. The Indian sepoys then dug themselves in around the approaches to the village of Tai Po and waited for an advancing Japanese column to blunder straight into a carefully laid ambush. Although the Indian battalion managed to smash an infantry unit and an artillery battery before withdrawing, this victory did not impede the Japanese advance and they recovered quickly and pressed on.

Private Francis Crabb of 2 Machine Gun (Scottish) Company, HKVDC, was mobilised shortly before the Japanese invasion. He spent 8 December finding his way from his home in Kowloon to the Volunteer HQ on Hong Kong Island. His company comprised 100 men, 90% of whom were Scottish. 'The companies were formed up and stores and gas masks issued as were rifles, Lewis guns and, in my case, a heavy .45 revolver, as I was a No. 1 on a Vickers machine gun,'[9] recalled Crabb. 'I had never seen a revolver before, let alone fired one, and being at the time a youth of tender years, I wasn't even able to pull the trigger of this monster.'[10] Private Crabb's unit was sent to guard against Japanese landings in Big Wave Bay, but were then switched to covering Sai Wan Bay and an artillery battery at Pak Sha Wan alongside the Royal Rifles of Canada and the Middlesex Regiment.

On 9 December a reconnaissance party from the Japanese 228th Regiment discovered that the British defences at '225 High Ground' near the Shing Mun Redoubt were weakly held. If the Japanese seized this high ground they could dominate all British positions to the west of the Line. At 9pm that evening, a lieutenant and ten men launched a surprise night attack on the Royal Scots holding the position. Japanese combat engineers blew holes in the barbed wire apron around the Redoubt and using special charges blew up several of the pillboxes. By 7am on 10 December the position was in Japanese hands and they had taken twenty-seven prisoners. Three British were killed and thirteen managed to escape. The Gin Drinkers Line had been fatally breached.

Later on 10 December, the Japanese launched a general assault on the Line and by the next day had captured Kam Shan and Tate's Cairn. By noon on the 11th Maltby decided to withdraw his remaining forces from the Line to Hong Kong Island in order to preserve the garrison. With the Redoubt gone, Mainland Brigade fell back on the town of Kowloon before crossing over to Hong Kong Island. Initially, the Royal Scots pulled back about 2,000 yards from the Gin Drinkers Line onto a position on Golden Hill, behind the Shing Mun Redoubt. On the 11th the advancing Japanese heavily engaged the two Royal Scots companies that were occupying the feature and the hill was wrested from them. The hill contained no prepared positions, just a few shell scrapes; and because the ground was rock hard Japanese mortar bombs exploded with devastating effect among the Royal Scots, causing heavy casualties. The survivors poured off the hill in considerable confusion. In a fierce counter-attack the battalion's 'D' Company retook the hill at the point of the bayonet but the Scots were too few in number to withstand repeated regimental-sized Japanese assaults on the hill and eventually they were forced to retire or face annihilation. The battalion had lost twenty-eight killed in the Golden Hill action.

With the fall of the Gin Drinkers Line the British had lost their best chance at stopping the Japanese in their tracks and forcing them into static fighting. Overhead, Japanese bombers and fighters constantly attacked the colony's main settlements and the remaining British warships, causing immense damage and great civilian suffering. The British had no way to respond as the few outdated aircraft at RAF Kai Tak had been destroyed on the ground on the first day of the Japanese offensive.

At the Royal Naval Hospital in Wanchai, Superintending Sister Olga Franklin had organised the relocation of all patients onto wards on the ground floor. The acute surgical and casualty departments had also been relocated to the ground floor in an effort to prevent casualties from the bombing and shelling. On the morning of 8 December incoming shells awakened the staff and patients. Over the next two days the hospital's upper floors were wrecked by repeated shell and bomb strikes. On 9 December, the 'Chinese staff took flight, looting as much of the hospital gear as they could on the way. More shells hit the hospital, shattering windows and doors, as staff took refuge in the strongest part of the building, the pharmacist's store.'[11] The hospital's gas, electricity and water supplies failed. The building was without heating, and sterilizers, kettles and X-ray machines were no longer functional. Even the emergency water tanks had been holed by shrapnel. 'When one bomb fell right outside Ward Five, shattered window-glazing flew in all directions; plaster, bits of masonry and parts of wooden shutters clattered on to patients' beds,'[12] recalled Sister Franklin.

The units holding the west side of the Gin Drinkers Line fell back on the ferries at Tsim Sha Tsui while the eastern defenders retired via Devil's Peak. Rioting broke out in Kowloon, and looting spread as the British lost control over the panicked Chinese population. Sappers busily destroyed anything in the town of military value and set fire to the massive oil depot sending huge black smoke clouds high into the air.

On 12 December, the Royal Navy was ordered to vandalise its own base to deny as much of the facility to the Japanese as possible. Armed with sledgehammers, dynamite and petrol, groups of young sailors and a few soldiers wrecked offices, machine shops and the headquarters vessel, HMS *Tamar*. She was the oldest naval ship in Hong Kong and had served as China Station Headquarters at Kowloon since 1897. The venerable ship was ignominiously scuttled in the harbour.

The Mainland Brigade fought its way to the waterfront through considerable chaos and lawlessness, Lieutenant Colonel R. Cadogan-Rawlinson's 5/7th Rajputs acting as a rearguard, furiously beating back Japanese attempts to get between it and the embarkation points on the quay. A group of Punjabis became separated from their battalion and eventually formed an *ad hoc* defensive position around the Star Ferry terminal in Kowloon. The Rajputs fought a final battle on Devil's Peak on 13 December, defeating the Japanese, before withdrawing across to the island with the assistance of the few remaining British warships, and some fast Motor Torpedo Boats. The Hong Kong Mule Company was forced to abandon most of its animals and escape across the harbour. In five days of fighting Maltby's forces had lost just sixty-six killed and his army remained intact.

Maltby had a few days grace once the evacuation from the mainland had been completed, before the Japanese would make an amphibious assault across the harbour and onto the island. Japanese aircraft and artillery began to furiously bombard Hong Kong's northern shoreline on 15 December, targeting British pill-boxes, gun emplacements and communication systems – a process known as 'softening up.' Hospitals were not immune from this general bombardment – Bowen Road Military Hospital and the Royal Naval Hospital at Wanchai each took over 100 artillery and bomb hits each. 'As the shelling from the mainland began there were several direct hits on our three-storey hospital,' recalled Canadian nurse Kay Christie at Bowen Road. 'We had to immediately evacuate the top two floors and crowd all the patients and equipment into the ground floor area.'[13]

General Sakai made surrender requests to Maltby on 13 and 17 December, but these were immediately rejected. The bombardment had wrecked many of Maltby's static defences and killed another fifty-four men.

Maltby rapidly reorganised his forces in preparation for the final assault. Mainland Brigade was renamed East Brigade, and Island Brigade became West Brigade. East Brigade's units were deployed as follows: the Rajputs covered the waterfront with the Royal Rifles of Canada and 1, 2, and 3 Companies, HKVDC in depth behind. Next to them were the units of West Brigade, the Punjabis on the waterfront, and the Winnipeg Grenadiers and 4, 5, and 7 Companies, HKVDC behind. The Royal Scots formed a bridge between the two frontline Indian battalions along with 6 Company, HKVDC, while the Middlesex Regiment manned the line of pillboxes that studded the north shore of the island.

The British had withdrawn three of the four destroyers from Hong Kong just before the Japanese attack. The last remaining destroyer, the 1,075-ton Admiralty S-class HMS *Thracian*, had its hands full fending off repeated Japanese dive-bomber and strafing attacks, its three QF 4-inch guns and single QF 2-pounder 'pom-pom' trying its best to harass Japanese aircraft. A small number of river gunboats also attempted to fend off repeated Japanese aerial assaults that resulted in several being damaged or sunk. A handful of Motor Torpedo Boats did manage to make several runs through the six battalions of Sakai's 38th Division as it crossed the narrow waters that separated Hong Kong from Kowloon on the night of 18 December, inflicting casualties, sinking several landing craft, but also suffering heavily themselves. The MTB assault was more of a nuisance raid than a serious attempt at stopping the Japanese landing.

The rest of the world believed that Hong Kong Island was 'Well protected by a honeycomb of shelters under "The Peak", the island's steeply rising gun-encrusted backbone,'[14] little realising that no such fortifications existed. In reality, only the hastily prepared positions thrown up by the Island Brigade would prevent the Japanese from quickly investing the island. The defence rested on under-trained, under-supplied and heavily outnumbered troops putting up a cohesive resistance through difficult terrain against an enemy riding high on victory, and with the sure knowledge of eventual success at the forefront of their minds.

On shore, British forces were soon heavily outnumbered by Japanese troops. The 5/7th Rajputs was annihilated in hand-to-hand fighting and the Japanese headlong advance inland was only stopped in this sector by HKVDC occupying high ground behind the landing zones, but the Japanese did manage to push south to the strategically important Wong Nai Chung Gap. This geographical feature divides Hong Kong Island into two halfs. On the 19th the fight for 'the Gap' began in earnest.

Private Crabb and the HKVDC's No. 2 Machine Gun (Scottish) Company found themselves cut off by Japanese patrols probing inland from the landing zones. They fought their first patrol actions in the 19th below Pottinger's Gap. 'It was then that we were introduced to the Japanese mortar which was extremely accurate and it was only because of the high percentage of duds that we were not wiped out,' recalled Crabb. 'We received our first casualties, including myself slightly wounded, but we gave as good as we got and they withdrew back to the Gap.'[15]

The Wong Nai Chung Gap was defended by Brigadier Lawson's West Brigade HQ, 3 Company HKVDC, elements of 5 Anti-Aircraft Battery, Royal Artillery and some men from the HK&SRA and HQ 'D' Company, Winnipeg Grenadiers. Later in the day the fighting would suck in the Winnipeg's 'A' Company, the entire Royal Scots and some Royal Engineers. Lawson lost 451 killed but he could not stop the Japanese advance. The Japanese intended to slice through the Wong Nai Chung Gap to Repulse Bay and cut Hong Kong Island, and the British defences, in half. Although Maltby could see what the Japanese were doing he lacked sufficient supplies and men to counter-attack strongly enough to prevent this disastrous outcome.

At the Salesian Mission religious buildings at Shau Kei Wan on Hong Kong Island an Advanced Dressing Station had been established under the command of Surgeon Major Barfill, Royal Army Medical Corps. A constant relay of ambulances, mostly driven by volunteers from the Royal Rifles of Canada, ferried in streams of wounded from the front lines. The hospital staff was a mixture of British Army doctors and medics, regular and volunteer army nurses, and St. John's Ambulance Brigade staff.

Japanese shells impacted close to the hospital, throwing up great clouds of dirt and rock, and the shelling seemed to increase around dawn on 19 December. There were a few armed sentries patrolling the grounds, but little to protect the hospital from attack. The hospital continued to function at full capacity, and Barfill refused to consider evacuation until he received a direct order from Brigade HQ, the British hoping that a hospital would be respected by the Japanese. 'No news of any landings had been received and some wounded Rajputs had just been sent off to Tai Tam by ambulance when at 06.00 hours a sentry reported that the Mission was surrounded by Japanese.'[16]

Japanese soldiers, ignoring the large Red Cross flags, climbed into the back of an army ambulance and bayoneted to death two wounded Rajput officers who were lying on stretchers. The medical staff was herded outside where the men were ordered to strip. They were searched for concealed weapons, and the Japanese soldiers also took this opportunity to loot wedding rings, watches and any money. The patients were left lying on stretchers or sitting on beds inside the dressing station under guard.

Five British Army doctors were made to kneel naked on the grass outside the hospital. A Japanese officer shot each doctor once in the back of the head. The nurses, sobbing uncontrollably, were forced to watch. Next, the Japanese officer shouted some instructions at his subordinates, and eight young soldiers from the Royal Rifles of Canada, who had been volunteering in the hospital or driving ambulances, were savagely kicked and beaten forward. Other Japanese officers drew their *katana* swords as the Canadians were forced to their knees and were beheaded one by one. Still the Japanese bloodlust was not satisfied. Ten medical corps orderlies were butchered, followed by three St. John's Ambulance Brigade volunteers. 'The Japanese then started butchering some of the wounded patients, forcing Major Barfill to watch.'[17] The nurses were untouched. They had been forced to watch the killings alongside Barfill, but when it was over a Japanese officer told them to go home. Barfill was left alive presumably to carry news of the massacre to the British front line – the Japanese hoping that such brutality would frighten the British into a swift surrender. They had done the same thing in China in the late 1930s, terrorising and murdering in the hope of reducing enemy morale.

Captain Osler Thomas, HKVDC medical officer, had been shot in the head but miraculously survived. Corporal Norman Leath of the RAMC was also alive, though he was seriously injured. A blow from a Japanese sword had partially decapitated the unfortunate soldier, but with the help of Thomas and Barfill he managed to survive. The three men fled into the nearby hills and separately hid for more than a week until they emerged to surrender after the fighting was finally over. The massacre at the Salesian Mission presaged even worse horrors to come when the Japanese captured the main British hospitals on Christmas Day.

Brigadier Lawson was killed when the Japanese got close enough to assault West Brigade HQ, which was only thinly protected by some Royal Scots. Lawson sent a final message to Maltby by radio saying that he was going outside to 'fight it out' with the Japanese, and with a service revolver clutched in each fist he dashed out of his HQ into the thick of the action where he was quickly cut down and killed. Lawson's chief-of-staff, Colonel Patrick Hennessey, was also killed, so command of West Brigade devolved to a part-time volunteer officer, Colonel H. B. Rose of the HKVDC.

Brigadier Wallis ordered the survivors of East Brigade to reform in the hills north of Stanley. On 20 December the Punjabis 'A' Company was ordered to relieve the Repulse Bay Hotel, the Japanese having almost succeeded in cutting the island in two. Simultaneously, East Brigade struck west along the same road. The Punjabis made it to Shonson Hill, but the peak was firmly in Japanese hands. East Brigade was halted at Eucliffe. On the same day Hong Kong's water supply fell into enemy hands when the Japanese captured the island's reservoirs, and the situation appeared dire.

The next day East Brigade tried again and attacked the Wong Nai Chung Gap but was halted at Red Hill. To the west, three platoons from the Winnipeg Grenadiers managed to retake Mount Butler, but were unable to hold the feature for long. During the battle 42-year-old Company Sergeant Major John Osborn showed tremendous courage in the face of the enemy. Although in a Canadian regiment, Osborn came from Norfolk in England. As 'A' Company was withdrawing off Mount Butler, Osborn single-handedly engaged the Japanese. 'With no consideration for his own safety he assisted and directed stragglers to the new Company position exposing himself to heavy enemy fire to cover this retirement.' Cut off and later surrounded, Osborn's company was showered with hand grenades by the Japanese. Osborn picked up several and threw them back. 'The enemy threw a grenade which landed in a position where it was impossible to pick it up and return it in time. Shouting a warning to his comrades this gallant Warrant Officer threw himself on the grenade which exploded killing him instantly. His self-sacrifice undoubtedly saved the lives of many others,' read Osborn's citation for the Victoria Cross. No matter how brave and resourceful the remaining defenders were, the Japanese attack was virtually irresistible.

The Middlesex Regiment stabilised the British line on Leighton Hill, preventing the Japanese from taking the waterfront and Victoria, the colony's capital. The Japanese changed their strategy and started forming a bulge in the hills south of the racecourse (Mount Nicholson and Mount Cameron). On 23 December, the Japanese bulge progressed into West Brigade's lines, while East Brigade began to be squeezed into the Stanley Peninsula. Maltby received a final message from Winston Churchill that read, 'Everyday that you are able to maintain your resistance, you help the Allied cause all over the world.' The day before in London the front-page headline of the *Daily Express* declared in bold black typeface: 'HONGKONG GARRISON FIGHT TO THE LAST'. The newspaper told its readers that Maltby's gallant command was, not untruthfully, 'Fighting to the death with swarms of Japanese who landed yesterday at many points on the island. Rejected with scorn a third offer of surrender terms, and then came silence'.[18]

Private Crabb's HKVDC unit fell back into the Stanley Peninsula. 'These withdrawals were something we had to get used to, but we were never able to understand the reasons especially as it seemed as at no time, except at the very end, were we actually forced to retire.'[19]

Street fighting continued in Wanchai throughout Christmas Eve, and the Japanese managed to push back Maltby's defences in the hills above Central. The 24th found Crabb's unit 'well pinned down in the valley by shell and machine gun fire. Our casualties gradually mounted so that the three platoons were getting rather thread-bare.' Company headquarters was now located in the

Stanley Police Station with one platoon on the Chung Hom Kok peninsula and the rest spread out in the foothills above the village. 'The Japs attacked in strength that night but we held our lines until midday on Christmas Day. 'We were now all mixed up,' recalled Crabb, 'Middlesex, ourselves, Stanley gaol warders and elements of the Volunteer batteries, all under control of our Company Commander.'[20]

At dawn on Christmas Day a strong Japanese assault managed to push the Stanley defenders back past the hospital at St. Stephen's College. At the hospital on Tun Tau Wan Road the Japanese perpetrated the worst war crime of the battle. Commanded by Captain George Black, a 65-year-old doctor and First World War veteran, assisted by a handful of British Army nurses, St. Stephen's was full to capacity with wounded British and Canadian soldiers. Two hundred Japanese infantry arrived on Christmas Day. Rifleman Alfred Babin, a 22-year-old serving in the Royal Rifles of Canada had been detailed as an ambulance driver but had been badly wounded while out collecting casualties. 'I was taking five wounded soldiers from Tai Tam Gap advance dressing station to Bowen Road Hospital in Victoria,' recalled Babin. 'With me was a British guide, supplied by RAMC. On the way, the ambulance was fired upon by the Japanese. Bullets from machine-guns shattered the windshield. I managed to run the ambulance between the wreckage of burned vehicles that lined the side of the road, sheltered somewhat from the Japanese, who were on top of the hill.' Everyone in the vehicle was in a bad way. 'I discovered that I had been wounded on the forehead and right hand, that Bickley (the guide) had received shattered glass from the windshield full in the face and was bleeding profusely, moaning that he could not see.'[21] The five wounded soldiers had been wounded again, and Bickley permanently lost his sight.

'At 7 o'clock they [the Japanese] knocked at the door with their rifle butts and shot the captain and took over,'[22] recalled Babin. Dr. Black and his second-in-command, Captain Whitney, tried to stop the Japanese entering the building. Both doctors were dressed in white lab coats, and they were wearing Red Cross brassards and carrying a white flag and a Red Cross flag as they walked slowly towards the heavily armed Japanese troops.

Black shouted at the leading Japanese soldiers: 'You can't come in here, this is a hospital.' A Japanese soldier leveled his rifle at the doctor's head and fired, killing Black instantly. Captain Whitney was gunned down shortly after as drunk Japanese soldiers piled through the open door stabbing at the two doctors' bodies with their bayonets as they lay in pools of their own blood. Japanese soldiers then embarked on a half hour killing spree. 20-year-old Sergeant Bob Clayton, another wounded Canadian, recalled that 'the Japanese entered downstairs and started bayonetting everybody.'[23] Captain James Barrett, chaplain to the Royal Rifles of Canada, witnessed some of the horrors. There had been approximately 160 patients in St. Stephen's when the Japanese entered. The Japanese ordered all walking wounded to their feet. 'They lined us all up at the bottom of the stairs,' said Babin. 'One soldier was counting us off and when he got to so many, he'd pull one out. When he got to me, I was holding onto a wounded man next to me, he hesitated, but he carried on. They marched us up to a room – it was very crowded, the temperature must have been 120 degrees.'[24] Those who had been selected from the line-up were shortly after bayoneted to death. The Japanese also went from bed to bed bayoneting or shooting all of the stretcher cases. Padre Barrett witnessed Japanese soldiers bayonet and/or shoot dead around twenty patients before he was herded into the store-room with those able to walk.[25] Barrett recalled: 'After we had been there [in the room] for about an hour the Japanese moved us up to a smaller room. Until then the nurses had been with me, but as we were being moved from the store room to the smaller room they were taken away.' The padre could not help the young women. 'I saw one of them beaten over the head with a steel helmet, kicked, and then slapped in the face by a Japanese soldier.'[26]

'In the small room ninety men were placed with me,' recalled Barrett, 'some of the hospital staff and some of the wounded men. The room was so small that we could not have all sat down together, and it was necessary for the very sick or wounded men to lie down as best they could and when they could.'[27] Barrett recalled that the Japanese regularly dragged men away. Sergeant Clayton recalled that 'Every once in a while they'd come in and pick someone out and that was it ...'[28] Barrett witnessed two young soldiers dragged from the room later that day, writing that

'Immediately afterwards we heard screams coming from the corridor outside.'[29] Barrett said that they 'remained in this room until 4 p.m. when a Japanese soldier entered and gave us to understand by sign language that Hong Kong had surrendered.'[30]

On Boxing Day Padre Barrett was released and discovered what had become of the army nurses. He stumbled about blood-soaked corridors looking for them. The hospital 'was in a dreadful state,' recalled Barrett. 'I found the two men who had been taken out of our room. Their bodies were badly mutilated, their ears, tongues, noses and eyes had been cut away from their faces. About seventy or more wounded men had been killed by bayonets while in their beds. Many more were seriously wounded ... I found the dead bodies of the commanding officer of the hospital, and his adjutant, on the ground floor. They had been badly mutilated.'[31]

'They were in a terrible state', said Barrett when he found the nurses. They walked with evident pain, and clung to one another for comfort. Shortly after they had been led away, they 'stripped them', recalled Kay Christie, 'they slapped their faces with their Red Cross arm bands and started raping them on top of the mattresses that had the corpses underneath. This went on and on.'[32] Padre recalled that Sister Elizabeth Fidoe 'told me she had been forced to lie on top of two dead bodies and had been raped several times.'[33] According to Sister Gordon's testimony the nurses were initially imprisoned in different classrooms on the first floor of the college. She was shut 'into a small room with four VADs Mrs Smith, Mrs Begg ..., Buxton and Simmons where there were five Chinese women.'[34] Five Japanese soldiers entered Gordon's room at 4.30pm and took Smith, Begg and Buxton away. These three women were never seen alive again. Sisters Gordon and Fidoe were then taken to a room that contained the five decomposing bodies of Red Cross workers butchered by the Japanese that were partially covered with mattresses. 'A little later two soldiers removed Mrs Fidoe and two removed me. I was taken to another room, where there were two dead bodies, and made to take off all my clothes whilst they removed theirs. Before touching me they apparently became afraid someone was coming and made me put on my clothes again and I was returned to the room where Mrs Simmons and Mrs Andrews-Levinge still were.' Sister Fidoe rejoined them almost immediately and told them that she had been raped. 'Three soldiers came in and took me to a small adjacent bathroom,' recalled Gordon, 'knocked me down and all raped me, one after another ... Mrs Fidoe was then taken and underwent a similar experience. Both Mrs Fidoe and I were taken out a second time and raped.'[35] Whilst this was going on the five Chinese nurses were also gang-raped.

Sister Christie says that after hours of gang raping the nurses the Japanese soldiers decided to kill some of them. 'Then for some reason, which the four girls who survived could never figure out, they took three of the volunteers and, after raping them, cut their heads off and piled their naked bodies outside.'[36] 'None of us had yet seen the three other nurses,' recalled Barrett in Tokyo, but added: 'Later in the morning one of the nurses came to me and said that a Japanese soldier wanted her to go with him out of the hospital into the grounds. She asked me to accompany her. I did and took a RAMC sergeant along with us. In the bushes, covered with branches, we found the bodies of the three dead nurses, one of whom had her head practically severed from her body ...'[37]

At nearly all of the other hospitals in Hong Kong the army nurses and female civilian volunteers all suffered to some degree or other at the hands of the Japanese. 'In one hospital,' recalled Sister Christie, 'the Japanese soldiers lined up all the females, many of whom were just young girls. The women were mostly British, who had been employed as secretaries, teachers and so on, or they were the wives of British business men or army officers. They were such a wonderful group who worked so hard at their volunteer duties in the hospital.'[38] Horrific acts of cruelty were once more played out as Japanese soldiers segregated the women from male prisoners. 'As one of the soldiers stood in the doorway with a machine gun, the others took the younger girls, laid them on the floor and raped them while the mothers could do nothing but stand by helplessly and watch.'[39]

The question remains as to why British nurses were not evacuated from Hong Kong when a Japanese attack became inevitable, when the behaviour of Japanese troops towards women had been well publicised around the world following the attack on China in 1937–38, particularly the appalling brutality of the Rape of Nanking.

Whilst the Japanese were murdering and abusing patients and staff inside St. Stephen's College, the remaining troops manning the shortened perimeter at Stanley continued to resist. 'By midday the position was pretty hopeless,' said HKVDC Private Crabb. 'The Company HQ had been wiped out ... and control was taken over by an officer who had been in gaol up to a few days before.'[40]

At 3.15pm on Christmas Day, General Maltby and the Governor of Hong Kong, Sir Mark Young, agreed to surrender. The Battle of Hong Kong officially ended at 6pm on Christmas Day 1941 when Governor Sir Mark Young signed the instrument of surrender at the Peninsula Hotel in Kowloon. It was the first time in history that a British colony had surrendered to an invading army.

Fighting continued on the Stanley Peninsula for a further eleven hours as the defenders were out of contact with higher headquarters. 'We pulled back to the hills just overlooking the gaol and then were relieved by the Royal Rifles of Canada who had been in Stanley Fort,' wrote Private Crabb. 'We were exhausted and retired to the Fort to sleep out that night. Next morning [26 December] we were advised that the Colony had capitulated the previous day and that the Stanley Peninsula area – or what was left of it – had surrendered early that morning.'[41] A quarter of the men in Crabb's unit had been killed, including the officer commanding and the company sergeant major, but they took some satisfaction from the fact that they had inflicted heavy casualties upon the Japanese.

Many Allied veterans of the battle recall that they only laid down their arms when instructed by higher command. 'We never gave up,' said former Company Sergeant Major George MacDonell, Royal Rifles of Canada, in 2005. 'They had to order us to surrender. If we hadn't run out of bullets, we'd have kept fighting them off for years.'[42] In view of the horrific imprisonment these men were to suffer at the hands of the Japanese, such fighting spirit was probably advisable.

The defenders had suffered up to 2,400 killed, including wounded soldiers, military medical staff and an unknown number of civilians who had been massacred by Japanese troops during the advance and *after* the surrender. Of the 1,975 inexperienced Canadians offered up for sacrifice by Churchill and Brooke-Popham, 290 were killed during the fighting and 493 wounded.

A further 260 would die in prisoner-of-war camps in Hong Kong and Japan. Overall, twenty-five percent of those taken prisoner in Hong Kong would perish in Japanese labour camps.

Britain would not be able to return to China until September 1945, except for a series of secret operations that were mounted during the war years. This 'secret war' got off to an appallingly bad start in Shanghai.

Chapter 8

Cloak and Dagger

OM telegrams to the Shanghai representative had to pass through the hands of the MI6 representative in Shanghai ... This representative was very anti-SOE.

In Shanghai on the morning of 8 December 1941 a group of extremely nervous middle-aged men had just been informed, through a contact at the British Embassy, that war was about to be declared. Most had been up all night, unable to rest, an unpleasant feeling churning through their guts. They had glanced at silver-framed photos of loved ones in their studies or atop drawing room pianos, and glanced out of the windows of their large and comfortable houses and apartments at the darkness, until official confirmation had arrived just after daybreak. The Japanese were at war with Britain and America.

William Gande was a 55-year-old wine and champagne sales-man, whose firm, W.J. Gande, was well-known throughout the International Settlement where it supplied all of high society's grandest parties and soirées. Gande was the leader of a covert group of patriots in Shanghai who were about to have their worlds turned upside down. John Brand was a 52-year-old businessman; Joseph Brister, 56, a company manager; George Jack, 55, a life insurance company manager; and Sydney Riggs, a 49-year-old surveyor. All middle-aged and used to comfortable lives, this unlikely gathering of men, who shared a common background and schooling, had been expected to open a new front in Shanghai against the Germans and Italians, who were present in the city in large numbers, and to keep a weather eye on the increasingly belligerent Japanese.

'Early in July, 1941, I was approached by W.M. Gande and asked if I would assist with certain Secret Service work,' recalled new agent Sydney Riggs, 'directed, of course, towards the war effort and aimed primarily against Axis interests.'[1] By such direct and almost schoolboyish methods Gande went about recruiting his agents. He knew he could rely on their patriotism, but clearly they did not really understand what they were getting themselves involved with. 'I willingly agreed to do all in my power in conjunction with others of the group,'[2] said Riggs, adding that he was offered £50 as an incentive – which he waived as he was paid well enough as a surveyor. The amateur nature of the organisation is revealed by Riggs: 'We were pledged each to the other to refer only to each other by codenames', even though they knew one another socially, adding that 'although other people were co-opted to assist the group, they acted in a strictly unofficial capacity and, although the official group knew of their existence, we adopted the policy of not allowing them to be known to each other.'[3] Two more agents were added: Edward Elias was a 41-year-old stockbroker and Irishman William Clarke was a former Deputy Commissioner of the Shanghai Municipal Police, and at 65 the oldest agent.

These seven men formed Britain's belated attempt at a military sabotage and intelligence group in Shanghai, and were called OM (Oriental Mission) Shanghai by their masters at Special Operations Executive in Singapore and London. For over a year these patriotic but largely untrained spies had lived double lives. By day they were respectable pillars of the International Settlement's British community, but in the shadowy hours of twilight they had banded together to plot and scheme – always hoping to strike a blow for King and Country in Shanghai, seemingly far removed from the war. It all seemed a million miles from the real shooting war in Europe and North Africa, and many in the British community had been stung by accusations from London that they were living 'high on the hog', safe in Shanghai, while their countrymen risked everything in the battle against Hitler and Mussolini. OM Shanghai had been formed specifically to counter such accusations.

But on that chilly December morning the seven members of OM Shanghai suddenly realised their inadequacies, their lack of tradecraft, and the danger of their being exposed. Safes were emptied and files burned, to cover their tracks and distance themselves from association with SOE. The Japanese reputation for brutality was well earned after the Rape of Nanking in 1937. The men of OM Shanghai all knew that they were now targets for the dreaded *Kempeitai*, the Japanese military police, whose use of torture was already infamous. They were trapped in Shanghai, far from any effective assistance from headquarters, and abandoned by their bosses in Japanese-occupied Shanghai. What was about to happen to them was worse than anything they could have imagined.

When Winston Churchill had ordered the formation of a new sabotage organisation with orders to 'Set Europe ablaze!' after the Dunkirk evacuations in 1940, the Special Operations Executive had been born. The group's task was to link up with resistance organisations inside Europe and carry out acts of subversion and sabotage against the Germans. SOE was placed under the auspices of the Minister for Economic Warfare, Hugh Dalton, and remained separate from Britain's existing pre-war intelligence departments, MI5 and the Secret Intelligence Service (MI6). The 'MI' stands for 'Military Intelligence', and today MI5 is tasked with dealing with intelligence threats inside the United Kingdom, whereas MI6 operates abroad. SOE was something new and untested, designed specifically for the war. It was viewed with great suspicion by the established intelligence organisations and their leaders.

By late 1940, it was obvious in London that the Far East was going to be an important new front. Dalton was asked to create an SOE section for the Orient. SOE had experienced great difficulties in establishing operations inside German-controlled France and decided to act quickly in creating a similar organisation on the ground in the Far East *before* an expected Japanese takeover became a reality. SOE agent A.E. Jones was dispatched to Singapore in January 1941 charged with establishing a headquarters and a regional organisation. Jones was ordered to appoint a 'No. 1' in Shanghai who would be responsible for all of Northern China, an area of great economic importance to Britain at the time.

In May 1941 a permanent head of OM was appointed and Jones became the organisation's second-in-command. SOE chose as head a man who was well known among the international business community in Shanghai, a former vice-chairman of Imperial Chemical Industries (ICI) and a former member of the exclusive Shanghai Municipal Council, Valentine Killery. Killery assumed the codename 'O.100' and set up his office in Singapore. He was commissioned a lieutenant colonel in the army and created what became known as Special Training School (STS) 101, but perhaps its former name best summed up its true purpose – The School of Demolitions.[4] The two top instructors in unorthodox warfare at the school were pre-war adventurer and mountaineer Major Freddy Spencer-Chapman and tough Royal Marine Colonel Alan 'Cocky' Warren. They created stay-behind parties of demolition and ambush specialists in Malaya should the Japanese capture the peninsula.

Killery's knowledge of the local expatriate business community led him to recruit his agents from among his contemporaries at the exclusive Shanghai Club. These men were very different from the young, tough and energetic soldiers being put through STS 101 in Singapore. It was perhaps not the best source from which to recruit personnel, as all would certainly attract the attention of the *Kempeitai* as soon as the Japanese captured the International Settlement, by dint of being prominent enemy personages. They could also expect to be swiftly interned as the Japanese relieved them of their business assets and their liberty. It was doubtful how useful these men would have proved to SOE, stuck inside an internment camp.

Killery faced many challenges in making OM a success, not the least of which was his complete lack of experience in espionage work. MI6 operated its own agents throughout Asia, and along with the British diplomatic community, it remained very wary of Killery's collection of amateur spies, gentleman adventurers and would-be saboteurs. According to the official, though unpublished, history of OM Shanghai, MI6 made life as difficult as possible for Gande and his associates. 'OM telegrams to the Shanghai representative had to pass through the hands of the MI6 representative in Shanghai ... This representative was very anti-SOE.'[5] The MI6 officer feared a breach in security by the amateurs that would have led to his own exposure to the Japanese. MI6 actively tried to destroy OM Shanghai through its control over communications and was quite successful in this regard.

The choice of targets for the new fledgling OM Shanghai to choose from was diverse. An unusual sight would have confronted visitors who arrived by ship in Shanghai in 1941. At the north end of the Bund sat the British Consulate, housing the Embassy since the Rape of Nanking, the Union Jack fluttering proudly in the stiff onshore breeze. A few buildings down the street visitors would have seen the Nazi swastika flag snapping out just as proudly in the wind. Enemies separated by only a few hundred yards of Settlement, Shanghai was neither colony nor Chinese city, but instead a neutral slice of territory controlled by a council dominated by the British and Americans, and peopled by a polyglot mixture of Europeans, Chinese, Japanese and Russians. No single power held sway, so although Britain and Germany were at war, diplomatic niceties were still being observed. Swinging on their anchor cables in mid-stream, the Italians maintained several warships on the Whangpoo River, easily observable from the many British businesses that lined the Bund and from the Shanghai Club.

Such proximity to one's enemies galvanised Gande's group to begin plotting a bold attack on the Axis. OM Shanghai had been issued with four main objectives by Killery in Singapore, the second of which read: 'Organize sabotage of enemy interests, such as shipping, enemy goods, wireless broadcast propaganda etc.'[6] Killery ordered Gande to start compiling lists of enemy goods in Shanghai and their destinations when moved. If these goods could then be sabotaged, so much the better. Enemy ships were also to be targeted for destruction, and a propaganda campaign was to be initiated against the Axis.

OM Shanghai seized upon the task of attacking enemy shipping, though quite how they expected to do this when none of the group had any commando or sabotage training was not addressed. Several plans were considered. Blocking the river was one idea, but although the Whangpoo is quite narrow, at least three ships would have been required to shut down traffic. Another idea was to sink ships as obstructions, while a final plan, which was

147

adopted much to the horror of the Foreign Office, was an attack on the Italian colonial sloop *Eritrea* that was moored close to the Bund. At the same time an effort was to be made to nobble a Nazi reporter named Karl von Wiegand who was filing articles for William Randolph Hearst's US publishing empire that were damaging Britain's reputation in the city.

OM Shanghai went ahead with planning an attack on the *Eritrea*, recently arrived from Kobe after the Japanese had refused her captain permission to intercept Russian convoys in the Pacific. The Royal Navy was behind Gande's plan, even though the RN's warship presence in Shanghai had shrunk to one partially manned gunboat and a tug, everything else having been evacuated to Hong Kong and Singapore in 1940. MI6, however, was annoyed at SOE muscling in on its field of operations and actively tried to block the scheme with the connivance of the FO. OM Shanghai's attempts at provoking a new war front in Shanghai were to be severely tested as the Foreign Office balked at launching military operations on what was effectively 'neutral territory'. The FO feared that attacking Japan's allies would provoke the Japanese into occupying Shanghai and beginning a war with Britain.

Gande's plan to sink the *Eritrea* had entered the final stages before suddenly the operation was abruptly cancelled by order of Killery in Singapore. Killery had been pressured by FO to stop the operation and complied with their wishes. 'We have very large interests there and no means of protecting them,' wrote the Foreign Office to OM headquarters in Singapore in reference to Shanghai. '[It] would therefore be rash for us to disturb the virtual truce now existing in the International Settlement, which though Chinese soil, has always enjoyed a quasi-neutral status.'[7] The diplomats had revealed themselves as men of straw, and MI6 had proved a greater danger to OM Shanghai than the local representatives of the Axis powers. Gande and his colleagues were devastated, but the cancellation probably saved their lives. Seven middle-aged men attempting to board and sink a fully armed warship in the midst of a peaceful city may have descended into farce, or more likely have resulted in a massacre.

The *Eritrea*, along with the other Italian vessels, remained untouched and safely moored on the Whangpoo River until the Italian armistice in September 1943, when Italy dramatically changed sides. The *Eritrea* dashed successfully to Colombo in Ceylon and surrendered to the British, while the crews of the other Italian vessels scuttled their ships and went into Japanese prisoner-of-war camps in Shanghai for the duration.

However, it was realised by SOE that when the Japanese took over the International Settlement and joined the Axis, Gande and his men would still not know the first thing about sabotage. With this disturbing fact at the forefront of his mind, John Brand travelled to Singapore in August 1941 to receive explosives and sabotage training at STS 101, and Gande was given £5,000 as a working budget for OM Shanghai. Incredibly, the money was remitted through the Hong Kong & Shanghai Bank on the Bund, and when the Japanese liquidated HSBC after their takeover of the city the entry was discovered in a ledger and the *Kempeitai* informed. The *Kempeitai* confiscated Gande's OM budget and used the cash to finance their operations in Shanghai. It was an astounding example of incompetence and indicative of the well-meaning but amateur nature of British intelligence operations in Shanghai.

Unfortunately, OM Shanghai completely underestimated the abilities of their arch-rivals, the *Kempeitai.* The Japanese had occupied all of Shanghai except the International Settlement and the French Concession since 1937. But even within the International Settlement, dominated by the British and Americans, the *Kempeitai* was running an efficient intelligence-gathering network, operating out of the Japanese concession located across Suzhou Creek in the Hongkew district. For several weeks prior to the Japanese takeover the *Kempeitai* had gathered information about OM Shanghai. The Japanese knew that OM was an intelligence organisation linked to the British Ministry for Economic Warfare, and this information had come to them through another elementary mistake made by an OM member. Gande kept certain secret files relating to his organisation in his safe at work, and, incredibly, other employees also had access to that safe. One employee, a Romanian, stole several of these files after recognising their value and sold them to the Japanese. The *Kempeitai* then covertly organised the tapping of Gande's telephone and recorded all of his conversations both with his superiors, and with his agents. OM Shanghai's days were numbered.

As the Shanghai Volunteer Corps and the Shanghai Municipal Police geared up for possible war in December 1941 and as the relocated British Embassy anxiously monitored events, the Foreign Office, MI6, and SOE's Far Eastern representatives did nothing. In an appalling piece of bureaucratic indifference, Gande and his associates were given no further instructions by London or Singapore and were abandoned to a terrible fate. Once the city was about to be overrun by the Japanese, it was too late to get Gande and his men out – their only hope was to keep a low profile and try to pass themselves off as what they appeared to be – pillars of settler society and leaders of expatriate business. Betrayal and arrest were now distinct possibilities for all seven men.

The tramp of army boots marching in unison up Nanking Road, Shanghai's main shopping street, matched the eerie squealing and grinding of tank tracks. From the river the last explosions died away as the British gunboat HMS *Peterel* lazily rolled over and sank, steam hissing from the water as her burning superstructure went under, following her futile last stand against the might of the Imperial Japanese Navy. Within the hour the Union Jack was being hauled down from the tower of the Customs House and the Rising Sun run up the flagpole. The British and other Allied nationals huddled inside their houses and apartments in disbelief, as short Japanese soldiers in dun-coloured uniforms, bayonets fixed to rifles that were almost as tall as their owners, started to take over businesses throughout the Settlement. Almost the only white people on the streets were Russian refugees and Germans eagerly sporting swastika armbands so as not to be confused with Japan's real Caucasian enemies. Behind the soldiers came the *Kempeitai* military police clutching lists of enemy aliens who should be investigated, arrested, executed.

SOE had made a ghastly mistake in organising OM Shanghai. All of its members were among the group the Japanese were most likely to intern early on during the occupation, the British ruling class. Gande knew that it was only a matter of time before he was hauled in for questioning. For he and the other six members of OM Shanghai, a terrible period of uncertainty followed. None felt able to withstand what would be a very unpleasant time in Japanese hands, but there was no way out of the city and any attempt to run would have signalled guilt more strongly than simply staying put and hoping for the best.

The methods employed by the *Kempeitai* to obtain information and confessions were brutally efficient and simple. The Japanese assumed that any initial answer to a question was a lie, and all interviewees were subjected to a beating, usually with a bamboo cane or a wooden club, that was designed to loosen the tongue. Questioning usually lasted several days, in some cases weeks and months, and beatings were interspersed with being hung from the ceiling by the thumbs, electric shocks being applied to the genitals, lit cigarettes mashed into yielding skin or thrust up nostrils, to the most dreaded torture of all – the water treatment. The subject was strapped down and a hosepipe forced into the mouth. Water was then pumped into the victim until drowning commenced and consciousness was lost. The questioner jumped on the victim's stomach or kicked the victim savagely and then evacuated the water. More questions would then be followed by more water treatment. Many men and women died under this sort of abuse.

The first member of OM Shanghai who was arrested by the *Kempeitai* was surprisingly not Gande, but the former senior policeman William Clarke, on 17 December 1941. Clarke was taken to the *Kempeitai* HQ at Bridge House located just across Garden Bridge at the north end of the Bund, and was tortured by Lieutenant Yamamoto and his men. American journalist John B. Powell, who shared a cell with Clarke, said that Clarke was unable to stand. Clarke said to Powell that he believed that he was going to die, and the two men prayed together and waited for the end. It is believed that Clarke cracked under torture and named some of the members of OM Shanghai. This would hardly have been surprising as Clarke and the others had received absolutely no training in withstanding interrogation. According to Powell, Clarke was pushed 'into the corner alongside me, and I saw he was in severe pain. He was suffering from several boils on his neck; they had become so infected and swollen, because of lack of medical attention, that his head was pressed over against his shoulder.'[8] However, Powell's representations to Yamamoto regarding Clarke's pitiful condition caused the Japanese to remove

Clarke to a local hospital for treatment, saving his life. Powell was not so lucky.

On 27 December, Yamamoto and his men struck again, this time arresting Gande, Brister and Jack. They were bundled at gunpoint into cars and driven to Bridge House.

The three SOE agents were extensively tortured until more names were forthcoming, then were thrown into overcrowded, rat-infested cells and denied medical attention. Under constant torture and dreadful sanitary conditions Gande developed infected toenails, among other things. A Japanese medical officer tore Gande's toenails off with a pair of pliers without administering any anaesthetic. The treatment dished out to Gande, Brister and Jack completely exposed the entire OM network in Shanghai, and would lead to the arrest of the final three men, John Brand, Sydney Riggs and Edward Elias. The Japanese had compelling evidence: telegrams between Gande and OM HQ in Singapore, phone tap records, references to the Ministry of Economic Warfare in London, and the evidence of torture. The arrested agents did not think that they would survive. The *Kempeitai* made sure that conditions inside Bridge House were as unpleasant as possible. Aside from fearsome interrogations, 'rats and disease-infested lice were everywhere, and no one was allowed to bathe or shower, so diseases from dysentery to typhus to leprosy ran rampant.'[9]

Many British and American journalists were swept up by the *Kempeitai* and extensively ill treated largely because they had had the temerity to publish articles condemning Japanese atrocities in China. The experience of John B. Powell was typical. According to the *North China Daily News* reporter Ralph Shaw, the 'Kempetai [sic] torturers wreaked their vengeance on the brave American [Powell] and subjected him to atrocious assaults, beating him unmercifully.' These beatings included 'kicking, usually in the genital region, beating – anything connected with physical suffering.'[10] Powell was the editor of the *China Weekly Review* and he was imprisoned and tortured alongside fellow American Victor Keen of the *New York Herald Tribune*. 'When the questioning began, they [the prisoners] had to remove all their clothing and kneel before their captors. When their answers failed to satisfy their interrogators, the victims were beaten on the back and legs with four-foot bamboo sticks until blood flowed.'[11] John Powell was left crippled. He was 'a permanent invalid, [and] was later shipped home to the United States aboard a repatriation vessel ... Gangrene set in and Powell had part of a leg amputated. He never recovered and died shortly later.'[12] A British journalist named Healey, who ran the XMHA radio station, was subjected 'to treatment which plumbed the depths of human depravity,' according to his friend Ralph Shaw. 'He went insane and died bloodied and crippled in his rat-hole of a cell in the Bridge House.'[13]

The greatest prize for the Japanese was a British writer and journalist named H.G.W. Woodhead, editor of *Oriental Affairs* and weekly columnist on the *Shanghai Evening Post and Mercury* who had spent years denouncing Japanese militarism in China. Woodhead had also broadcast twice weekly a strong anti-Japanese message on Shanghai's XMHC and XCDN radio stations at the direct behest of the British government. On 5 December 1941, just days before Pearl Harbor, the British Embassy had advised Woodhead to get out of Shanghai as fast as possible, and the frightened journalist had booked passage on a Panamanian ship scheduled to sail four days later. This delay meant that Woodhead was still in Shanghai on 8 December. He took refuge in a friend's house in the French Concession, but eventually emerged and registered as an enemy alien, as all British, American, Free French, Dutch, Norwegian, Greek and other nationals were required to do by the Japanese.

London was becoming concerned, for OM Shanghai appeared to have dropped off the face of the earth. Nothing was heard from them. SOE dispatched a Chinese agent codenamed 'Dr. Chang' to Shanghai on 21 April 1942 in an effort to find out what had become of them. SOE was still in operation in the rest of China, and unlike OM, had sensibly utilised local Chinese as agents. Chang managed to discover, at great risk, that Gande and the others, minus Clarke who was in hospital, were being held in terrible conditions at Bridge House. This information came from Hugh Collar, local head of ICI and pre-war friend and colleague of Valentine Killery. Chang visited several other British businessmen in Shanghai, but they were all afraid and most realised that they were probably under *Kempeitai* surveillance. Chang could not contact Gande's group and returned to Kunming in Free China on 11 September to report to London. By this stage London had already been appraised of the fate of OM Shanghai, which had been reported in the Shanghai press in June.

By early 1942 the *Kempeitai* appeared to have been satisfied that it had captured all of the members of the British sabotage group. The Japanese decided that a prosecution would be made against the men and that this should have at least the veneer of legality. For the members of OM Shanghai who fully expected to have their heads cut off any day, the sudden news of a trial at least offered a reprieve from any more torture, and perhaps even survival for some of their number.

For several weeks Gande and his compatriots had lived a terrifying existence marked by brutality and horrific living conditions, during which the men had become emaciated through lack of food, were covered in cuts and bruises from the ill-treatment they had suffered, and sported straggly beards and unkempt hair full of lice. These men had had a glimpse of hell, but with a sudden jerk they were ordered out of Bridge House by the *Kempeitai*. As each man left, the Japanese forced them to sign a document stating that they had been reasonably treated and were in good health – the Japanese being almost as pedantic record keepers as the Nazis. Loaded aboard a truck, they were driven to Kiangwan and pushed into fresh cells. Kiangwan is about ten miles from Shanghai, and in 1942 was the headquarters of the Japanese 15th Army. At this point the Japanese held off on any further ill treatment, and the men's wives were permitted to send in food parcels – which the Japanese pilfered before handing over. Clarke appears to have been overlooked by the *Kempeitai*, and was left in a hospital in Shanghai recuperating from his experiences of torture.

William Gande's health was rapidly deteriorating at Kiangwan when it was announced that all six men would be placed on trial before a military tribunal on 28 April 1942 charged with 'having operated a secret organisation whose activities were detrimental to the interests of Japan and to local law and order.' The *Kempeitai* charge did not mention SOE or OM explicitly, probably indicating that the Japanese never fully understood the full significance of the group. The trial was a mockery. Gande received the harshest sentence – four years imprisonment, while the rest received lesser terms. The sentences were to be served at Ward Road Jail in Shanghai.

Thankfully this large, modern prison was run by the Shanghai Municipal Police and not by the Japanese. Strangely, some of the British prison warders had been permitted by the Japanese to continue in their duties. Britons ended up guarding Britons! These brave prison warders risked severe punishments by passing messages to and fro between the OM Shanghai members and their families, as well as getting them extra food and cigarettes. The Japanese eventually interned all of the warders when they decided to remove all enemy aliens from posts throughout the city.

In the autumn of 1942 Riggs, Brister, Jack and Brand were suddenly freed and bundled aboard a repatriation ship bound for Lourenco Marques in Mozambique, part of an exchange of Allied personnel for Japanese who had been interned in Britain. Riggs was to write a report exposing exactly what had happened to OM Shanghai that ruffled many feathers in Whitehall. The 'Riggs Report', as it has become known, did not make for happy reading in London. The report was believed to be so damaging to the reputation of SOE, already quite self-conscious in front of the established intelligence organisations, that the version released to the Foreign Office was considerably watered down. Lord Selborne, the minister responsible for the SOE, called it 'ghastly to read, restrained and vivid'.[14] Questions were naturally asked, for example why were a group of men with no training and little practical support permitted to represent SOE in Shanghai, and what did they achieve other than their own capture and imprisonment? Valentine Killery was criticised for permitting such a foolish venture to occur in the first place, along with several other highly placed officials.

MI6 was not overly upset at the swift demise of OM Shanghai, an organisation that could have exposed all British intelligence operations in Shanghai. Suspicions have continued that MI6 may have had a hand in the destruction of OM Shanghai. All of this was not helped by the fact that it was obvious that the Japanese had had an agent close to OM Shanghai virtually from the beginning. The whole episode was incredibly embarrassing for SOE, and they were determined to bury the fiasco as fast as possible.

Riggs, Brister, Jack and Brand were free, but Gande, Elias, and Clarke remained in Japanese hands. In October 1943 Edward Elias was suddenly released from Ward Road Jail. His subsequent activities in occupied Shanghai have generated a great deal of suspicion since the war. He set himself up as a freelance spy. It seems he was also a double agent by this time – trying to recruit young foreigners into his organisation with the intention of betraying them to the Japanese. Elias was named several times as a Japanese spy, which might have some bearing on the earlier arrest and imprisonment of OM Shanghai.

When William Clarke was released at the end of 1942, he too chose to remain in Shanghai. He could have sought repatriation as he was above military age and had suffered considerable ill health as a result of his association with OM Shanghai. Nevertheless he stayed put. Perhaps he stayed because his wife was Indian, and therefore socially unacceptable in Britain at the time, or perhaps he had cracked under *Kempeitai* torture and feared that he would be punished if he returned to Britain. There is also the tantalising possibility that Clarke had been an MI6 agent and stayed in Shanghai to continue working for military intelligence. When this author requested the SOE personnel files at Kew only Clarke's was still classified, for *77 years*. Elias' file had only been declassified in 2007.

SOE learned a valuable lesson from the OM Shanghai debacle, one that impinged directly upon further operations in China. Gifted amateurs were always welcome in SOE, but never again would a team be left to its own devices and then completely abandoned at the critical hour. Much bitterness and recrimination was generated by the affair, especially when SOE tried to downplay the embarrassing events it had created in Shanghai.

SOE was quick to rebuild its operations in occupied and Free China, working closely with the American Office of Strategic Services (OSS) and with the corrupt Chinese Nationalist regime of Chiang Kai-shek (whom the Americans referred to as 'Cash My-check'). Some great successes were achieved later in the war using Chinese personnel as agents, though operational control remained in the hands of the British in India. The contribution to the ultimate defeat of Japan was significant.

One of the best examples of a patriotic Englishman with SOE in China was Walter Fletcher, a larger-than-life character who managed to create a massive smuggling network in occupied China through his close relationship with Chinese criminal gangs. Through smuggling and currency speculation this one man managed to raise the staggering sum of £77 million for SOE. This made OM financially independent for the rest of the war, and allowed it to provide assistance to British internees when Japan was defeated, as well as a host of other legal and illegal projects.

After the war, Lord Selborne was one of many British officials who had been appalled at the treatment handed out to Gande and his group, and one of several who suggested an official apology and compensation be offered to the former SOE men. For example, Gande eventually was remitted £5,000 for his trouble, and given a written apology. But it was not a public apology: SOE was not prepared to allow its reputation to suffer. The whole affair leaves one with a bad taste in the mouth, and smacks of a payoff.

As a 'stay-behind' force, OM Shanghai was an unmitigated disaster. Probably more useful as a propaganda exercise the negligible results of OM Shanghai's operations negated this value as well. But the men deserved better than to be left untrained, compromised by their recruitment into an organisation the Japanese wanted to smash, and then cynically abandoned to their fates when the British position in Asia unravelled in the face of the Japanese onslaught. OM Shanghai represents the ugly side of an otherwise glorious SOE history, which perhaps explains why it is hardly ever mentioned in the histories of that organisation, and why several of its files remain top secret nearly seven decades after the end of the war.

Chapter 9

'Am Under Heavy Fire'

Suddenly we saw a line of splashes rip across the water just astern of us, followed by an inoffensive pop, pop, pop, popping noise. Bater gasped 'I'm scared P.O.' and doing my best not to look scared said, 'That makes two of us.'

Petty Officer Terry Currie, HMS *Consort*, 1949

On the open bridge of the sloop HMS *Amethyst*, Lieutenant Commander Bernard Skinner raised his binoculars and searched the banks of the wide Yangtze River, his Chinese river pilot calling out small course corrections to avoid the many sandbars and navigation hazards. Skinner's other officers also scanned the banks, all looking for the origin of the artillery shells that tore overhead with a whine or threw up great geysers of water close to the ship.

The *Amethyst* was on her way to Nanking from Shanghai, wending her way along China's greatest river as her predecessors had been doing for over a hundred years. It was April 1949 and China was in the grip of a horrific civil war. Britain's position in the Middle Kingdom was extremely unsteady.

Skinner turned to his second-in-command: 'No. 1, action stations.' The young lieutenant quickly relayed the command, the ship's electric warning bell ringing insistently as all hands ran to their assigned posts, the gunners dragging on white anti-flash hoods and gauntlets as they manned the turrets forward and aft.

'No. 1, get the Union Jacks unfurled, starboard first.' The crew quickly unfurled huge British flags on both sides of the ship, clearly marking the vessel as neutral. 'Full ahead both', ordered Skinner down the voice pipe to the wheelhouse beneath the bridge, the coxswain repeating his order. The *Amethyst* picked up speed, but still the shells kept coming at them. 'Yeoman, break out battle ensign,' ordered Skinner, and atop the radar tower the White Ensign proudly snapped out into the wind. 'It's coming from the north bank, sir,' said No. 1, as they all trained their binoculars onto the Communist-held side of the river. 'I saw the flash that time.'

Skinner did not hesitate. 'Tell Director, train on bearing Green 70.' The gunnery officer ordered the turrets to turn onto the north bank, and the guns were loaded. The gunnery officer could not yet see the enemy guns, and could only estimate their position and range whilst he looked for their smoke.

'Open fire!' said Skinner. A moment later the *Amethyst's* 4-inch guns started pumping shells into the riverbank, as Chinese shells started to get the range and began to batter the British ship. 'Tell Wireless Office – make from Amethyst to all ships: Am under heavy fire'. Seconds later a Chinese shell struck the bridge, killing or wounding everyone on it. Britain was fighting its last battle in China.

The Western domination of China formally came to an end in 1943 when the governments of the Allied powers agreed to relinquish control over their many concessions and enclaves. With the exception of Hong Kong, a crown colony, all other British concessions were signed over to Chiang Kai-shek's Nationalists. Any future trading with China would be conducted under Chinese laws, foreigners losing their rights to extraterritoriality. Of course, this was all rather a moot point as the concessions were then all under Japanese occupation. It was only in September 1945, following the Japanese surrender, that British armed forces returned to a very changed China.

Postwar China was in turmoil. The uneasy truce that had largely held between Chiang's Nationalists and Mao Zedong's Communists had completely broken down once the common Japanese enemy had been removed from the picture. A civil war based on a conflict between two political ideologies had swiftly broken out, a disaster not just for war ravaged China, but also for Western hopes of re-establishing lucrative trade now that the Japanese were gone. The situation was complicated because the Nationalist capital, then recognised as the legitimate government of China, was located in Nanking, far up the Yangtze River from the coast, and British traders and diplomats were isolated and increasingly vulnerable as Communist forces approached the city. In order to protect British interests in Nanking, the Royal Navy stationed a guard ship there with orders to evacuate British and Commonwealth nationals if the Communists threatened the city. The days of the China gunboat were over, these useful vessels having become casualties during the war or handed over to the Nationalists as bribes to keep them on the Allied side. But the Yangtze is a huge river, easily navigable for large ships for hundreds of miles into the Chinese interior.

In April 1949 the guard ship at Nanking was HMS *Consort*, a 1,885-ton C-class destroyer built in 1944. With a full complement of 186, including embarked Royal Marines, the *Consort* was due to be relieved by another ship coming up from Shanghai, HMS *Amethyst*. The *Amethyst* was a smaller vessel than the *Consort*, officially designated a Modified Black Swan-class sloop of 1,350-tons, though with a larger crew numbering 192 men under skipper Bernard Skinner. A sloop was a large corvette designed primarily as a convoy escort and anti-aircraft vessel. Built in Scotland in 1942, the *Amethyst* had scored some successes as an anti U-boat patrol vessel during the war. She was armed with six quick-firing Mk. XVI 4-inch anti-aircraft and dual-purpose guns housed in three twin turrets, two fore, and one aft. These guns fired 35lb high explosive shells and the vessel was also armed with heavy machine guns.

No one on board the *Amethyst* expected a fight – her mission was routine, though the crew expected to see some fighting between Nationalist and Communist troops, for Mao's forces had reached the north bank of the Yangtze River and dug in while more troops moved on Nanking. It was only a matter of time before the Communists crossed the river and the *Amethyst* would be called upon to evacuate British and Commonwealth citizens from the Chinese capital. The British certainly underestimated the degree of ingrained hostility towards them harboured by Communist troops who looked upon the British and other foreigners as having abused, robbed and cheated China for over a hundred years for their own profit and power. The Communists did not want to see 'imperialist' ships on the Yangtze.

In Nanking, the *Consort* was tied up to pontoons secured to the riverbank adjacent to a dried egg powder factory. 'If, or when civil disorder occurred, all British nationals were told to make for the dried egg powder factory where Jolly Jack would defend them by turning the egg factory into a kind of fort; armed with Lanchesters, Bren guns, rifles and pistols, with Consort on its river flank with its heavier arms,' recalled Petty Officer Terry Currie, who was serving on the *Consort* at the time. 'Every day large junks passed Consort jam-packed with what I took to be refugees. They all looked very poor and dirty in their padded quilted jackets.'[1]

Ordinary British sailors understood little of the situation in China, and perhaps cared even less. 'Civil war was raging in China at this time,' recalled Currie, 'yet I cannot recall being unduly worried – it was their war – nothing to do with us. Such was the effect of my cocooned and controlled life [aboard ship] I thought that Mao's Army was a rabble of peasants armed with pitchforks and staves.'[2]

On 20 April, HMS *Amethyst* was making her way up the Yangtze when, at 8.31am, a burst of small arms fire from the north bank passed close to the ship. Ten shells in quick succession followed this from a People's Liberation Army (PLA) artillery battery, the shells all dropping well short of the *Amethyst*, throwing up great plumes of muddy river water. Skinner was not alarmed – he assumed that the Communists were firing at the Nationalist bank of the river and had misjudged their fall of shot. Skinner ordered speed to be increased and two very large Union Jacks to be unfurled on both sides of the ship to make sure that those ashore knew her nationality and neutral status. The firing stopped immediately.

At 9.30am the *Amethyst* was passing the town of Kiangyin (now Jiangyin), approximately 100 miles east of Nanking by river. The boom of artillery startled the crew as PLA batteries on Low Island opened fire. This time there was no doubt that the gunners' target was the British ship. The first shell tore over the *Amethyst* with a whine and exploded in the river. The crew was at action stations.

A shell struck the wheelhouse, causing extensive damage and mortally wounding Commander Skinner and injuring his first lieutenant, Geoffrey Weston. The coxswain was also wounded, but he clung on to the ship's wheel. During the following few minutes the *Amethyst* was repeatedly struck by PLA shells. One tore through the sick bay; and one the port engine room, reducing the ship's power. The injured coxswain grounded the *Amethyst* on Rose Island, the vessel coming to rest in a manner that prevented her two forward turrets from engaging the shore battery. PLA shells slammed into the stationary ship, killing and wounding dozens. Lieutenant Weston managed to send a frantic radio message to all nearby vessels: 'Under heavy fire. Am aground in approx position 31.10' North 119.50' East. Large number of casualties.' A shell struck the radio room, knocking out the ship's communications, while another smashed the generator, disabling the vessel's electrics, including power to the gun turrets. The *Amethyst* was helpless and stuck fast.

On the quarterdeck the ship's doctor, Surgeon Lieutenant John Alderton, ran out to try and tend to the many wounded accompanied by Sick Berth Attendant Owen Aubrey. A Chinese shell instantly killed both men.

Although the two forward turrets could not be brought to bear on the enemy, the aft turret managed to fire thirty rounds before a Chinese shell hit home, disabling one of the two barrels. The other barrel fired off a few more shells until the wounded Lieutenant Weston, who had assumed command from the dying Skinner, ordered it to ceasefire in the hope that this would encourage the Chinese to do likewise. Weston now ordered as many of the crew as possible over the side. As shells continued to hammer the stricken *Amethyst* everyone who could swim, swam to Rose Island, all the time under a fearsome barrage of artillery shells and machine gun bullets. Several were killed. The walking wounded and non-swimmers managed to get away in the only ship's boat that was still undamaged.

A total of fifty-nine ratings and four Chinese mess boys made it alive to the Nationalist-controlled south bank. They were taken to a Nationalist Army field hospital for treatment before being trucked back to Shanghai. Forty unwounded sailors remained aboard, along with twelve wounded and fifteen dead. Weston ordered the unwounded to arm themselves with Lee Enfield rifles and Bren light machine guns and to prepare to repel boarders.

One member of the crew who was not evacuated was Simon, the ship's cat. In March 1948, when the *Amethyst* had been moored in Hong Kong, Ordinary Seaman George Hickinbottom had befriended the young stray that was hanging around the docks. The 17-year-old Hickinbottom had smuggled Simon aboard ship and before long the crew, who appreciated Simon's ratting expeditions below decks, had adopted the friendly cat. Simon would leave dead rats as presents in sailors' bunks and had taken to sleeping in skipper Commander Ian Griffiths' cap inside his cabin. Simon was considered a lucky mascot and when Bernard Skinner took over command in late 1948 he soon took a liking to the affable feline.

On 21 April 1949 Simon was in Skinner's cabin when it took a direct hit from a Chinese shell. As the evacuation of the crew was underway a badly wounded Simon crawled out onto the deck where sailors immediately took him to the sick bay for treatment. Four pieces of shrapnel were removed from the cat and it did not look as though the plucky animal would survive.[3]

By 11.00am the Communist shelling had stopped, but any movement on the battered British ship attracted deadly accurate Chinese snipers. By now, a total of twenty-two British sailors had been killed and another thirty-one wounded. On the following day Bernard Skinner, their mortally wounded skipper, also died.

Aboard the *Consort*, quietly anchored in Nanking, the morning routine was about to be rudely shattered. 'I noticed Hutch, the Petty Officer Yeoman of Signals approaching the Captain with his signal board in his hand,' recalled Petty Officer Currie. 'He saluted the Captain, who returned his salute and then he read his signal. The Captain turned and … hurriedly made for the gangway. We were told that HMS Amethyst had come under fire. She was aground, and had suffered casualties.'[4]

'In no time all lines were let go and the ship swung around to head down stream at thirty knots, the fastest a British warship had ever travelled on the Yangtze at that time.' In order to make her neutral status abundantly clear to the Chinese, special precautions had been taken. 'We had two white sheets, flags of truce

– flying from both yardarms,' recalled Currie. 'On either side of the bridge large canvas squares were lashed upon which were painted Union Flags. Our white ensign streamed rippling from our stern.'[5]

The *Consort* intended to take the battered *Amethyst* in tow and aboard the *Amethyst* towing cables were hastily prepared. Unfortunately, the entire plan was doomed to failure as the *Consort* immediately attracted considerable fire from the north bank. Currie and Able Seaman Bater were standing by the un-manned 'Y' gun shield, the *Consort* having a reduced peacetime complement that meant that some guns were missing crews. 'Suddenly we saw a line of splashes rip across the water just astern of us, followed by an inoffensive pop, pop, pop, popping noise,' wrote Currie. 'Bater gasped "I'm scared P.O." and doing my best not to look scared said, "That makes two of us." '[6] Bater was called forward and Currie requested a Bren gun and ammunition, which was granted. 'By now the three 4.5-inch guns had opened up, also I could hear the twin Bofors thumping away – all hell had broken loose.'

The *Consort* steamed past the *Amethyst*, preparing to take her under tow. 'The river at this point was about one third of a mile wide, ideal for a crossing,' said Currie. 'I could see one of their sandbagged gun positions and when they fired, three or four guns together, the blast from the guns lifted the dust in an arc in front of the position.'[7] Currie lay in the prone position on the deck and loaded his Bren gun. 'I put my sights on 300 yards and as taught squeezed off a short burst and saw my fall of shot hit the water just in front of the sandbags. I raised the sight to 350 yards and squeezed off another burst (I had no tracers), no hits on the water so I was either hitting the sandbags or at least worrying the Chinese gunner.'[8]

The *Consort* turned about and made another pass, firing as she went but was unable to stop and take the *Amethyst* in tow. 'Our 4.5-inch shells were exploding on the banks of the river, the shells from the gun batteries were screaming overhead or hitting the water, some exploding and scattering shrapnel across the surface,' recalled Currie. 'I could see a gun battery fire and instantaneously the shells either hit or roared overhead.' The *Consort* took an almighty battering as she was fired on at virtually point blank range on the river. 'I decided to go for'rd and as I reached the starboard door at the break of the foc'sle I saw young Able Seaman Bater, he looked shocked and was plastered with, what looked like, mince. I asked if he was ok. He made a shaky gesture with his thumb "I'm ok – it's from them in there."' The horrific nature of the fighting soon revealed itself to Currie. 'I stepped over the dwarf bulkhead slotted into the bottom of the door and I looked down. An electrician lay dead, his lower jaw shot away, the dirty water from a shattered fire main ran across Consort's slightly rolling deck and covered his face and body. A stoker lay dead, there was a hole in his side; his liver gleamed wetly on an ammunition box. On the portside lay a messmate, the P.O. Telegraphist, disembowelled and one leg off, hit by two 75mm shells – I made my way to the bridge; it was at this time that I think action had been broken off.'[9]

Currie was among many veterans of this battle who later questioned the common sense of placing British warships in such a dangerous situation. 'While Consort was making a turn, and was virtually a stopped target in the river, the Chinese gunners, in military terms "boxed us." They put a hole in the barrel of "A" gun and killed an ordinary seaman. "B" gun received a hit removing the gun trainer's seat and taking most of his backside with it. He died later.' The Consort narrowly avoided the same fate as the Amethyst. 'The wheelhouse was hit killing the C.P.O. Coxswain and Consort raced for the bank out of control – the Captain steered her by using the twin screws,' wrote Currie. 'The gun transmitting station was hit killing the petty officer and a young A.B. The radio office was also hit. Many 37mm solid anti tank shells passed right through the ship wounding many sailors.'[10]

The Consort gave up and signalled the Amethyst that she was heading for Shanghai. The destroyer had taken fifty-six hits from shells, with ten crew killed and thirty wounded.

The Amethyst remained stuck fast. Any movement on the ship's superstructure attracted Chinese sniper fire, but the Communists had at least stopped shelling the vessel. It seemed clear that the Chinese did not wish to sink the British warship: they could have pounded her to pieces with impunity had they wanted to. Instead the Amethyst was being held hostage. But the Chinese had underestimated both Lieutenant Weston's resourcefulness and the determination of the Admiralty to rescue the *Amethyst*. For several days Weston had tried to free the *Amethyst* from the sand bank until, on the night of the 22nd, he finally succeeded, after pumping twenty tons of oil fuel aft to lighten the vessel. Earlier in the afternoon, Weston had received a heartening signal from China Station HQ: 'HM Ships London and Black Swan are moving up river to escort the Amethyst downstream. Be ready to move.'

The *Consort*, instead of heading directly for Shanghai, had instead rendezvoused with HMS *London*, a 9,750-ton County-class heavy cruiser dating from 1927. During the war *London* had been part of the task force that had hunted and destroyed the German battleship *Bismarck* as well as undertaking the hazardous task of escorting convoys to Murmansk in northern Russia. Armed with 8-inch guns capable of delivering a 256lb high explosive shell up to fifteen miles away, she was the most formidable vessel on the Yangtze in 1949. The *Black Swan* was *Amethyst*'s sister ship, built in 1939. She had been the first British ship into Shanghai in September 1945 in company with the cruiser HMS *Belfast*, following the Japanese surrender.

When the captain of the *Consort* heard that the *London* and *Black Swan* were going to try and reach the *Amethyst*, he volunteered his battered vessel. 'As we were so badly damaged in areas vital to our fighting ability he was ordered to return to Shanghai by the commanding officer of London,' wrote Petty Officer Currie. 'This we did and on our arrival, ambulances were waiting on the jetty to take our wounded to hospital. We carried our dead shipmates ashore on stretchers. They had been sewn up in canvas and each body was wrapped in a white ensign. As we carried our dead, a group of American sailors who had collected on the jetty, formed a sort of impromptu mourning party by dividing into two ragged ranks and then saluting as we filed past them to awaiting trucks. This gesture was more respectful than the headline in Time Magazine a few weeks later "Limey's kicked out of Chinese River." Who needed enemies when you had friends like these?'[11]

HMS *London* and *Black Swan* were greeted by a storm of fire. The Chinese were not intimidated by the large British cruiser and liberally plastered her and the *Black Swan* with both high explosive and anti-tank shells from batteries near Bate Point. The *London* was holed twelve times on her port side, her two forward 8-inch turrets and 'X' after turret were damaged and rendered inoperable, and her bridge was hit several times. The *London* suffered fifteen killed and thirty wounded while the *Black Swan's* superstructure was severely damaged, twelve men being wounded. Reluctantly, the order was given to withdraw down the river lest the *London* and *Black Swan* ended up in a similar condition to the *Amethyst*.

This action revealed the limitations of using large warships as gunboats on a river against an enemy well armed with modern artillery. The *London*, for all of her size and armament, just ended up as a larger target for the Chinese. Because of the narrowness of the river she was unable to stay out of range of the Chinese guns while hitting them with impunity with her big 8-inch main armament. The much smaller pre-war Yangtze River gunboats had never had to face such a well armed and determined opponent as the PLA was proving to be.

Captain Cazaler of the *London*, in his Captain's Report of the action, noted that the vessel had fired 132 8-inch shells, as well as 449 4-inch and over 2,000 light anti-aircraft shells during the brief but very violent river battle. 'All damage to the ship was quickly and efficiently dealt with by the Damage Control Parties,' wrote Cazaler, 'whose performance I consider to be outstanding, taking into consideration the difficulty of providing realistic training in these duties. The bearing and conduct of the Ship's Company, a large proportion of whom are very young and were experiencing action for the first time, was beyond praise.' Cazaler singled out the gun crews for particular praise. 'As an instance, the 4in Gun Crews and Supply Parties suffered 38% casualties, who were not replaced as they fell.'

Later on the 22nd an RAF Sunderland flying boat flew up from Hong Kong carrying Flight Lieutenant Michael Fearnley, an air force doctor, and some urgently needed medical supplies. The huge white aircraft landed in the river near to the *Amethyst* and quickly off-loaded the doctor and supplies just as the PLA opened fire. Shells landed as close as 100 yards away from the Sunderland and the pilot could not linger. A boat also arrived from Nanking carrying Lieutenant Commander John Kerans, the British Embassy's

Assistant Naval Attaché, who had been ordered to assume command of the *Amethyst*.

Some members of the crew later returned to the *Amethyst* on the 22 April. Vice Admiral A.C.G. Madden, Commander in Chief Far East Station reported to the Admiralty that the vessel had three Royal Navy officers, an RAF doctor, fifty-two ratings and eight Chinese mess attendants embarked. Madden sent a message to the *Amethyst*: 'In a splendid performance by all on board ship the work of your sole telegraphist evokes my admiration. I cannot be grateful enough to him for his help.' Madden was also busy organising assistance for the wounded crew members who were arriving in Shanghai overland. The American hospital ship USS *Repose* arrived off Woosung and offered her assistance, which Madden gratefully accepted.

In the meantime, the strategic situation in Eastern China had changed dramatically, making the *Amethyst*'s rescue even more perilous an undertaking. On the same day that HMS *London* and *Black Swan* attempted to rescue the *Amethyst*, the Communists had launched a general offensive along a 250-mile front. One column penetrated as close as forty-five miles from Shanghai. Nationalist forces evacuated the town of Chinkiang, and the Shanghai–Nanking Railway was cut. Kiangyin Navy Base, eighty-five miles below Nanking on the Yangtze River, went over to the Communists. Another column threatened the city of Wuxi, seventy miles from Shanghai.

By the 23rd the battered *Amethyst* was anchored close to Chinkiang. In Shanghai, a memorial service was held at Holy Trinity Cathedral for the twenty-three dead sailors who had been sent by train and the British Resident's Association started a relief fund to raise money for the dead men's dependents.

On 26 April, the Communists occupied Nanking. There was no resistance as the Nationalist 28th Army had already evacuated the city along with its positions on the Yangtze River. It had joined up with the 45th Army and the 100,000 soldiers had begun to march towards Hangchow (now Hangzhou) near Shanghai. Widespread civilian looting had broken out in the Chinese capital. 'While the looters were at work,' reported a British newspaper, 'military demolition squads were blowing up Hsiakwan railway station and setting fire to ammunition dumps, aircraft and aviation fuel, lorries, jeeps, stores of weapons, and river craft.' Order had completely broken down. 'Policemen stripped off their uniforms and disappeared from the streets.' Former general Ma Qing Yuan contacted the Communists and arranged for them to enter once his men had brought the looting under control, and he eventually imposed some semblance of order. Over 900,000 Communist troops had crossed the Yangtze in several places, and the *Amethyst* was now deep inside hostile territory.

The Communist media had begun to report on the *Amethyst* situation, though for propaganda purposes its reportage was distorted and inaccurate. 'On Wednesday "two enemy war vessels" suddenly opened fire on Communist positions on the north bank,' ran one report. 'The Communists ... returned fire and hit one of the vessels [*Amethyst*], which subsequently sunk, while the other [*Consort*] steamed to the West and was "half sunk" near Chinkiang. Then another enemy war vessel [*London*], steaming east from Chinkiang, reached the spot and opened fire.'

In Shanghai, the British Consul General R.W. Urquhart stated to the press: 'Every possible means of rescuing them [the crew of the *Amethyst*], either by an operation or a cease-fire order, will be taken.' But in reality the mighty Royal Navy was running out of options. Vice Admiral Mallen was loath to expose any more of his vessels to shore bombardment on the river, so some other way would have to be found to obtain the *Amethyst*'s release. In the meantime, the *Repose* moved down to the Whangpoo River, anchoring off the Shanghai Bund a safe distance from Communist shore batteries. American Consul General John Cabot urged the 2,500 US citizens who remained in Shanghai to leave. The US Navy had enough ships to evacuate all of them before the city fell to the Communists, and also space to take off many other foreigners.

John Kerans was a 33-year-old Second World War veteran and he wasted no time in organising the evacuation of the remaining wounded men and getting the *Amethyst* sea-worthy again. Soon afterwards, the PLA made contact, requesting a meeting between Kerans and the local PLA political officer, a Colonel Kung. Kung acted as a representative for Colonel Ye Fei, the local military commander. At their first meeting on 30 April, Kung demanded that Kerans sign a statement in which the British admitted to having 'invaded' Chinese territorial waters by steaming warships up the Yangtze, and having fired first on the PLA. Kerans refused, stating repeatedly that the *Amethyst* was going about her lawful business under the various treaties that had been signed between China and the Western Powers when she had been fired on by the PLA without warning or provocation. Naturally Kung refused to accept this. The Communists consistently refused to recognise any of the treaties that had been made under the Qing Dynasty or those by the subsequent Nationalist government, declaring them all to be 'unequal' and therefore unlawful. Only in 1989 did retired General Ye Fei finally admit that the PLA had fired first.

Kung and Kerans found themselves at an impasse. The Chinese informed Kerans that as long as the British behaved themselves the PLA batteries would not fire on the *Amethyst*, but if he tried to move the ship they would do so. Kerans and the *Amethyst* were now to be Chinese hostages, the PLA intention being to starve the crew into submission and force them to sign the face-saving admission of guilt. Kerans never wavered and instead settled down to a long siege.

The *Amethyst* remained at anchor and under PLA guns for ten weeks. The Chinese denied the vessel most supplies, but because only a small steaming party had manned the ship since the 21 April battle and evacuation, the ship's stores were sufficient to last. The Chinese played a cat-and-mouse game with Kerans. They made demands, sometimes offered concessions, such as permitting outgoing mail or supplying oil for cooking, but all the time trying to persuade or bully Kerans into signing a statement admitting that the *Amethyst* had opened fire first. The Chinese strategy was designed to lower the British sailors' morale, but Kerans was wise to their tricks and he determined to make a run for Shanghai and the open sea when the opportunity presented itself.

British morale was much boosted by the activities of Simon, the ship's cat. He had miraculously survived his ordeal by shellfire and had resumed his extremely useful duties killing rats aboard the stationary ship. 'There was a particularly large and ferocious rat on board that the crew nicknamed Mao Tse Tung. Mao and his followers were wreaking havoc on the ship's dwindling supplies. The crew felt that Simon in his weakened state would be no match in a one-on-one with Mao.'[12] They underestimated Simon, and in a duel to the death, Mao the rat was killed. Although Kerans did not have the same affinity for the animal as the crew, Simon had nonetheless helped to prevent a disease outbreak by killing off the vermin that infested the *Amethyst*, and his contribution to the struggle was recognised by his promotion to the rank of 'Able Seacat'.

During the early hours of 30 July 1949, the *Amethyst* slipped her chain and quietly moved downriver towards Shanghai, beginning a hazardous 104-mile dash for freedom. By now, the Communists had crossed the river and established gun batteries on both banks. If Kerans's escape attempt was discovered his ship would have been blown out of the water by PLA guns. Kerans's preparations had included greasing the anchor cable to deaden the noise, and changing the ship's silhouette with black-painted canvas screens erected forward to confuse the Chinese gunners as to her identity. The crew were all dressed in dark colours and all white parts of the ship's superstructure had been painted out.

Just before Kerans gave the order to slip, a well-lit Chinese passenger ship, the *Kiang Ling Liberation*, came around a bend in the river heading for Shanghai. She was carrying refugees. Kerans decided to follow the *Kiang Ling*, using her as a pilot to navigate the treacherous shoals, and the Chinese vessel's lights would also distract the PLA gunners, leaving the blacked-out *Amethyst* trailing in the shadows. However, this plan did not last long as the movement was spotted by the PLA and parachute flares shot into the night sky. Kerans immediately ordered 'full ahead both' and the *Amethyst* surged past the *Kiang Ling* as the Chinese batteries opened fire. Perhaps distracted by the lights on the *Kiang Ling*, the Chinese gunners failed to hit the *Amethyst*, though she returned fire with alacrity. The unfortunate *Kiang Ling* was pounded by Chinese shells, caught fire and eventually sank, and an unknown number of refugees were killed.

Two forts, Woosung and Par Shan, had protected the entrance to the Yangtze River for over a century. They were thirty-eight miles from the East China Sea and Shanghai. These forts, which had a long history of battles with the British, mounted modern

8-inch guns. If the forts opened fire on the *Amethyst* she would be destroyed.

In order to help the *Amethyst* reach the open sea, Admiral Brind ordered another C-class destroyer, HMS *Concord*, to enter the Yangtze and sit off the Woosung Fort with orders to bombard it if necessary.[13] This was a very risky action, for the *Concord* was only armed with 4.5-inch guns. Now that the cruiser *London* had been sent for urgent repairs in Hong Kong following her battering up the Yangtze, the *Concord* would have to do. But the *Concord*'s skipper, Commander Ian Robertson, was prepared to do his duty, come what may.

Late on the evening of 20 July, *Concord* proceeded upriver. She was challenged by a Nationalist Chinese gunboat, but unmolested. The *Concord* anchored at 1.45am on 21 July, but shortly afterwards weighed and proceeded up the Yangtze for twenty miles. At 2.20am the *Concord* spoke briefly with another Nationalist warship near the Tungshan bank buoy, anchored again, and after another brief period, set off once more. The telegraphist picked up a message from the *Amethyst*: 'Woosung in sight.' This was followed a little while later by 'Concord in sight.'[14] The time was 5.25am, and the *Concord* spotted the battered *Amethyst* at a distance of three miles. *Concord* signalled the *Amethyst*: 'Fancy meeting you again', to which the *Amethyst* replied: 'Never, repeat never, has a ship been more welcome.'[15]

Commander Kerans signalled Admiral Brind, with a copy to the Admiralty in London: 'Have rejoined the fleet, no damage or casualties. God save the King.'[16]

Travelling in concert, at 7.15am the ships 'secured from action stations', which meant they were no longer ready to fight, and at 12.12pm the main engines rang off. They were kept at two hours notice for steam. *Concord* transferred stores and discharged 147 tons of fuel oil to the *Amethyst* – after so long under siege, the *Amethyst*'s tanks only contained seven tons of fuel. At 6pm Lieutenant T.J.D. Grant was drafted onto the *Amethyst* on temporary loan along with one signalman and one telegraphist. At 10pm that night the *Concord* slipped from *Amethyst* and in company they set off for Hong Kong. A short while later they encountered the destroyer HMS *Cossack*. *Concord* was ordered to proceed on patrol leaving the *Cossack* to escort the *Amethyst* to Hong Kong.

Due to the very sensitive nature of her mission, the *Concord*'s log book was taken out of service and replaced. The British were keen that there would be no trace of *Concord*'s 'invasion' of the Yantgze River. This has led to the part played by *Concord*'s crew being minimised or ignored, even though they placed themselves at great risk under the guns at Woosung. This would also lead to the denial to the crew of the Naval General Service Medal with bar *'Yangtse 1949'* that was given to the ship's companies aboard the *Amethyst, London, Black Swan,* and *Consort*.

Of the forty-six British sailors who were killed during the Yangtze Incident, twenty-three were buried with full military honours in Shanghai. Unfortunately, during the 1960s their graves were desecrated and eventually completely destroyed. Lieutenant-Commander Bernard Skinner was buried at sea off Shanghai as per the wishes of his widow in Hong Kong, while the remaining dead were buried in the Yangtze River.

It was perhaps only natural that an animal loving people like the British should seize upon the story of Simon, the ship's cat, to help them come to terms with the *Amethyst* disaster. Simon was lauded in both the national and international press after the *Amethyst* returned to Plymouth in November 1949. At each and every port that the ship visited Able Seacat Simon was lauded and honoured alongside the *Amethyst*'s brave crewmen. He was given the premier award for animal bravery, the Dickin Medal, as well as a medal from the Blue Cross. He was also given the Naval General Service Medal alongside his shipmates. One crewman from the *Amethyst* was given the full-time job of responding to the thousands of letters that people from all over the world wrote to the cat. On arrival in England, Simon was placed into routine quarantine at an animal centre in Surrey but he developed an infection caused by his war wounds and died on 28 November. His tiny coffin, draped in the Union Jack, was interred in a cemetery in Ilford, East London. Hundreds, including the entire crew of HMS *Amethyst*, attended his funeral.

Chapter 10

The Immortal Memory

I think the armed forces will be remembered for having provided the infrastructure ... which allowed Hong Kong to flourish.

Major General Bryan Dutton,
Last British Commander, Hong Kong, 1997

In pouring tropical rain, Pipe Major Steven Small, 1st Battalion, The Black Watch, stood at attention, playing on his bagpipes a sad lament appropriately named 'The Immortal Memory'. Drawn up before a huge crowd stood a company from the Black Watch, the RAF Regiment's Queen's Colour Squadron and a contingent of Royal Navy sailors. The date was 30 June 1997, the last day of British rule in Hong Kong before its transfer to the People's Republic of China. For the British military, it was closing day.

Most of the units that formed Hong Kong's garrison had already departed or been disbanded. The four regiments of Gurkhas had been amalgamated in 1994 into the Royal Gurkha Rifles and split between bases in England and Brunei. The Gurkha Training Wing in Hong Kong had also closed in 1994 and found a new home at Church Crookham in Hampshire. The brigade's support units, the Queen's Gurkha Engineers, the Queen's Gurkha Signals and the Queen's Own Gurkha Logistic Regiment, had been drastically cut and the surviving squadrons transferred to the UK. Responsibility for guarding the border had been handed over to the Royal Hong Kong Police – itself shortly to lose its illustrious prefix. The same year that the Gurkhas amalgamated, the colony's dedicated

174

Army Air Corps unit, 660 Squadron, was redeployed elsewhere. 28 (Army Cooperation) Squadron RAF flew the last British military helicopters in Hong Kong until shortly before the handover in 1997.

The successor unit to the famed Hong Kong Volunteer Defence Corps, which had fought so courageously in the defence of the colony in December 1941, was the Royal Hong Kong Regiment (The Volunteers). They were stood down for the last time in 1995 after 141 years of unbroken service. The Hong Kong Military Service Corps, the only unit of the regular British Army that recruited among the local Chinese population, survived until 1997 until disbanded. There were many sad parades, followed by the laying up of colours and speeches of thanks and remembrance. A feeling of finality was everywhere, tinged with uncertainty about the future, post-1997.

Hong Kong had been an important Royal Naval base for 156 years, but that came to an abrupt halt on 11 April 1997, when HMS *Tamar*, no longer a ship but what the navy called a 'stone frigate', was decommissioned at Stonecutters Island in a moving ceremony attended by the First Sea Lord. The three Peacock-class patrol ships of the 6th Patrol Craft Flotilla, HMS *Peacock*, *Plover* and *Starling*, would remain in Asia after the handover – sold for just $20 million to the Philippines. The modern Prince of Wales Building, headquarters of the British Garrison in Hong Kong was to have new tenants in the form of Chinese Communist troops who would cross the border into the territory at the stroke of midnight on 30 June 1997. The building's name would linger on until 2002, when it became the Chinese People's Liberation Army Forces Hong Kong Building and the royal crest was removed. The last British line infantry regiment to serve in Hong Kong, 1st Battalion, The Staffordshire Regiment, had departed in 1996.

In 1997, Britain returned to China a territory of immense riches, an economic powerhouse and one of the world's most prominent port cities. It was an extraordinary transformation in just over 150 years, and the nation was rightly proud of what Hong Kong had become under British control. Its future as a Special Administrative Region of China is perhaps less assured, but British values and practices have proved able to endure far beyond the handover and Hong Kong still feels very different from Mainland China.

When Britain returned to Hong Kong in September 1945, shortly after the Japanese surrender, the colony was a shadow of its former self. The Japanese had stripped all of its assets, victimised and murdered its citizens, and imprisoned its administrators. Hong Kong had suffered from Allied bombing raids, food shortages, and much else besides. Its population had decreased dramatically, and its once famous manufacturing industries lay mostly silent.

There was no guarantee that British sovereignty could be re-established in the immediate postwar period, but the British government moved fast lest the Nationalist Chinese annexed the territory in the power vacuum after the defeat of Japan. A group of former British officials led by Colonial Secretary Frank Gimson had been imprisoned for three years and eight months in Stanley Prison, a Japanese civilian internment camp in Hong Kong. On 15 August, the day Emperor Hirohito surrendered, the Japanese were still responsible for maintaining public order in the colony, which was a completely unsatisfactory situation. Sir Horace Seymour-Conway, the British Ambassador to Nationalist China based in Chungking (now Chongqing), sent a message to Gimson on the eve of the Japanese surrender. Gimson received instructions from Sir Horace, which came from the top in London, to exercise sovereignty on behalf of the British government as the Governor, Sir Mark Young, was still incommunicado in a Japanese prison camp in Manchuria. Gimson immediately left the prison with all of the former colonial officials in tow, including the Commissioner of the Royal Hong Kong Police, the director of public works, and other top officials, and speedily organised a provisional government. Gimson appointed himself 'Acting Governor' in Sir Mark's absence.

On 27 August, Gimson broadcast by radio to the people of Hong Kong, informing them that the provisional government was firmly in control and that orderly British rule had been re-established. Three days later, a Royal Navy flotilla led by Rear Admiral Cecil Harcourt sailed into Victoria Harbour charged with taking the surrender of the Japanese occupation forces and forming a military government. Gimson handed over control to Harcourt, who briefly appointed him Lieutenant Governor, and the navy remained in charge of the colony until Sir Mark Young returned from convalescing in England following his release from captivity.

Over the next few years the situation inside Hong Kong improved rapidly. New construction projects and a thriving manufacturing base fuelled by cheap labour soon made Hong Kong an integral part of the world economy.

By 1956, after a decade of peace, the garrison had been reduced to an internal security force. But on 10 October, 'Double Ten Day' to the Chinese, many local people were celebrating the 1911 October Revolution and the foundation of the republic, and an officious British resettlement officer ordered Kuomintang (Chinese Nationalist) flags to be removed from buildings inside refugee camps. This sparked off anti-Communist rioting as mobs rampaged through Kowloon attacking properties belonging to Communist sympathisers. There was no official intervention at this point as colonial officials hoped the violence would quickly burn itself out. By the following day, there were particularly violent attacks at Tsuen Wan, five miles from Kowloon. Kuomintang supporters stormed the clinic and welfare centre and four people were murdered. Others were hauled off to the Nationalist headquarters and tortured.

Chinese Communist owned factories were attacked and there were some brutal murders committed. In Kowloon a foreign car was attacked and the Swiss consul's wife died from the injuries that she sustained. Colonial Secretary Edgeworth David now took action, and armoured cars of the 7th Queen's Own Hussars, based at Sek Kong Camp, were deployed onto the streets and the soldiers given orders to shoot rioters without hesitation. Communists were given sanctuary in police compounds while the police and the army tried to contain the trouble. By 12 October, the riots had subsided. The rioters had murdered fifteen people, while forty-four troublemakers had been shot dead by the police and army. Four rioters were later found guilty of murder and sentenced to death. Peace was restored to Hong Kong.

Garrison duty in Hong Kong between the 1950s and the Handover was a much sought after posting for British soldiers. Families could go with them, and the social, travel and shopping opportunities in

Hong Kong were unrivalled anywhere else in the world at the time. 'Life was very pleasant,' recalled a regimental historian. 'There was no need to be bored, a trip on the ferry to watch the world go by was of constant interest. Plenty of time for window shopping and meeting friends and taking meals out in Kowloon and in Hong Kong. Hong Kong was a fun place, full of colour and excitement.'[1] The nature of the duties performed by garrison battalions changed little between 1948 and 1997; but the challenges did, as the People's Republic of China attempted various ways to disrupt life in Hong Kong.

It is not possible here to tell the stories of every single British battalion that served in Hong Kong during the postwar period, but what follows is a selection of experiences of individual units through the different decades, demonstrating both the un-changing nature of garrison life in the colony, and also the duties and challenges faced by British soldiers.

The 1st Battalion, the Queen's Royal Surrey Regiment arrived in Hong Kong aboard the troopship HMT *Oxfordshire* on 5 March 1962 following a tour of duty in Aden. At that time the British Garrison in Hong Kong consisted of only one British infantry battalion supporting the three battalions of 48 Gurkha Brigade, with a Royal Artillery regiment at Gun Club Hill Barracks, Kowloon. The Queen's were based at Stanley Barracks at the extreme southern end of Hong Kong Island with a company outstation at Lyemun overlooking Victoria Harbour.

The first problem the Queen's encountered was the extreme heat when they stepped off the ship. Being winter, the Adjutant had ordered thick battle dress to be worn. It turned out that the temperature in Hong Kong that day was in the high nineties Fahrenheit with 100% humidity. So the next day olive green was adopted. But just twenty-four hours later the temperature had dropped to fifty-five degrees and 'the Stanley Peninsula gave a good imitation of Dartmoor in winter.'[2] The weather in Hong Kong is very fickle and changeable, presenting acclimatisation challenges for freshly arrived troops.

The men and their families were more than satisfied with Stanley Barracks. 'Built in the 1930s, [they] were among the best in the world, with an all-round view of the coastline. Beautiful trees and shrubs were planted round the buildings.' C Company was detached and based at Lyemun Barracks, which it shared with various other units. 'This suited the men as they were nearer the fleshpots of Wanchai and of course further away from the management. The companies changed round every six months.'[3]

The battalion was almost immediately called upon to perform ceremonial duties, an important part of garrison service in Hong Kong. The Queen's Birthday Parade was held in Kowloon on 12 April, followed by the battalion firing a *feu-de-joie*, and Beating Retreat at Stanley Fort on 2 May.

On 9 May, fifty Chinese other ranks joined the Queen's. They were the first locally recruited Chinese soldiers to join a British line infantry battalion and they arrived just in time to replace the last batch of conscripted National Servicemen, who had completed their two years service and were about to be discharged at the end of May. The Queen's Commanding Officer, Lieutenant Colonel M.A. Lowry MC, 'sent a message to Officer Commanding A Company informing him that he held the last National Serviceman to leave the Battalion and should this not be marked with an appropriate farewell. Major D.R. Bishop, being a wise officer, sent for his Company Sergeant Major, CSM Wilson. He put the point to him and had a prompt reply in 'CSM language' which being translated was 'Course you know why he's the last to leave. He's had to make up so much time spent in the nick.' There was no farewell gesture, except a few well chosen words from the CSM.'[4]

The Chinese soldiers proved to be a mixed blessing. 'Two members of the Chinese increment were attached to [Training] company and proved to be willing soldiers from 0700 to 1300 but thereafter lost interest as they went off to "No. 2 jobs". One lost his rifle, which was never found.'[5]

The Queen's battalion was given some opportunity to do some patrolling up on the frontier with China. In May and June 1962, Battalion HQ and A and B Companies were placed under the command of 48 Gurkha Brigade. They formed part of the force that took part in what was known as Operation Seal. The Chinese had opened the border and they were attempting to flood Hong Kong with refugees (including many released criminals) in a deliberate attempt to destabilise the colony. The British Army and the Royal Hong Kong Police worked hard to capture the refugees and return them to the Chinese side of the line. This work involved intensive patrolling and guarding of the frontier. 'The Companies were issued with radio sets, one to each section, so the Platoon Commanders were able to keep in touch by remote control,' wrote the regimental historian. 'We are told that CSM Wilson and C/Sgt. Riley did not need these modern inventions to keep in touch as they could clearly be heard over the length of the frontier and beyond!' Two officers and ten ratings from the aircraft carrier HMS *Ark Royal* volunteered to patrol the border on attachment to the Queen's. 'Some soldiers thought they were barmy to inflict so much discomfort on themselves.'[6]

The patrol and apprehension method was simple in theory, though, in practice, far from so. Patrols would capture and bring Chinese into the company position, and then they were taken down the mountain in trucks to a holding camp at the railhead and from there returned to China. 'We soon found out for ourselves how hard was the terrain and how exposed to the searing heat of the sun were the mountainsides,' recalled the regimental historian. 'It did not help that you might be able to see a Chinese across a valley. By the time you had clambered down and then back up through the thorny undergrowth, he had probably gone to ground in some inaccessible thicket and you had a tedious search on your hands. It was hot and tiring work and your water had to be carefully conserved.'[7] Once Operation Seal was completed, C Company remained on Hong Kong Island to train and mount guard. Lieutenant P. Gray took Support Platoon to the frontier in July to man observation posts, but all was quiet.

One of the greatest threats to life on the China coast is not armed military conflict but the weather – particularly deadly typhoons. Hong Kong is regularly struck by these awesome displays of Nature's power, and during the Queen's tour Typhoon Wanda made landfall in the colony. No one at Stanley Barracks was injured but considerable structural damage was done to the buildings and many trees blown down. 'C/Sgt Riley remembers Captain Jimmy Kemp the Quartermaster asking him when he had last seen the company dustbins and his reply "Heading out to the China Seas, Sir."'[8]

On a more serious note, great damage had been done to many of the Chinese residential areas; people had been killed and injured, while others had lost their homes or their possessions.

The Queen's were mobilised to provide disaster relief, and also set up a fund to collect donations for the destitute.

Training Company had nearly been caught in the open up in the hills of the New Territories. They had just reached the Nissen huts at Sai Kung Camp when a sharp-eyed NCO spotted a typhoon warning signal flying from a special tower. The huts actually survived Wanda very well, but the windows were blown in and the camp water towers collapsed. 'After the storm had passed the scene was pretty awe-inspiring. There were bits of trees everywhere and bent water pipes gushing water in all directions.'[9]

The remainder of the Queen's Hong Kong tour was spent in exercises both with and against the Gurkhas, sporting competitions, social activities and A Company went back up onto the border to hunt for illegal immigrants. One hundred Territorial Army soldiers from the regiment's reserve battalion spent their annual summer camp attached to the regulars in Hong Kong, getting a taste of border soldiering and the fantastic lifestyle in the colony before boarding a twenty-five hour flight back to the UK.

The 1960s proved to be turbulent times in Hong Kong as the events of China's Cultural Revolution spilled over the border into the territory. In 1966 there was a severe dispute concerning Star Ferry prices that quickly escalated into widespread rioting. On 6 April, the garrison was called out to patrol the streets of Kowloon with fixed bayonets, and enforce a curfew. The worst trouble occurred a year later when Mao's Red Guards attempted to seriously undermine Britain's control of the colony. On the border, several Hong Kong policemen were killed during violent cross-border attacks, while Communist agitators took over buildings in Hong Kong and organised an eighteen-month long bombing campaign that took many lives. The army defused over 8,000 homemade bombs during this period and the violence only came to an end when Chinese Prime Minister Zhou Enlai ordered leftists to stop, indicating just how much of the violence was being orchestrated from Beijing.

At one point the People's Liberation Army Commissar Huang Yongsheng, who controlled Guangdong Province bordering Hong Kong, secretly suggested invading the colony. Zhou Enlai vetoed this plan, but when Margaret Thatcher was negotiating Hong Kong's future with Deng Xiaoping in 1982, an invasion was once again secretly suggested.[10] In all probability, such an invasion would have succeeded, with British forces having to replay the events of December 1941.

The Black Watch played an important role representing the British Army in the handover of Hong Kong to China in 1997, but it was not the first time that the regiment had served in the colony. In 1972 the 1st Battalion had arrived to begin a routine three-year posting and its experiences are representative of the roles and activities of infantry regiments in Hong Kong during the period.

In 1972 the offensive element of the Hong Kong Garrison consisted of five infantry battalions. The Black Watch was based at Gun Club Hill Barracks in Kowloon while the 1st Battalion, Irish Guards were at Stanley on Hong Kong Island. Guarding the border and providing internal security were three battalions of Gurkhas.[11] Supporting the infantry was an armoured squadron of the 14th/20th King's Hussars and the part-time Royal Hong Kong Regiment (The Volunteers).

'Mainly it was all ceremonial,' recalled Regimental Sergeant Major Bob Ritchie when interviewed in 2008. 'We had had Hong Kong island for a long, long time and what we were really doing was showing we still had a presence in Hong Kong right up to two or three years ago when we'd to hand it back.'[12]

Ceremonial was an important part of what the British garrison in Hong Kong was all about. 'It was mainly all parades; Queen's Birthday parades; running about with Pipes and Drums; Military Bands and just keeping the people of Hong Kong sweet,'[13] recalled Ritchie. But there was also the equally important job of guarding the border with China. 'Three times a year we had to go up to the Chinese border; we were up there three weeks at a time and we guarded all the points the trouble could flash.' Traffic across the border was almost entirely one way. 'Nothing was leaving us to go through on the Chinese side,' said Ritchie. 'All the Chinese wanted to come to us, to Hong Kong because of the bright lights and everything else that Hong Kong had and mainland China didn't.'[14]

The young soldiers called the border excursions 'snake patrols', as they walked in groups of seven or eight, often accompanied by an officer from the Royal Hong Kong Police, along the barbed wire fences that marked the frontier, and through the small villages that in some cases actually straddled the border line. 'On the border ... we'd monitor the Communist Chinese,' recalled Sergeant Ronnie Proctor. 'What they were doing and where they were and sometimes, one of the jobs, I was in charge of the reconnaissance platoon, and we would live in the ground and watch the North Chinese Army.'[15]

One location that offered both an up close and personal look at the People's Liberation Army and a potential flash point was Sha Tau Kok village in the northeast of the New Territories. This settlement actually straddled the border and had a white line painted through its centre – on one side was Hong Kong and on the other Communist China. The British and Chinese had guard posts facing each other in the village and both sides mounted regular foot patrols along the frontier. 'At some of the observation posts we had, you could see the Chinese soldiers going about and what they used to do,' recalled Private Jim Sandilands, who had first visited Hong Kong as a merchant navy seaman before he joined the Black Watch in 1972. 'They always had, sort of like, green boiler suits; a green hat with a red star in the centre and the white canvas shoes and carrying the Russian Kalashnikov rifles.'[16] If the British observed eight or more Chinese soldiers together the entire battalion was stood to, as a constant worry was a Chinese invasion.

One day when Sandilands was tail end Charlie on an eight-man foot patrol through Sha Tau Kok, the men passed extremely close to the border. Opposite them was a young Chinese soldier watching them intently. 'By this time he's getting himself ready with a mouthful of spit, ready to draw out; just to spit on me as I'm the last man leaving,' recalled Sandilands. In the event the Chinese soldier mistimed his assault and ended up with spit all down his tunic instead. 'I thought, "Up you, pal,"'[17] said Sandilands.

The desperate people that attempted to flee China for the freedoms of Hong Kong faced perilous journeys that many did not survive, and horrific sights often greeted British troops. Many Chinese tried to enter Hong Kong by swimming over from outlying Chinese islands, particularly Ping Chau in Mirs Bay to the northeast of Hong Kong. 'There were quite strong currents and tides,' recalled Sandilands. 'They would cover themselves in goose fat and various other stuff and they'd get anything that would float, like bicycle tubes ... anything that was inflatable and they would strap that to them and make their way across,' said Sergeant Proctor. 'And many of them did. But many of them didn't.'[18]

One incident in particular stuck in the minds of several Black Watch soldiers. 'On one occasion we had a patrol on the beach and we actually found a body washed up on the beach,' recalled Proctor. 'After, we found another person who was quite well and a third one who was badly injured and had been eaten by a shark.'[19] A helicopter was called for to take the men to hospital. The Hong Kong Auxiliary Air Force, a mostly Chinese manned reserve unit, operated the chopper. After collecting the injured Chinese the pilot, who was low on fuel, decided to set the helicopter down in Sha Tau Kok village to refuel. Unfortunately, he landed on the wrong side of the line, in Chinese territory. 'Both sides stood to,' remembered Sandilands. Chinese troops 'just dragged the boy [who had been injured by a shark] out of the helicopter and left him there and he just lay and bled to death probably. It took a massive amount of negotiations and I think they stripped the helicopter bare and took photographs and put it back together again before they eventually got it back, a day or so [later].'[20] The occupants of the helicopter, including the pilot, were badly beaten by Chinese troops and the military personnel were only released after the British had applied intense diplomatic pressure. Incidents like this demonstrated that the border between British Hong Kong and Communist China was a place of tense Cold War rivalries and deep suspicions. It was a frontier in the West's continuing battle against Communism. At the same time that British troops were guarding the Hong Kong border, their comrades were doing the same in West Berlin against the Soviet Union.

On a lighter note, another important job performed by resident infantry battalions like the Black Watch was providing sentries at the white-painted Government House, official residence of the Governor of Hong Kong. In 1972 the Governor was Sir Murray MacLehose. An element of farce soon crept into the proceedings, as Private Sandilands recalled. The sentries at the entrance to the Government House drive could not see when the Governor's car was leaving because the road incorporated a blind corner and heavy foliage. Sentries had to be at the present when the Governor passed through the gates, so they required some signal to warn them to present arms in time. 'So his chauffeur would give two toots of the horn. Knowing this was a car coming round the corner, you were up and ready saluting the Governor as he drove by,'[21] said Sandilands. Comedy soon ensued. 'The Chinese taxi driver population all knew about this as well. So it was every five minutes, you'd hear "Toot, toot", and you were up at the present arms and there was some Chinese or Yank or something sticking their heads out with their camera, taking your photograph, as you're giving them a salute.'[22]

At Government House on the last day of June 1997, a moving scene was played out as Governor Chris Patten watched the Union Jack slowly hauled down for the final time, to the sound of The Last Post played by a Royal Hong Kong Police bugler. A police colour guard, armed with Second World War-era Lee-Enfield rifles, performed a superb display of drill before Patten, and then the flag, carefully folded, was solemnly presented to Patten, who bowed his head deeply. At that moment the first drops of the day's heavy rain began to fall. Climbing into a black Rolls Royce, the gate guard presented arms for the last time as the Governor made his way down to the new convention centre for the formal handover ceremony with China.

After the soldiers, sailors and airmen had paraded, the speeches had been made, the Union Jack hauled down for the last time at the stroke of midnight, and Pipe Major Small had piped his haunting lament, British rule in Hong Kong had passed into history. Gathering his wife and daughters, Governor Patten had sailed away aboard the royal yacht *Britannia*, itself shortly to be mothballed, and for many observers it seemed that the day's dignified and sad proceedings marked the close of Britain's military relationship with the Far East. But this has not been the case. There are no more British armed forces in China, apart from an occasional goodwill visit from the Royal Navy to its old haunts in Shanghai and Hong Kong; but there is still a British presence in the Far East, which may well become more significant as time passes and the region's problems become more overt.

Although Hong Kong was handed back sixteen years ago, in 2013 there are still over 1,000 members of the armed forces who are permanently stationed in Asia. This figure does not include over 10,000 troops currently on active war fighting operations in Afghanistan. Britain's largest post-Hong Kong garrison in Asia is in the tiny oil-rich Sultanate (and former colony) of Brunei, located on the island of Borneo, where, since 1961, a sizeable number of British troops have been based at the request of the Sultan. British Garrison Brunei, numbering 900 personnel, is based in the town of Seria and looks every inch a colonial-era barracks with its neat and whitewashed accommodation blocks and officers' bungalows arranged around a spotless parade ground, the Union Jack fluttering in the humid tropical air. At Seria some flavour of Hong Kong-style soldiering 'East of Suez' has managed to survive the endless rounds of defence cuts that have radically altered Britain's military relationship with Asia since 1971.

The majority of the troops based at Seria are not Britons but Gurkhas, contract soldiers from Britain's oldest Asian ally, Nepal, who have been volunteering since 1816 and who have played such an important role in Britain's military relationship with China. One battalion from the Royal Gurkha Rifles is stationed in Brunei, on a three-year rotation with the other battalion in the UK, providing Britain with an acclimatised jungle warfare unit stationed in Asia. In recent years, the resident Gurkha battalion has seen service in Afghanistan and East Timor, and even gone as far as Sierra Leone in West Africa. Supporting the infantry is a rear link detachment from the Queen's Gurkha Signals, an Army Air Corps helicopter flight, and a detachment from the Royal Military Police. Another important purpose of the Brunei Garrison is its Jungle Warfare Training School, enabling Special Forces, primarily the SAS but other units as well, to retain vitally important military tracking and survival skills. With the closure of a similar facility in the Central American country of Belize, the Brunei school remains the British Army's last dedicated tropical training base.

The Gurkhas also man another series of small British bases in Asia known as British Gurkhas Nepal (BGN). Due to the importance of selecting and recruiting young Nepalese men each year for the

British Army, the UK maintains its own apparatus inside Nepal at three locations. At Kathmandu are HQ BGN and a transit camp supported by a Queen's Gurkha Signals rear link detachment. Two recruiting bases are maintained at Pokhara and Dharan. Sixty-one British military personnel man these three bases.

British Indian Ocean Territory near the Seychelles is an important base for the American military, which has a huge airbase on the island of Diego Garcia hired under the terms of a defence agreement with London. The Royal Navy is responsible for administering the islands and liaising with the Americans, and the forty-person Naval Party 1002 does this vital job as well as providing training facilities for visiting British military forces.

Britain's smallest military unit remaining in Asia is Naval Party 1022 in Singapore. Just three Royal Navy personnel oversee some forty locally recruited workers in refueling and resupplying warships from Britain and her allies at the old British naval base. Destroyers and frigates from Britain regularly visit Asia, including China, on goodwill voyages and are also engaged in international efforts to suppress piracy in the Strait of Malacca and Horn of Africa. In fact, the British presence in Asia is likely to increase over the coming years rather than decrease with the recent announcement that Japan may permit a British submarine to be based there, and with continued regional problems including China's increasingly belligerent stance over island disputes with its neighbours.

At the beginning of the 21st Century, Britain remains as militarily engaged with Asia as at any time in the previous two hundred years. For good or ill, the British military's activities in China opened that ancient nation to the international trade system and the world economy. Britain's victory in the First Opium War, though morally reprehensible, led directly to the creation of China's greatest port metropolises, Shanghai and Hong Kong. British military operations during the Boxer Rebellion led to the weakening of the corrupt and venal Qing Dynasty, and actually encourage republicanism, leading to the creation of a new China in the second decade of the 20th century. British naval power in China assured trade along the coasts and the inland waterways for half a century, allowing both Westerners and Chinese to trade in safety and to grow rich while the nation was in turmoil all around them. Britain entered China to acquire markets and territory, and grew rich from the opium trade and, later, from a myriad of other ventures. But it also changed China by association, helping to modernise and introduce new ideas and technology that have endured in many aspects of China today. That this opening and modernisation was initially carried out at the point of a gun cannot be ignored, but when Britain closed up shop in Hong Kong in 1997 all that was ancient history. We left with our heads held high; knowing that what we left was infinitely better than what we found on that barren island in 1841. Trade may have created Shanghai, Hong Kong and a multitude of other great port cities the length of the China coast, but it was the British military that provided the security for that trade that allowed it to have germinated and then flourished with such phenomenal consequences for modern China.

Appendix 1

Order of Battle
Anglo-Tibet War 1903–04

British Commissioner to Tibet – Major Francis Younghusband
Escort Commander – Brigadier General James Macdonald, CB

British Army
5th Royal Dragoons
7 Mountain Battery, Royal Garrison Artillery
Maxim Gun Detachment, Royal Irish Rifles
1st Battalion, Royal Fusiliers
1st Battalion, Norfolk Regiment
1st Battalion, Devonshire Regiment
1st Battalion, King's Own Royal Lancashire Regiment
3rd Battalion, Rifle Brigade
Supply and Transport Corps
Army Veterinary Department
Survey Department
Telegraph Department

British Indian Army
27 Mountain Battery, Royal Indian Artillery
30 Mountain Battery, Royal Indian Artillery
23rd Sikh Pioneers
2nd Madras Sappers and Miners
8th Gurkha Rifles
40th Pathans
19th Punjab Regiment
55th Coke's Rifles (Frontier Force)

5th Mule Corps
6th Mule Corps
9th Mule Corps
11th Mule Corps
12th Mule Corps
19th Mule Corps
24th Mule Corps
Peshawar Coolie Corps
Sikkim Coolie Corps

Appendix 2

Order of Battle
Shanghai Volunteer Corps
21 November 1941[1]

I. **Corps Headquarters** (50 British)

II. **Corps Cavalry** (160 British & Americans, partly mounted)
   1. Headquarters Troop
   2. Light Horse Troop
   3. Light Horse Troop

III. **Corps Troops** (560 mixed nationalities)
   1. Headquarters Company
   2. Signals Company (British)
   3. Field (Engineers) Company (British)
   4. Chinese Company
   5. Japanese Company (110 – but not available)
   6. Transport Company

IV. **'A' Battalion** (350 British)
   1. Headquarters Company
   2. A (British) Company
   3. B (British) Company
   4. C (British) Company
   5. Shanghai Scottish Company
   6. Light Artillery (Air Defence) Company

V. **'B' Battalion** (190 American, Filipino & Russian)
   1. Headquarters Company
   2. American Company
   3. Filipino Company
   4. White Russian Regiment
   5. American Machine Gun Company

VI. **'C' Battalion**
   1. Portuguese Company
   2. Armoured Car Company (British) (8 vehicles)

Appendix 3

China Command 1900–1997
British Garrisons
Hong Kong

Royal Navy

1934–97	Operations and Training Base
1945–92	China Squadron (various vessels and units)
1969–71	6th Mine Countermeasures Squadron
1971–97	6th Patrol Craft Squadron
1967–96	Hong Kong Royal Naval Volunteer Reserve

British Army

1900s

1908–09	2nd Battalion, Queen's Own Cameron Highlanders

1910s

1914	2nd Battalion, Duke of Cornwall's Light Infantry
1917–18	1st Battalion, Middlesex Regiment

1920s

1923–26	1st Battalion, East Surrey Regiment
1926–28	2nd Battalion, Scots Guards

1930s

1930–34	1st Battalion, South Wales Borderers
1932–36	1st Battalion, Royal Lincolnshire Regiment
1937–38	1st Battalion, The Seaforth Highlanders
1937–41	1st Battalion, Middlesex Regiment

1937–39	1st Battalion, Kumaon Regiment
1937–39	19th Hyderabad Regiment
1938–41	2nd Battalion, Royal Scots (The Royal Regiment)
1939–41	2nd Battalion, 14th Punjab Regiment
1939–41	5th Battalion, 7th Rajput Regiment

1940s

1941	1st Battalion, Winnipeg Grenadiers
1941	1st Battalion, Royal Rifles of Canada
1948–50	2nd Battalion, 6th Gurkha Rifles
1948–50	2nd Battalion, 10th Princess Mary's Own Gurkha Rifles
1949–50	1st Battalion, Argyll and Sutherland Highlanders (Princess Louise's)

1950s

1950	4th Hussars
1950–52	1st Battalion, Wiltshire Regiment
1951–52	1st Battalion, Argyll and Sutherland Highlanders (Princess Louise's)
1952–62	1st Battalion, 7th Duke of Edinburgh's Own Gurkha Rifles
1953–57	2nd Battalion, 2nd King Edward VII's Own Gurkha Rifles
1953–54	A Sqn., 16th/5th Lancers
1954–56	1st Battalion, The Essex Regiment
1954–57	2nd Battalion, 7th Duke of Edinburgh's Own Gurkha Rifles
1956	7th Hussars
1956–59	1st Battalion, Green Howards
1957–60	1st Battalion, 10th Princess Mary's Own Gurkha Rifles
1957–60	1st Royal Tank Regiment
1958–61	1st Battalion, Royal Northumberland Fusiliers

1960s

1960–63	17th/21st Lancers
1962	2nd Battalion, 7th Duke of Edinburgh's Own Gurkha Rifles
1962	C Sqn., Royal Scots Greys

1962–63	2nd Battalion, 6th Queen Elizabeth's Own Gurkha Rifles
1963–66	1st Battalion, South Wales Borderers
1965–67	1st Battalion, The Queen's Own Buffs, The Royal Kent Regiment
1965–73	1st Battalion, 6th Queen Elizabeth's Own Gurkha Rifles
1966–68	2nd Battalion, 2nd King Edward VII's Own Gurkha Rifles
1966–68	1st Battalion, The Welch Regiment
1967–69	1st Battalion, Lancashire Fusiliers
1968–70	1st Battalion, Duke of Wellington's Regiment (West Riding)
1969–72	1st Battalion, Royal Welch Fusiliers
1969–73	1st Battalion, 10th Princess Mary's Own Gurkha Rifles

1970s

1970–72	1st Battalion, Irish Guards
1970–73	14th/20th King's Hussars
1972–75	1st Battalion, The Black Watch
1972–75	2nd Battalion, 2nd King Edward VII's Own Gurkha Rifles
1972–77	1st Battalion, 7th Duke of Edinburgh's Own Gurkha Rifles
1973–75	C Sqn., 16th/5th Lancers
1974–76	C Sqn., 1st Royal Tank Regiment
1975–77	1st Battalion, Light Infantry
1975–78	1st Battalion, 6th Queen Elizabeth's Own Gurkha Rifles
1975–79	1st Battalion, 10th Princess Mary's Own Gurkha Rifles
1977–79	1st Battalion, 2nd King Edward VII's Own Gurkha Rifles
1977–80	1st Battalion, Royal Green Jackets
1977–81	2nd Battalion, 2nd King Edward VII's Own Gurkha Rifles
1979	1st Battalion, Argyll and Sutherland Highlanders (Princess Louise's)
1979–83	1st Battalion, 6th Queen Elizabeth's Own Gurkha Rifles

1980s

1980–82	1st Battalion, Queen's Own Highlanders (Seaforth & Cameron)
1981–83	1st Battalion, 10th Princess Mary's Own Gurkha Rifles
1981–85	1st Battalion, 2nd King Edward VII's Own Gurkha Rifles
1982–84	1st Battalion, Scots Guards
1983–85	2nd Battalion, 2nd King Edward VII's Own Gurkha Rifles
1983–87	1st Battalion, 7th Duke of Edinburgh's Own Gurkha Rifles
1984–86	1st Battalion, Cheshire Regiment
1985–87	1st Battalion, 6th Queen Elizabeth's Own Gurkha Rifles
1985–89	1st Battalion, 10th Princess Mary's Own Gurkha Rifles
1986–88	1st Battalion, Coldstream Guards
1987–89	1st Battalion, 2nd King Edward VII's Own Gurkha Rifles
1987–91	2nd Battalion, 2nd King Edward VII's Own Gurkha Rifles
1988–90	1st Battalion, Duke of Edinburgh's Royal Regiment
1989–91	1st Battalion, 7th Duke of Edinburgh's Own Gurkha Rifles
1989–93	1st Battalion, 6th Queen Elizabeth's Own Gurkha Rifles

1990s

1990–93	1st Battalion, Royal Regiment of Wales
1991–92	1st Battalion, 2nd King Edward VII's Own Gurkha Rifles
1991–93	1st Battalion, 10th Princess Mary's Own Gurkha Rifles
1993–94	1st Battalion, Black Watch (Royal Highland Regiment)
1993–94	1st Battalion, 7th Duke of Edinburgh's Own Gurkha Rifles
1994–96	1st Battalion, Royal Gurkha Rifles
1996	1st Battalion, The Staffordshire Regiment
1997	1st Battalion, The Black Watch (Royal Highland Regiment)

APPENDIX 3

Reserve Forces
1854–1941 Hong Kong Volunteer Defence Corps
1951–95   The Royal Hong Kong Regiment (The Volunteers)

Support & Ancillary Units (not exhaustive)
Army Air Corps
- 1978–94   660 Squadron Army Air Corps

Royal Engineers
- 67, 68, 69 & 70 Squadron Queen's Gurkha Engineers
- 50 Field Engineer Regiment, Royal Engineers

Royal Corps of Signals
- 246, 247 & 248 Squadron Queen's Gurkha Signals
- 252 Squadron, Royal Corps of Signals

Royal Corps of Transport
- 28 & 31 Squadron Gurkha Transport Regiment
- 29 & 56 Squadron, Royal Corps of Transport

Others
- 50 Hong Kong Workshop, Royal Electrical & Mechanical Engineers
- Defence Animal Support Unit, Royal Army Veterinary Corps
- 1948–97 – Hong Kong Military Service Corps
- 1971–94 – Training Depot, Brigade of Gurkhas
- British Military Hospital Kowloon

Royal Air Force
1978–97   28 (Army Cooperation) Squadron

Shanghai
1927 (Shanghai Defence Force)
2nd Battalion, Coldstream Guards
1st Battalion, Devonshire Regiment
2nd Battalion, Suffolk Regiment
1st Battalion, Bedfordshire & Hertfordshire Regiment
2nd Battalion, Gloucestershire Regiment
1st Battalion, Border Regiment

2nd Battalion, Border Regiment
2nd Battalion, Durham Light Infantry
1st Battalion, Green Howards
1st Battalion, Middlesex Regiment
12 Royal Marine Battalion

1927 (reinforcements to Shanghai Defence Force)
2nd Battalion, Scots Guards
1st Battalion, Queen's Regiment
2nd Battalion, Northamptonshire Regiment
2nd Battalion, Welch Regiment

1929–33	1st Battalion, The Wiltshire Regiment
1937–39	2nd Battalion, The Loyal Regiment (North Lancashire)
1939–40	2nd Battalion, The East Surrey Regiment
1939–40	1st Battalion, The Seaforth Highlanders

Tianjin

1939–40	1st Battalion, Durham Light Infantry

Appendix 4

Order of Battle Hong Kong Volunteer Defence Corps, 8 December 1941

I.   **Corps Headquarters**

II. **Corps Artillery**
     1. 1st Battery
     2. 2nd Battery
     3. 3rd Battery
     4. 4th Battery
     5. 5th (Anti-Aircraft) Battery

III. **Corps Troops**
     1. Field Company Engineers
     2. Signals Company
     3. Armoured Car Platoon
     4. Army Service Corps Company

IV. **Infantry**
     1. No. 1 Company
     2. No. 2 (Scottish) Company
     3. No. 3 (Eurasian) Company
     4. No. 4 (Chinese) Company
     5. No. 5 Company
     6. No. 6 (Portuguese) Company
     7. No. 7 Company
     8. The Stanley Platoon
     9. The Hughes Group (Hughsiliers)

199

Notes

Chapter 1: Foreign Mud

1. William Hall & William Bernard, *Narrative of the Voyages and Services of the Nemesis from 1840 to 1843* (2nd ed.), (London: Henry Colburn, 1844), 342
2. Niall Ferguson, *Empire: How Britain Made the Modern World*, (London, Penguin Books, 2004), xxiv
3. 'Ch'ien lung's Letter to George III,' web.jjay.cuny.edu/~jobrien/ reference/ob41.html, accessed 30 October 2012
4. John Ouchterlony, *A Statistical Sketch of the Island of Chusan, with a Brief Note on the Geology of China*, (London: Pelham Richardson, 1841), vii
5. Jocelyn, Viscount Robert, *Six Months with the Chinese Expedition; or, Leaves from a Soldier's Note-book*, (London: John Murray, 1841), 59
6. Bingham, John Elliot, *Narrative of the Expedition to China* (2nd ed.), Volume 1, (London: Henry Colburn, 1843), 398
7. William Hall & William Bernard, *Narrative of the Voyages and Services of the Nemesis from 1840 to 1843* (2nd ed.), (London: Henry Colburn, 1844), 126
8. The Asiatic journal and monthly register for British and foreign India, China and Australasia, 1841, Vol.35, 106

Chapter 2: Harrying the Coast

1. William Hall & William Bernard, *Narrative of the Voyages and Services of the Nemesis from 1840 to 1843* (2nd ed.), (London: Henry Colburn, 1844), 342
2. *Bulletin of State Intelligence 1841*, (London: F. Watts, 1841), 359
3. Ibid: 359–360
4. Ibid: 688
5. Ibid: 689
6. Ibid: 689
7. Ibid: 691

8. Ibid: 691
9. Ibid: 691
10. *Bulletins and Other State Intelligence 1842*, (London: F. Watts, 1842), 573
11. Ibid: 576
12. Ibid: 580
13. Ibid: 577
14. Ibid: 581
15. Ibid: 582
16. Ibid: 577
17. Ibid: 585
18. Ibid: 589
19. Ibid: 587–588
20. Ibid: 588
21. Ibid: 588
22. Ibid: 589
23. Ibid: 915
24. Ibid: 915
25. Ibid: 916
26. Ibid: 917
27. Ibid: 918
28. Ibid: 809
29. Ibid: 811
30. Ibid: 812
31. Ibid: 776–777
32. Ibid: 778
33. Ibid: 779
34. Ibid: 779
35. Ibid: 780
36. Ibid: 780

Chapter 3: The Arrow War

1. *Bulletins and Other State Intelligence Compiled and Arranged from the Official Documents Published in the London Gazette*, (London: Harrison & Sons, 1859), 101
2. Ibid: 102
3. Ibid: 104
4. Ibid: 104
5. Ibid: 106–107
6. Ibid: 98–99
7. *Papers Relating to the China War, 1856–58*, (London: Harrison & Sons, 1857), 100
8. Father Chapdelaine was canonised by Pope John Paul II in 2000, much to the anger of the Chinese government

9. 4-gun vessels: HMS *Plover, Banterer, Forester, Haughty, Janus, Kestrel, Lee, Oppossum* and *Starling*. 6-gun vessels: HMS *Nimrod* and *Cormorant*

10. *'Taku Forts 1860'*, queensroyalsurreys.org.uk, accessed 10 December 2012

11. *Supplement to the London Gazette*, Issue 22412, November 27, 1860, 4770

12. Ibid: 4771

13. Ibid: 4771

14. Ibid: 4771

15. Ibid: 4771

Chapter 4: 'Destroy the Foreigners'

1. *'With Brave Hearts and Bright Weapons'* by Mark Henry, 1 March 2000, Osprey Publishing

2. Ibid.

3. Bryan Perrett, *Against All Odds: More Dramatic Last Stand Actions*, (London: Brockhampton Press, 1999), 129

4. Richard O'Connor (1973) *The spirit soldiers: a historical narrative of the Boxer Rebellion* (Putnam 1973), 85

5. Ibid: 130

6. *'With Brave Hearts and Bright Weapons'* by Mark Henry, 1 March 2000, Osprey Publishing

7. Ibid.

8. Bryan Perrett, *Against All Odds: More Dramatic Last Stand Actions*, (London: Brockhampton Press, 1999), 132

9. British Indian Army units involved in the Relief of Peking, 1900:
    – 1st Duke of York's Own Lancers (Skinner's Horse)
    – 15th Cavalry
    – 7th (Duke of Connaught's Own) Rajput Regiment
    – 51st Sikhs (Frontier Force)
    – 24th Punjabis
    – 2nd Queen Victoria's Own Rajput Light Infantry
    – 2nd Queen Victoria's Own Sappers and Miners
    – 6th Jat Light Infantry
    – 20th (Duke of Cambridge's Own) Punjabis (Brownlow's Rifles)
    – 57th Wilde's Rifles (Frontier Force)
    – 63rd Palamcotta Light Infantry
    – 91st Punjabis (Light Infantry)
    – 122nd Rajputana Rifles (God's Own)
    – 4th Gurkha Rifles
    – 33rd Queen Victoria's Own Light Cavalry
    – 1st Sappers and Miners

- 3rd Sappers and Miners
- 14th King George's Own Ferozepore Sikhs
- 34th Pioneers
- 1st Madras Infantry (Pioneers)
- 88th Carnatic Infantry
- 98th Cavalry
- 30th Baluchis

10. A. Henry Savage Landor, *China and the Allies*, (New York: Scribner's Son's, 1901), 356–357
11. *'With Brave Hearts and Bright Weapons'* by Mark Henry, 1 March 2000, Osprey Publishing
12. Ibid.

Chapter 5: Slaughter in Shangri-La

1. Sir Francis Younghusband, *India and Tibet: A History of the Relations which have Subsisted Between the Two Countries From the Time of Warren Hastings to 1910; With a Particular Account of the Mission to Lhasa of 1904*, (London: John Murray, 1910), 172
2. Ibid: 172
3. *'Across the North-East Frontier'* by Colonel H.C. Wylly, CB, The United Service Magazine, Vol. 29 New Series April 1904 to September 1904, 642
4. Sir Francis Younghusband, *India and Tibet: A History of the Relations which have Subsisted Between the Two Countries From the Time of Warren Hastings to 1910; With a Particular Account of the Mission to Lhasa of 1904*, (London: John Murray, 1910): 174
5. Ibid: 174
6. Ibid: 174
7. Ibid: 175
8. Ibid: 176
9. Ibid: 177
10. Ibid: 178
11. Ibid: 178
12. Ibid: 178
13. Ibid: 178
14. Orville Schell, *Virtual Tibet: Searching for Shangri-La from the Himalayas to Hollywood*, (Metropolitan Books, 2000), 195
15. Sir Francis Younghusband, *India and Tibet: A History of the Relations which have Subsisted Between the Two Countries From the Time of Warren Hastings to 1910; With a Particular Account of the Mission to Lhasa of 1904*, (London: John Murray, 1910), 179
16. Ibid: 178
17. Ibid: 179

18. Ibid: 179
19. Ibid: 182
20. Ibid: 182
21. Ibid: 184
22. Ibid: 186
23. Ibid: 187
24. Ibid: 187
25. Ibid: 187
26. Ibid: 188
27. Ibid: 189
28. Ibid: 189
29. Ibid: 189
30. Ibid: 190
31. Ibid: 194
32. Ibid: 196
33. Ibid: 196
34. Ibid: 215
35. Ibid: 219
36. Ibid: 219
37. John Parker, *The Gurkhas: The Inside Story of the World's Most Feared Soldiers*, (London: Headline Book Publishing, 1999), 93–94

Chapter 6: Showing the Flag

1. The Regiment amalgamated with the East Surrey Regiment in 1959 to become The Queen's Royal Surrey Regiment. In 1966 it was amalgamated with three other regiments to become the The Queen's Regiment. In 1992 the Queen's was amalgamated for a final time into its present incarnation, The Princess of Wales' Royal Regiment (Queen's and Royal Hampshires)
2. *The Queen's rejoin the China Station – 1930*, The Queen's Royal Surrey Regimental Association, queensroyalsurreys.org.uk, accessed 16 February 2012
3. Ibid.
4. Ibid.
5. Shaw: 16
6. Ibid: 16–17
7. Ibid: 17
8. *The Queen's rejoin the China Station – 1930*, The Queen's Royal Surrey Regimental Association, queensroyalsurreys.org.uk, accessed 16 February 2012
9. Ibid.
10. Shaw: 17
11. Ibid: 17–18

12. Ibid: 18
13. Ibid: 18
14. Ibid: 18
15. Ibid: 22
16. *The Queen's rejoin the China Station – 1930*, The Queen's Royal Surrey Regimental Association, queensroyalsurreys.org.uk, accessed 16 February 2012
17. Ibid.
18. Ibid.
19. Ibid.
20. Ibid.
21. Ibid.
22. Ibid.
23. Ibid.
24. Ibid.
25. Ibid.
26. Ibid.
27. Ibid.
28. *The Daily Province*, 8 September 1937, 1–2
29. Ibid: 1–2
30. Shaw: 23
31. Ibid: 23
32. Ibid: 23
33. Ibid: 23
34. Ibid: 23
35. Ibid: 23
36. Ibid: 24
37. Ibid: 24
38. Ibid: 25
39. Ibid: 25

Chapter 7: Christmas in Hell

1. 'City of Terror: The Japanese Takeover of Shanghai 1941' by Mark Felton, *That's Shanghai*, December 2012
2. Ibid.
3. Ibid.
4. *Toronto Globe and Mail*, 10 December, 1941
5. 'Granite Memorial Recalls Hong Kong Sacrifices' by Sharon Adams, *Legion Magazine*, 3 November 2009
6. The Hong Kong Volunteer Defence Corps and the remnants of the Hong Kong Chinese Regiment were amalgamated in 1949 to form the Hong Kong Regiment (The Volunteers), a reserve forces infantry battalion and later reconnaissance regiment. 'The Volunteers' played

an important role in safeguarding the internal security of the colony, including dealing with the 1967 riots, illegal immigration from China, guarding the border alongside British forces, and running refugee camps for a flood of Vietnamese illegal migrants known as 'Boat People'. The Queen granted the Regiment the prefix 'Royal' in 1970 and 'The Volunteers' continued in existence until disbanded in September 1995 as the British cut troop numbers in Hong Kong before the formal handover of the colony to China in June 1997

7. Nicola Tyrer, *Sisters In Arms: British Army Nurses Tell their Story*, London: Weidenfeld & Nicolson, 2008, 42
8. *Toronto Globe and Mail*, 10 December, 1941
9. 'The Fall of Hong Kong' by Crabbies, WW2 People's War, Article ID: A4279331, 26 June 2005, bbc.co.uk/history/ww2peopleswar, accessed 18 January 2013
10. Ibid.
11. Eric Taylor, *Front-line Nurse: British Nurses in World War II*, London: Robert Hale Ltd, 1997, 167
12. Ibid: 167
13. *A Nursing Sister's Story: In Memory of Lieutenant Kay Christie*, Hong Kong Veterans Commemorative Association, hkvca.ca, accessed 2 June 2008
14. *Toronto Globe and Mail*, 16 December 1941
15. 'The Fall of Hong Kong' by Crabbies, WW2 People's War, Article ID: A4279331, 26 June 2005, bbc.co.uk/history/ww2peopleswar, accessed 18 January 2013
16. Ron Taylor (Ed.), *Hong Kong – Invasion*, Far East Prisoners of War Association, fepow-community.org.uk, accessed 3 June 2008
17. Ibid.
18. *Hongkong Garrison Fight to the Last*, Daily Express, December 20, 1941, front page
19. 'The Fall of Hong Kong' by Crabbies, WW2 People's War, Article ID: A4279331, 26 June 2005, bbc.co.uk/history/ww2peopleswar, accessed 18 January 2013
20. Ibid.
21. Veterans Affairs Canada, vac-acc.gc.ca, accessed 14 January 2013
22. Ibid.
23. Ibid.
24. Ibid.
25. Brereton Greenhous, *'C' Force to Hong Kong: A Canadian Catastrophe*, (Ottawa: Dundurn Group Ltd, 1997), 114
26. Lord Russell of Liverpool, *The Knights of Bushido: A Short History of Japanese War Crimes*, (London: Greenhill Books, 2002), 97
27. Ibid: 97

28. Veterans Affairs Canada, vac-acc.gc.ca, accessed 14 January 2013
29. Lord Russell of Liverpool, *The Knights of Bushido: A Short History of Japanese War Crimes*, (London: Greenhill Books, 2002), 97
30. Ibid: 97
31. Lord Russell of Liverpool, *The Knights of Bushido: A Short History of Japanese War Crimes*, (London: Greenhill Books, 2002), 98
32. *A Nursing Sister's Story: In Memory of Lieutenant Kay Christie*, Hong Kong Veterans Commemorative Association, hkvca.ca, accessed 13 January 2013
33. Lord Russell of Liverpool, *The Knights of Bushido: A Short History of Japanese War Crimes*, (London: Greenhill Books, 2002), 98
34. Nicola Tyrer, *Sister's In Arms: Complete citation*, 55
35. Ibid: 56
36. Ibid.
37. Lord Russell of Liverpool, *The Knights of Bushido: A Short History of Japanese War Crimes*, (London: Greenhill Books, 2002), 98
38. *A Nursing Sister's Story: In Memory of Lieutenant Kay Christie*, Hong Kong Veterans Commemorative Association, hkvca.ca, accessed 13 January 2013
39. Ibid.
40. 'The Fall of Hong Kong' by Crabbies, WW2 People's War, Article ID: A4279331, 26 June 2005, bbc.co.uk/history/ww2peopleswar, accessed 18 January 2013
41. Ibid.
42. *'Pilgrimage for veterans of the battle of Hong Kong'*, 10 November 2005, canada.com, accessed 20 January 2013

Chapter 8: Cloak and Dagger

1. *Report of Mr. S.C. Riggs*, November 1942, HS1/181, The National Archives (Public Record Office), Kew
2. Ibid.
3. Ibid.
4. Colin Smith, *Singapore Burning: Heroism and Surrender in World War II*, (London: Penguin Books Ltd, 2005), 78
5. *SOE Operations China, 1941–1944*, HS1/226, The National Archives (Public Record Office), Kew
6. Bernard Wasserstein, *Secret War in Shanghai: Treachery, Subversion and Collaboration in the Second World War*, (London: Profile Books Ltd, 1998), 118
7. Ibid: 121
8. John B. Powell, *My Twenty-Five Years in China*, (New York, 1945), 386
9. Ibid: 272
10. Ralph Shaw, *Sin City*, London: Warner Books, 1997, 207

11. Stella Dong, *Shanghai: The Rise and Fall of a Decadent City*, (New York: Perennial, 2001), 272–273
12. Ralph Shaw, *Sin City*, London: Warner Books, 1997, 208
13. Ibid: 208
14. *A.DU to C.D.*, 1 November 1942, HS1/181, The National Archives (Public Record Office), Kew

Chapter 9: 'Am Under Heavy Fire'

1. *'Send a Gunboat'* by Terry Currie, MaritimeQuest, maritimequest.com, accessed 22 October 2012
2. Ibid.
3. *'The Dickin Medal'* by Joe Knight, *Military History Monthly*, February 2013, Issue 29, 36
4. *'Send a Gunboat'* by Terry Currie, MaritimeQuest, maritimequest.com, accessed 22 October 2012
5. Ibid.
6. Ibid.
7. Ibid.
8. Ibid.
9. Ibid.
10. Ibid.
11. Ibid.
12. *'The Dickin Medal'* by Joe Knight, *Military History Monthly*, February 2013, Issue 29, 36
13. *'HMS Concord: Our part in the Yangtse Incident'* by Derek Hodgson, britains-smallwars.com, accessed 1 January 2013
14. Ibid.
15. *'HMS Concord and the Escape of the Amethyst'* by William Leitch, maritimequest.com, accessed 14 November 2012
16. Ibid.

Chapter 10: The Immortal Memory

1. *China and Hong Kong* by Les Wilson, The Queen's Royal Surrey Regimental Association, queensroyalsurreys.org.uk, accessed 2 January 2013
2. Ibid.
3. Ibid.
4. Ibid.
5. Ibid.
6. Ibid.
7. Ibid.
8. Ibid.
9. Ibid.

10. *'Revealed: the Hong Kong invasion plan'* by Michael Sheridan, *The Sunday Times*, 24 June 2007
11. 1st Battalion, 10th Princess Mary's Own Gurkha Rifles, 2nd Battalion, 2nd King Edward VII's Own Gurkha Rifles (The Sirmoor Rifles) and 1st Battalion, 7th Duke of Edinburgh's Own Gurkha Rifles
12. *Interview with Bob Ritchie*, 2 December 2008, YMCA Perth Museum of the Black Watch, Remembering Scotland at War, Exhibition: Hong Kong – the lion of Asia, rememberingscotlandatwar.org.uk, accessed 21 January 2013
13. Ibid.
14. Ibid.
15. *Interview with Ronnie Procter*, 9 December 2008, YMCA Perth Museum of the Black Watch, Remembering Scotland at War, Exhibition: Hong Kong – the lion of Asia, rememberingscotlandat-war.org.uk, accessed 21 January 2013
16. *Interview with Jim Sandilands*, 9 December 2008, YMCA Perth Museum of the Black Watch, Remembering Scotland at War, Exhibition: Hong Kong – the lion of Asia, rememberingscotlandat-war.org.uk, accessed 21 January 2013
17. Ibid.
18. *Interview with Ronnie Procter*, 9 December 2008, YMCA Perth Museum of the Black Watch, Remembering Scotland at War, Exhibition: Hong Kong – the lion of Asia, rememberingscotlandat-war.org.uk, accessed 21 January 2013
19. Ibid.
20. *Interview with Jim Sandilands*, 9 December 2008, YMCA Perth Museum of the Black Watch, Remembering Scotland at War, Exhibition: Hong Kong – the lion of Asia, rememberingscotlandat-war.org.uk, accessed 21 January 2013
21. Ibid.
22. Ibid.

Appendix Order of Battle – Shanghai Volunteer Corps, 21 November 1941

1. *Note on Shanghai Volunteer Corps*, 21 November 1941, WO106/2393, (The National Archives (Public Record Office)), Kew

Bibliography

Archives

National Archives (Public Record Office), Kew
Report of Mr. S.C. Riggs, November 1942, HS1/181
SOE Operations China, 1941–1944, HS1/226

Books
Bingham, John Elliot, *Narrative of the Expedition to China* (2nd ed.), Volume 1, London: Henry Colburn, 1843
Bulletin of State Intelligence 1841, London: F. Watts, 1841
Bulletins and Other State Intelligence 1842, London: F: Watts, 1842
Bulletins and Other State Intelligence Compiled and Arranged from the Official Documents Published in the London Gazette, London: Harrison & Sons, 1859
Daws, Gavan, *Prisoners of the Japanese: POWs of the Second World War*, London: Pocket Books, 1994
Dong, Stella, *Shanghai: The Rise and Fall of a Decadent City*, New York: Perennial, 2001
Hall, William & Bernard, William, *Narrative of the Voyages and Services of the Nemesis from 1840 to 1843* (2nd ed.), London: Henry Colburn, 1844
Jocelyn, Viscount Robert, *Six Months with the Chinese Expedition; or, Leaves from a Soldier's Note-book*, London: John Murray, 1841
Landor, A. Henry Savage, *China and the Allies*, Scribner's Son's, 1901
Ouchterlony, John, *A Statistical Sketch of the Island of Chusan, with a Brief Note on the Geology of China*, London: Pelham Richardson, 1841
Papers Relating to the China War, 1856–58, London: Harrison & Sons, 1857
Parker, John, *The Gurkhas: The Inside Story of the World's Most Feared Soldiers*, Headline Book Publishing, 1999
Perrett, Bryan, *Against All Odds: More Dramatic Last Stand Actions*, Brockhampton Press, 1999
Powell, John, *My Twenty-Five Years in China*, New York, 1945
Schell, Orville, *Virtual Tibet: Searching for Shangri-La from the Himalayas to Hollywood*, Metropolitan Books, 2000
Shaw, Ralph, *Sin City*, London: Warner Books, 1997

Smith, Colin, *Singapore Burning: Heroism and Surrender in World War II*, London: Penguin Books Ltd, 2005
Wasserstein, Bernard, *Secret War in Shanghai: Treachery, Subversion and Collaboration in the Second World War*, London: Profile Books Ltd, 1998
Younghusband, Sir Francis, *India and Tibet: A History of the Relations which have Subsisted Between the Two Countries From the Time of Warren Hastings to 1910; With a Particular Account of the Mission to Lhasa of 1904*, London: John Murray, 1910

Newspapers and Journals
American Heritage
Hansard
London Gazette
Military History
Military History Monthly
Naval History
Proceedings (US Naval Institute)
That's Shanghai
The Daily Province
The Straits Times
The Sunday Times
The Times
United Service Magazine

Internet
'HMS Concord: Our part in the Yangtse Incident' by Derek Hodgson, britains-smallwars.com
'HMS Concord and the Escape of the Amethyst' by William Leitch, maritimequest.com
Letter about the Chinese Civil War 1927 by Harold Vermont, A History of the World, BBC History, bbc.co.uk/ahistoryoftheworld
YMCA Perth Museum of the Black Watch, Remembering Scotland at War, Exhibition: Hong Kong – the lion of Asia, rememberingscotlandatwar.org.uk
'Send a Gunboat' by Terry Currie, MaritimeQuest, maritimequest.com
The Queen's Royal Surrey Regimental Association, queensroyalsurreys.org.uk

Index

Alderton, Surgeon-Lt. John, 162
Algerine, HMS, 12–13, 23, 28, 36
Alligator, HMS, 11–12, 19, 20
American Volunteer Group,
    118–119
Amethyst, HMS, 158–159, 160–161,
    162–173
Ampthill, Lord, 103
Anglo-Tibetan Agreement, 103
Ariadne, HMS, 35
Ark Royal, HMS, 180
Armstrong, Commodore James, 46

Arrow, 42–43, 46
Banterer, HMS, 52
Barracouta, HMS, 45
Barrett, Capt. James, 138–139
Bartholomew, Maj.-Gen. Arthur,
    117–118
Bingham, Lt. John, 14
Bishop, Maj. D.R., 179
Black, Surgeon-Capt. George,
    137–138
Black Swan, HMS, 166–167, 168
Blenheim, HMS, 15, 19, 20
Blonde, HMS, 34, 36
Bowring, Sir John, 43, 46–47
Boyd, Lt.-Col. J.D., 112
Boxers see 'China'
Boxer Protocols (1901), 84–85

Brand, John, 143, 149, 155, 156
Brander, Col. Herbert, 89, 95, 97,
    98–99
Bremer, Commodore Sir James,
    12, 13, 15, 16, 18, 21, 24
Brister, Joseph, 143, 152, 155, 156
British Army:
    8 Gurkha Infantry Brigade, 178
    1st King's Dragoon Guards, 58
    7th Queen's Own Hussars, 177
    14th/20th King's Hussars, 182
    Royal Artillery, 15, 81, 80, 96,
        133, 178
    Corps of Royal Engineers, 59,
        99, 106, 109, 111, 118, 133
    Royal Corps of Signals, 109, 111
    Army Air Corps, 175
    Royal Army Service Corps, 106,
        111
    18th (Royal Irish) Regiment of
        Foot, 13, 25–26, 28, 30, 31,
        34, 38
    26th Regiment of Foot, 13, 15,
        20, 30, 31, 38
    31st (Huntingdonshire)
        Regiment of Foot, 55
    44th (East Essex) Regiment of
        Foot, 55, 56
    49th Regiment of Foot, 13, 15,
        20, 25, 29, 30, 31, 38

55th Regiment of Foot, 29
67th Regiment of Foot, 56
Black Watch, 174, 182–185
Durham Light Infantry, 106
Irish Guards, 182
Middlesex Regiment, 126, 127, 128, 132, 136
Norfolk Regiment, 90
Royal Fusiliers, 100, 101, 102
Royal Gurkha Rifles, 174, 186
Royal Scots, 126, 127, 128, 129, 132, 133
Royal Welsh Fusiliers, 78
Staffordshire Regiment, 175
Queen's Royal Regiment (West Surrey), 105–106, 107, 108–111
Queen's (Second) Royal Regiment of Foot, 55
Royal Army Medical Corps, 106, 133, 135
Royal Military Police, 111
Queen's Gurkha Engineers, 174
Queen's Gurkha Signals, 174, 187
Queen's Own Gurkha Logistic Regiment, 174
British Colonial Units:
Hong Kong Chinese Regiment, 126
Hong Kong Military Service Corps, 175
Hong Kong Mule Company, 131
Hong Kong & Singapore Royal Artillery, 126, 128, 133
Hong Kong Volunteer Defence Corps, 126, 128, 129, 132, 133, 135, 140, 175
Royal Hong Kong Regiment (The Volunteers), 175, 182

Shanghai Volunteer Corps, 111, 114, 121, 122, 150
Tientsin British Volunteer Corps, 109
British Indian Army:
Bengal Lancers, 80, 81
Madras Artillery, 30
Madras Sappers & Miners, 13, 90, 99
2/14th Punjab Regiment, 126, 127, 132, 135
5/7th Rajput Regiment, 126, 127, 128, 131, 133
7th Duke of Connaught's Own Rajput Regiment, 83
8th Gurkha Rifles, 90, 96, 97, 98, 100, 101, 102
23rd Sikh Pioneers, 90, 99
29th Punjab Regiment, 100
32nd Sikh Pioneers, 96
36th Madras Native Infantry, 31
37th Madras Native Infantry, 15, 20, 25, 26–27
40th Pathans, 100, 101, 102
Bengal Volunteers, 13, 14, 15, 20
Brooke-Popham, Air Chief Marshal Sir Robert, 124, 125, 141
Brown, Margaret, 115
Burrell, Brig.-Gen. George, 12
Butler, Lt. Smedley, 82

Cabot, John, 169
Cadogan-Rawlinson, Lt.-Col. J., 131
Calliope, HMS, 16, 19
Cambridge, 20–21
Canadian Army:
Winnipeg Grenadiers, 126, 128, 132, 133, 135
Royal Rifles of Canada, 126, 128, 132, 138, 141

Carnatic, 7
Chaffee, Brig.-Gen. Adna, 81–82
Chiang Kai-shek, 115, 156, 159
China:
  Behaviour of citizenry, 34–35,
    39
  Boxers, 63–65
  Cultural Revolution, 181
  Military effectiveness, 17–18
  Opening to foreign trade, 4–5
  Opium trade, 5–7, 10–11, 41–42
  Self-Strengthening Movement,
    60
  Taiping Rebellion, 42–43
Chinese Army:
  Imperial:
    Gansu Fighting Braves,
      31–32, 67, 68, 73, 84
    Green Flag Regiments, 68
    Imperial Guards, 31, 32, 67
    Manchu Bannermen, 68
    Mongolian Cavalry, 58
  Nationalist:
    28th Army, 168–169
    36th Division, 116
    86th Division, 116
    87th Division, 115, 116
    88th Division, 115
  Communist:
    People's Liberation Army,
      161–162, 166, 168,
      169–170, 171–173, 175,
      183
Christie, Sister Kay, 131, 139, 140
Churchill, Winston, 136, 141
Cixi, Empress Dowager, 64, 66–67,
  68, 70, 72, 84, 85
Clarke, William, 144, 151, 156
Clayton, Sgt. Bob, 138
Clio, HMS, 36
Collar, Hugh, 153
Columbine, HMS, 17, 36

Concord, HMS, 172–173
Consort, HMS, 160, 163–164, 166
Cossack, HMS, 172
Convention of Peking (1860), 60,
  61
Conway, HMS, 11
Coromandel, HMS, 45
Cornwallis, HMS, 34, 36, 38, 39
Cousin-Montauban, Lt.-Gen.
  Charles, 55, 56
Crabb, Pvt. Francis, 129, 133,
  136–137, 140
Cruizer, HMS, 12–13
Cuming, PO James, 123–124
Currie, PO Terry, 161, 163–165
Curzon, Lord, 89, 93, 95, 96

Dalai Lama, 13th, 88, 89, 91, 94, 99,
  102, 103, 104
Dalai Lama, 14th, 104
Dalton, Hugh, 145
Daoguang, Emperor, 6–7
David, Edgeworth, 177
Dong Fuxiang, Gen., 68, 73, 85
Druid, HMS, 14, 17, 20, 26, 28
Dunlop, Maj. Wallace, 93

East India Company, 5–6
Elgin and Kincardine, Earl of,
  47–48, 56, 59
Elias, Edward, 144, 152
Elliot, Rear-Adm. Charles, 7–8, 9,
  10, 11, 13–14, 15, 18, 26, 39
Enterprise, HMS, 14
Eritrea, 148, 149

Fame, HMS, 71, 86
Fearnley, Fl. Lt. Michael, 167
Fletcher, Capt. John, 11–12
Fletcher, Walter, 157–158
Foley, St. George, 57
Foote, Cdr. Andrew, 46

Franklin, Sup. Sister Olga, 130
Fukushima, Maj.-Gen. Yasumasa, 78

Gande, William, 143–144, 148, 149, 150, 152, 154–156
Gandon Tri Rimpoche, Regent, 104
Gaselee, Maj.-Gen. Sir Alfred, 79, 82, 85
Gimson, Frank, 176
Gladstone, William, 10
Gong, Prince, 58, 60
Gordon, Capt. Charles, 59
Gros, Baron, 60
Gough, Maj.-Gen. Hugh, 22, 24–25, 27–28, 29, 31, 34, 36–37, 38
Grant, Lt.-Gen. Sir James Hope, 55–56, 58
Grant, Lt. John, 101–102
Griffiths, Cdr. Ian, 163
Guan Tianpei, Adm., 8, 9, 10, 16, 20
Guangxu, Emperor, 64, 85
Gutzlaff, Karl, 12, 14
Gwynnes, Maj. Timothy, 118

Hadow, Lt. Arthur, 93
Halliday, Capt. Lewis, 76, 85
Harcourt, Rear-Adm. Cecil, 176–177
Haughty, HMS, 53
Hennessey, Col. Patrick, 135
Herald, HMS, 19, 24
Herbert, Capt. Sir Thomas, 16, 19, 21
Hong Lu, Gen., 50
Hong Xiuquan, 43
Hoover, Herbert, 78
Hope, Rear-Adm. James, 50, 51
Huang Yongsheng, 181
Hyacinth, HMS, 8, 9, 10, 14

Ignatiev, Count, 60
Indian Army see 'British Indian Army'
Izumo, 115, 120, 123

Jack, George, 143, 152, 155, 156
Japan:
  Imperial Japanese Army:
    3rd Infantry Division, 116
    8th Infantry Division, 116
    11th Infantry Division, 116
    38th Infantry Division, 126, 132
    21st Infantry Regiment, 128
    23rd Infantry Regiment, 128
    38th Infantry Regiment, 128
    228th Infantry Regiment, 129
    Kempeitai Military Police, 118, 145, 146, 149, 150, 151–152, 154–156
  Imperial Japanese Navy:
    Shanghai Special Naval Landing Force, 115, 124
Jellicoe, Capt. John, 66, 85–86
Jocelyn, Viscount, 11–12, 13

Kerans, Lt.-Cdr. John, 167–173
Kestrel, HMS, 53
Ketteler, Klemens, Baron von, 67, 72
Keyes, Lt. Roger, 71, 86
Killery, Lt.-Col. Valentine, 146, 148, 153

Macartney, Lord, 6, 11
MacDonald, Sir Claude, 64, 69, 79–80, 82, 85
MacDonald, Brig.-Gen. James, 89–90, 91, 93, 94, 99, 100, 101, 103
MacDonell, CSM George, 141
Mackenzie, Lt. Colin, 71

MacLehose, Sir Murray, 184–185
Madagascar, 21, 23
Madden, Vice-Adm. A.C.G., 168
Ma Fulu, Gen., 73
Ma Fuxiang, Gen., 73
Ma Qing Yuan, Gen., 169
Maitland, Rear-Adm. Sir
    Frederick, 12
Maltby, Maj.-Gen. Christopher,
    124–127, 131–133, 135, 136,
    141
Mao Zedong, 87, 104, 159
McCalla, Capt. Bowman, 65–66
McDougall, Pvt. John, 56
Melville, HMS, 13–14, 15, 19, 20
MI6, 148, 155
Modeste, HMS, 17, 20, 21, 23, 35
Montgomerie, Lt.-Col. P., 30, 32
Mountain, Lt.-Col. Armine, 30, 34

Nankin, HMS, 45
Nemesis, HMS, 16, 18, 19, 21, 22, 33,
    35, 36
Neuralia, HMT, 105–106
NieShicheng, Gen., 66, 69, 72–73

Office of Strategic Services, 156
Opossum, HMS, 51, 52, 53
Osborn, CSM John, 135–136
Osborne, RSM G., 111
Oxfordshire, HMT, 178

Palmerston, Viscount, 7, 10, 15,
    46–47
Parker, Rear-Adm. Sir William,
    28, 31, 36, 37
Parkes, Harry, 44–45, 56, 59
Peacock, HMS, 175
Peterel, HMS, 120–121, 122–123,
    150
Phlegethon, HMS, 33, 36
Plover, HMS, 51, 52, 53, 175

Pluto, HMS, 35
Polkinghorn, Lt. Stephen, 120–121,
    123
Ponsonby, Lt.-Col. H.C., 106
Portsmouth, USS, 46
Pottinger, Sir Henry, 39
Powell, John B., 151–152, 153
Pratt, Maj. Simson, 15–16, 20
Pun, HavildarKarbir, 101–102
Pu Yi, Emperor, 66, 85
Pylades, HMS, 28

Qianlong, Emperor, 11
Qi Shan, 15, 18
Queen, HMS, 16, 19

Rattlesnake, HMS, 11–12
Repose, USS, 168, 169
Riggs, Sydney, 143–144, 152, 155,
    156
Ritchie, CSM Bob, 182–183
Rogers, Lt. Robert, 56
Ronglu, Gen., 66, 68, 84
Rose, Col. H.B., 135
Royal Air Force:
    28 (Army Cooperation)
        Squadron, 175
    Hong Kong Auxiliary Air Force,
        184
    RAF Kai Tak, 130
    Queen's Colour Squadron, 174
Royal Hong Kong Police, 174,
    179–180, 185
Royal Marines, 1–2, 13, 14, 15, 20,
    23, 25, 31, 37, 38, 45, 50, 55, 62,
    65, 76, 79
Royal Navy:
    6th Patrol Craft Flotilla, 175
    China Station Headquarters,
        131, 175
    Naval Party 1002, 187
    Naval Party 1022, 187

INDEX

Royal Naval Hospital, Wanchai, 130–131

Royal Saxon, 3, 8, 10

Russell, Lord John, 57

Sakai, Maj.-Gen. Takashi, 126, 132

Saltoun, Maj.-Gen. Lord, 12, 38

Samarang, HMS, 16, 17, 19, 20

Sandilands, Pvt. Jim, 183–184

Selbourne, Lord, 157

Senhouse, Capt. Sir Humphrey, 19–20, 25

Sesostris, HMS, 34, 36

Seymour, Vice-Adm. Sir Edward, 65, 66, 73, 74–75, 77, 85

Seymour, Rear-Adm. Michael, 43–44, 45, 48, 50

Seymour-Conway, Sir Horace, 176

Schoedde, Maj.-Gen. T.H., 29, 30, 31, 38

Scott, Capt. James, 16–17, 22

Shaw, Pvt. Ralph, 106–107, 108, 116–117, 152–153

Skinner, Lt.-Cdr. Bernard, 158–159, 162, 173

Small, Pipe Major Steven, 174, 185

Smith, Capt. Henry, 8–9, 14–15

Special Operations Executive, 144, 145–146, 156, 157

Starling, HMS, 23, 175

Strouts, Capt. R.M., 79

Sugiyama, Akira, 67

Sulphur, HMS, 21–22

Sydenham-Clarke, Lt. Monty, 113

Symonds, Lt. Richard, 22

Tamar, HMS, 131, 175

Tattnall, Commodore Josiah, 52–53

Tenasserim, HMS, 36

Terrible, HMS, 78

Thatcher, Margaret, 181–182

Thomas, Surgeon-Capt., Osler, 135

Thracian, HMS, 132

Titus, Pvt. Calvin, 83

Toey-Wan, USS, 52

Treaty of Aigun (1858), 49

Treaty of Nanking (1842), 40, 41–42, 43

Treaty of Tientsin (1858), 49, 55

Urquhart, R.W., 169

Victoria, Queen, 7, 24, 25, 28

Vixen, HMS, 37

Volage, HMS, 3, 8, 9, 10

Wake, USS, 120, 121

Waller, Capt. Littleton, 73

Wallis, Brig. Cedric, 127

Watts, James, 74–75

Wellesley, HMS, 11, 13, 15, 20, 28

Weston, Lt. Geoffrey, 162, 165–166

Whiting, HMS, 71

Wiegand, Karl von, 147

Willes, Capt. George, 51, 53

Woodhead, H.G.W., 153

Xianfeng, Emperor, 58, 64

Ye Fei, Col., 169–170

Ye Mingchen, 43–44, 47, 48

Ye Puyun, Gen., 31

Yi Kong, 31

Yilibu, 39

Young, Sir Mark, 140, 176–177

Younghusband, Maj. Francis, 89, 90, 91–94, 95–98, 100, 102–103, 104

Zhao Erfeng, Gen., 103

Zhang Mingfeng, 47

Zhang Zhizhang, 115, 116

Zhou Enlai, 181